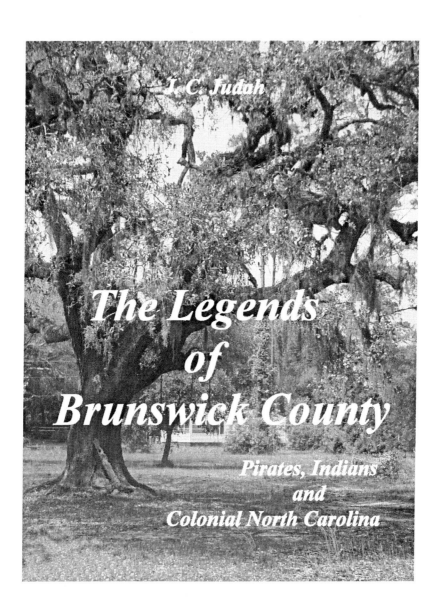

J. C. Judah

The Legends
of
Brunswick County

Pirates, Indians
and
Colonial North Carolina

The Legends of Brunswick County
Pirates, Indians and Colonial North Carolina

By J. C. Judah

ISBN: 978-0-6151-7586-7
Published by Coastal Books
C. 2008 by Joyce C. Judah

Photographs by John Muuss, Photographic Artist, Inc.,
www.johnmuuss.com, and the author, J. C. Judah

Additional Books by this Author

An Ancient History of Dogs: Spaniels through the Ages
Building a Basic Foundation for Search and Rescue Dog Training
Search and Rescue Canine Training Log & Journal
Search and Rescue Training Log & Journal
Brunswick County: The Best of the Beaches
The Faircloth Family History:
A Compilation of Resources and Genealogy
Available at www.heritagebooks.com

For a complete listing of books written by this author, visit
www.lulu.com/spaniels

Contact Information: (910) 842-7942
www.lulu.com/spaniels or
www.geocities.com/springers2020
carolinakennels@2khiway.net
2690 Ocean Station SW, Supply, NC 28462

The cover page book is an actual book located in the Brunswick County Courthouse listing Last Wills and Testaments, Deeds and other legal documents from the colonial settlers of Brunswick County, North Carolina.

Printed in the United States of America

Dedication & Acknowledgements

I would like to thank my family for their support in my writing adventures. Thanks Dad, Mom, Jenny and Jonathan for listening to idea after idea as I wrote this book and helping to edit the book.

Thank you to Birdie Frink, her husband Barry, and Francis Williams for touring the southern part of the county with me. Thanks to Lynn and Judy Holden, Ouida Hewett, Bertha Bell, and the many, many other folks who gave of their knowledge and time to help create this book sharing their family lore and historical knowledge. Thank you to Nathan Henry and Richard Lawrence, Underwater Archaeologists, who guided me on my Indian searches, and all the other residents and agencies of Brunswick and New Hanover County who endured my questions and curiosity during the course of my research. Perhaps together, we have documented a piece of our local history.

As always, my love to all my family, especially my grandsons, Isaih and Jacob.

Christy Judah

v

Table of Contents

Preface

Quite a few years ago I decided to obtain my first English Springer spaniel. In the course of getting "a dog", I quickly became enthralled with the idea of obedience training and dog activities. Several more spaniels soon followed, along with a new canine venture; training search and rescue dogs. My interest in this field grew to include the formation of the Brunswick Search and Rescue Team and national involvement in search and rescue related activities.

Over the course of many searches for missing persons, "Bailey" and "Gypsy" (two of my spaniels), were trained to locate buried persons. Requested by local, state and national law enforcement agencies to find missing persons, both dead or alive, these dogs and others like them on the Brunswick Search and Rescue team began to assist the residents of Brunswick County to locate historic burial sites which dated into the 1700's.

As a result of this volunteer work, and a newspaper article, the SAR dogs and handlers from the Brunswick Search and Rescue team were asked to locate the final resting places of individuals in a little known Slave Cemetery on Stone Chimney Road. This cemetery had all but disappeared into the landscape with only one headstone remaining. It was a vague memory for two eighty-year old gentlemen who remembered the sole remaining monument. Canine crews from BSAR ultimately identified the final resting place of 47 individuals.

This Slave Cemetery project followed a like project identifying burials at the Job Holden Cemetery and the Hewett Cemeteries, both located just a few miles south of the Slave Cemetery. It soon became apparent that the Hewett, Holden and Slave cemeteries were intimately connected. Several colonial records, including the Last Will and Testament of

Mary Hemingway, linked them together and began to paint a picture of colonial life in southeastern North Carolina.

It didn't take long to realize that some of the slaves buried in the Stone Chimney Slave Cemetery were most likely the slaves of Mrs. Mary Hemingway. In her Last Will and Testament each slave was noted by name and bequeathed to subsequent owners. Mrs. Hemingway's gravesite was located and flashes of her life story emerged. This adventure soon became a tale of some of the earliest known residents in the Holden Beach area. Just blocks from my own residence, and next to modern-day beach businesses and a high-rise access bridge, colonial settlers had left their mark. It was up to us to protect and revere these archaeological remains.

Over 150 years ago, Mary Hemingway ran an enormous plantation, with census records attributing over 200 slaves to her employ. Part of her bequeaths included property to "Job Holden", who lay just down the road in a cemetery surrounded by a modern residential development. I was beginning to feel like I "knew" these folks. I was given a brief glimpse into their lives and their deaths.

I knew that this historical information needed to be collected and recorded. It didn't take long for me to realize that one of the slaves mentioned in Mrs. Hemingway's Last Will and Testament was the great-great grandmother of the person who sought out our services to identify gravesites at the Slave Cemetery. The historic epic of a long ago ancestor turned into the heritage of my neighbor and friend. Her interest in the past is now channeled into efforts to restore and preserve the Slave Cemetery where her ancestors are likely buried. Best wishes to Mrs. Bertha Bell.

The book continued to evolve when my interest and my heart were so moved by the Mary Hemingway story and the efforts of some other citizens working to preserve and protect her burial site. Mrs. Ouida Hewett and Mr. Grover Holden, with other local residents, continue to seek remedies to preserve this historical site. It is with this taste of

Brunswick County history that I began to collect and record the stories and heritage of the earliest developments in the county.

As the original settlers came to the coast of North Carolina they were met by the American Indian natives who long ago lived and visited the great lands of Chicora (the likely native name for North Carolina). It is with a quest to record this data in a methodical manner that this book is offered. This work does not go into detail regarding the military battles and skirmishes that were held in Brunswick County, nor does it detail the military leaders who are so richly represented in other writings. This book was not intended to be an all-inclusive historical essay, nor a complete account of past events, but a historic representation of the figures and events in southeastern North Carolina that shaped the area. Although not an all-inclusive history, it does attempt to portray life in southeastern North Carolina through real people in real places. This book is my contribution to preserve that past for future generations. Although not finished, I conclude this work, for now.

Christy Judah

The Legends of Brunswick County

Pirates, Indians and Colonial North Carolina

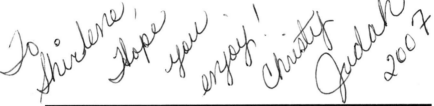

J. C. Judah

Introduction

The southern tip of North Carolina has long been a vacation destination of families across the United States. It's pristine beaches, excellent fishing, challenging golf courses, and family atmosphere have made it the choice of many desiring the ultimate escape.

Few know the fascinating history of this sleepy coastal region full of tradition reaching back into the 16th century. This book was written to provide a peek into the past through the eyes of its early residents, historical documents, seafaring pirates, well-known spirits, Indian predecessors, notable cemeteries (including known Slave Cemeteries), local facts, and legends. It provides a momentary look into the rich tradition and culture of Brunswick County. In the course of the research, information about the surrounding region, including New Hanover County, was included to create this southeastern North Carolina legacy.

Brunswick County was established on March 9, 1764 when Governor Arthur Dobbs appeared before the General Assembly of the province and gave approval "to an Act for erecting part of St. Phillip's Parish in New Hanover County and the lower part of Bladen County into a separate county to be known as Brunswick County." It was named after the town of Brunswick, which was named in honor of King George I, who was the Duke of Brunswick and Lunenberg. It is located in the southeastern portion of North Carolina and bounded by the Atlantic Ocean, the Cape Fear River, the State of South Carolina, and, Columbus, Pender and New Hanover Counties.

The town of Brunswick was the original county seat, established in 1745. The county seat was moved to John Bell's plantation in 1779. That was located near the Lockwood Folly Bridge. In 1808, the courthouse was moved from Lockwood Folly to Smithville. Smithville was named for Benjamin Smith and established in 1792. Smith later becomes the Governor of North Carolina from 1810-1811.

In 1887 Smithville's name was changed to Southport and it became the county seat until 1977. In 1977 the county seat was moved to Bolivia where it remains today, a central location for the citizens.

Brunswick County currently consists of about 856 square miles. It is the seventh largest county in North Carolina and boasts a current population of over 90,000, growing extremely fast. With 19 municipalities, is has more municipalities than any other county in the state.

Former woodlands, farms and plantations are fast becoming residential developments and commercial centers. Long forgotten cemeteries are being discovered and preserved by caring communities who are taking steps to preserve history. As development continues to expand throughout the county, the history of Brunswick County continues to be exposed through building excavations and concentrated efforts by the citizens desiring to record and maintain its rich heritage. Residents are encouraged to continue to preserve our history and landmarks.

While all efforts have been taken to verify the accuracy of the information contained herein, the specificity of some topics do not easily lend to a verification of details from multiple sources. It is with an earnest attempt that the integrity of all tales has been recorded. This book is intended to document the facts and legends of our ancestors lest we forget.

The Legends of Brunswick County

Pirates, Indians and Colonial North Carolina

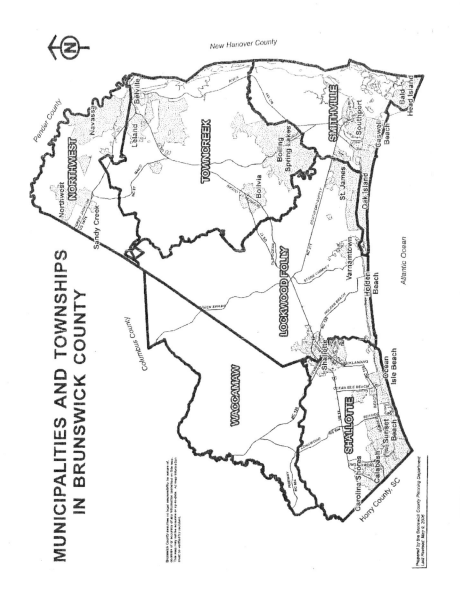

MUNICIPALITIES AND TOWNSHIPS IN BRUNSWICK COUNTY

BRUNSWICK COUNTY, N.C.
2000 CENSUS TRACTS

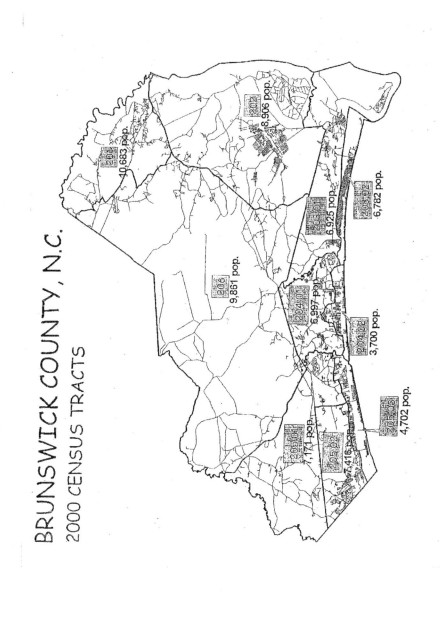

201
10,683 pop.

202
8,906 pop.

203.01
6,925 pop.

203.02
6,782 pop.

206
9,861 pop.

204.01
6,997 pop.

204.02
3,700 pop.

205.03
4,702 pop.

205.01
7,171 pop.

205.02
4,416 pop.

Chapter 1

The Indian Legacy Of Southeastern North Carolina

Brunswick County has a strong heritage in it early inhabitants, the American Indian. To best understand the nature of these original residents, one needs an understanding of the history of the American Indian and how they evolved in culture, habits and life style. The North Carolina Museum of History provides an excellent overview of the American Indian in the United States from the pre-sixteenth century era to the present. Summarizing, we find that: Circa 40,000 to 15,000 B. C., people migrated on the Bering Land Bridge to North America from Asia. By 10,000 – 8,000 B.C. American Indians were nomadic and hunted large animals for food. These people left no evidence of permanent homes in North Carolina. By 8,000 to 1,000 B. C., the nomadic Indians began to change their lifestyle due to climate conditions. They gradually began hunting for smaller animals, fishing for food, and first collected plants for nourishment.

1. By 8,000 B. C., the American Indians left either a permanent or seasonal habitation site in Wilson County, North Carolina. Around 1200 B. C. the southeastern N. C. Indians began growing crops, including squash and other gourds.

2. About 1000 B. C. to about 1550 A.D., the Woodland Culture American Indians settled in permanent

locations, often beside streams. They used hunting, gathering and some agriculture to sustain themselves. They created pottery and developed elaborate funeral procedures to honor their dead. Among those procedures was the practice of building mounds. By 200 B. C. Indians were growing corn.

Around 700-1550 A.D. American Indians began creating populations, groups, called Chiefdoms. They began to construct flat-topped pyramidal mounds to serve as foundations for temples, mortuaries, chief's houses, and other important dwellings. Those Chiefdoms living in North Carolina at this time included the Chowanoke, Croatoan, Hatteras, Moratoc, Secotan, Weapemeoc, Machapunga, Pamlico, Coree, Neuse River, Tuscarora, Meherrin, Cherokee, Cape Fear, Catawba, Shakori, Sissipahaw, Sugeree, Waccamaw, Waxhaw, Woccon, Cheraw, Eno, Keyauwee, Occaneechi, Saponi, and Tutelo tribes.

3. By 1492 A. D. when Italian explorer Christopher Columbus landed in America, the Indians had their first interactions with the Europeans.

4. The Ancient Waccamaw Indians were river dwellers that lived along the Waccamaw River covering an area that reached from North Carolina's Lake Waccamaw to Winyah Bay near Georgetown, South Carolina. They may have been one of the first native groups visited by Europeans as early as 1521. In that year the Spaniards Francisco Gordillo and Pedro de Quexos took several shiploads of Indian people and carried them off into slavery. One became known as *Francisco de Chicora* who identified over twenty tribes living in the Cape Fear and Waccamaw areas. The Waccamaw tribe kept domesticated animals including deer. They made cheese from the does'

milk. They also raised chickens, ducks, geese and other domestic fowl. They were gardeners who kept individual and community plots containing corn, pumpkins, kidney beans, lima beans, squash, melons, gourds, and tobacco.

Europeans introduced disease and nearly eliminated the Waccamaw tribes. The early Europeans also forced the Waccamaw Indians into slave labor. However in 1752 the King of England ordered all owners to free their Indian slaves. This caused the owners to label them "black" in order to maintain the free labor. After the Emancipation Proclamation, thousands of Indians walked away from the cotton fields along with the blacks.

5. By the Sixteenth Century, about 1540, Hernando de Soto, a Spanish explorer, entered the western portions of the present day North Carolina in search of gold. His crews are suspected of introducing smallpox into the Indian population.

   Spanish explorer Juan Pardo, also seeking gold, entered western North Carolina about 1566-67 and visited the Catawba, Wateree, and Saxapahaw Indians.

   Sir Walter Raleigh sent explorers Philip Amadas and Arthur Barlowe into North Carolina in 1584. They met Native American Chief Wingina in the Roanoke area while looking for settlement sites. Two Indians returned to England with Amadas and Barlowe, namely Manteo and Wanchese. These Indians eventually learned English.

   In 1585 Roanoke Island was established and local Indians soon began to see the colonists as a drain on their food supply and resources. In 1586 Sir Francis Drake arrived at Roanoke Island and took most of the colonists back to England. Drake is thought to have left Africans and South American Indians in the area that he had previously captured from the Spanish. A relief ship arrived at Roanoke Island and, finding none of the colonists, left fifteen men to hold the area for England.

By 1587, John White led a new group of settlers to Roanoke. The colonists discovered the bones of the previous 15 men left to hold the area. Even though White and Manteo built a relationship with some of the Roanoke and Croatoan Indians, most of the Indians left the colonists to fen for themselves.

When White returned to the Island, he found the colony deserted. That settlement is now forever known as the *Lost Colony.*

Jamestown leader, John Smith, finds nothing conclusive when he sent expeditions to the Roanoke Island to find the missing settlers. He again found nothing in 1608.

There are those who think that some of the descendents of the Lost Colony currently reside in Brunswick County. (Several informational sources suggest this conclusion, which will be discussed in more detail throughout this manuscript.)

By 1650, more settlers began to arrive along the coast of North Carolina. In 1675 there were reports of Chowanoc Indian attacks on white settlements in the Carolinas. The uprising was quelled with many losses on both sides.

6. By 1709 North Carolina is described by surveyor John Lawson in A New Voyage to Carolina. He describes

4

the flora and fauna and various groups of American Indians living in the state.

7. Reports in 1711 recorded many white deaths by the hands of Indians and the colonists requested assistance from Virginia. They are denied manpower but were sent 1,000 pounds in financial assistance.

About this time more than 130 colonists died in the Tuscarora Wars. Eventually South Carolina colonists assisted the northern North Carolina settlements in their battles with the Tuscarora. After 10 days of fighting, a truce was announced. However, the Indians continued to fight and defend their hunting grounds and resources. Most of them eventually gave up and migrated north by 1715.

8. In 1754, Governor Arthur Dobbs received a report of 50 Indian families living along the present-day Lumber River (then called Drowning Creek).

9. In 1755 there were about 356 Indians living in the eastern portion of North Carolina. Most were the remaining Tuscarora Indians. By 1758 a few Cherokee Indians had attacked the North Carolina colonists.

10. In 1759, the French and Indian Wars raged. At about this time, Typhus and smallpox devastated some Indian tribes such as the Catawba, cutting their population by half.

11. In 1760, the NC Assembly permitted residents to enslave Indian captives. Indians responded with further attacks along the Yadkin and Dan Rivers. By 1761 the British militia destroyed 15 villages ending Cherokee resistance, and by December, the Cherokee

signed a treaty to end the war with the colonists.

12. In 1838, over 17,000 North Carolina Cherokees were forcibly removed from the state and taken to Oklahoma, the state with Indian Territory, on the *Trail of Tears* where over 4,000 Cherokee died during this 1,200-mile trip. Several hundred refused to go and hid in the mountains. This group established the current eastern band of North Carolina Cherokee.

In 1885, the state recognized the Croatan Indians, now known as the Lumbee, as an official tribe. Some believe that the Lumbee are the descendents of the ill-fated settlers from Roanoke Island. The name of the Croatan Indians was changed in 1911 to the Indians of Robeson County. This is later changed to Cherokee Indians of Robeson County in 1913.

Carolina Indian Tales

Natives, that we call the Cape Fear Indians, originally inhabited Brunswick County. We are not sure what they called themselves, but they were probably connected to the Waccamaw and Choctaw Indians. James Sprunt called them the Sapona Indians. Others felt the Sapona Indians were located further north, not as far south as the Cape Fear River areas of Brunswick and New Hanover Counties.

Some of the local coastal Indians were but visitors in the summer months that came to gorge on fish and seafood but remained inland most of the year. The Indians were said to have drunk tea from the Yopon (sic) plant, with its' bright berries and evergreen leaves for the medicinal qualities. These plants are still evident today along the waterways of the creeks and rivers, growing near salt water. (Note: The Yopon (Yaupon) plant contains a high caffeine count.) Some of the southern Indians were said to come in "droves" to gather leaves for their "black drink" made from the Yopon leaves.

This tea caused them to vomit profusely, which they continued for several days in order to cleanse themselves. They then gathered an ample harvest of the leaves and returned to their inland home.

David Bushnell, Jr., noted archaeologist of the early 1900's, believed that the Woccon, Saxapahaw and Cape Fear Indians were all Siouan as noted by their associations with the Sioux Indians. He believed that the population of the southeastern NC Indians may have reached a couple of hundred during that time.

Some of the early Indians called southeastern North Carolina "Chicora". Chicora also extended into Columbus County, NC, and Horry County, SC.

William Hilton Arrives in 1663

William Hilton explored the Cape Fear area and the coast below it. On his second trip to North Carolina, his vessel the *Adventure*, sailed from Barbados on August of 1663. He entered the Charles River, which was later named the Cape Fear. His first expedition to this area found few Indians. His second found more natives, especially in the northeast branch where he stated he saw numerous Indians, as well as their fields and places of habitation. He reportedly met with over forty or more warriors on that trip. He also encountered Indians below the Forks and referred to the two places where they lived as Smith Island and Necoes, an Indian Plantation (which may be the Sachoms Plantation of Shapley's map).

Hilton reported the Indians friendly with only one unpleasant incident noted. According to Lawrence Lee in The History of Brunswick County, North Carolina, "On the Northwest branch a lone Indian shot an arrow at the small boat in which the English were traveling, but the whites found revenge by locating and destroying his hut and other property. At the same time, they found dubious satisfaction in a peace offering of two young Indian women, which were made by *other* Indians of the tribe. Not willing to offend the givers, but unwilling to accept the gift, the English pacified the natives with presents of beads and other trinkets and a promise to return. The ladies were left behind to find happiness among their own people."

One account is noteworthy providing a glimpse into the aboriginal culture of the Cape Fear Indians. Hilton and his crews were examining land from the ship's long boat when a solitary Indian shot an arrow into the ship. The shooter was one of the four Indians previously encountered, just a short time earlier, which had appeared friendly as they bought acorns from him. The Hilton crew was unable to catch the shooter. Several miles downstream, his canoe was tied to the bank. The Hilton crew went to his hut, pulled it down, broke his pots, platters, and spoons, and tore his deerskins and mats in pieces, and took away a basket of "acorns." He was most likely Siouan or perhaps a part of the Waccamaw tribe.

These southeastern North Carolina Indians left behind remnants of their existence, which can be seen today in local museums. The North Carolina Maritime Museum in Southport displays a 2,000-year-old Indian canoe fragment, as well as other treasures from local shipwrecks. These artifacts help preserve the Native American lore of Brunswick County.

The Cape Fear Indians of the 1600's

A Small tribe of Indians lived on the Cape Fear River, possibly Siouan. The settlers called them the Cape Fear Indians, however, it is unknown what they called themselves. Their population was estimated to be around 1000 in the year 1600.

In 1661, an English colony settled near that area and an upheaval soon occurred. The colonists began seizing the Indian children under the pretense of instructing them in the ways of the civilized man. This was a *supposed* attempt at introducing the Indian children to Christianity. In essence, slavery was more likely the correct term to describe what the new settlers were doing. The enslavement of the American Indian was a custom adopted by Europeans and brought much dissension among the whites and Indians. Outraged at the treatment of their people, the Indians turned against the colonists. They used bow and arrows; the English used rifles. Angry, the Indians destroyed the new settlers livestock, a mainstay of their existence and the colonists were soon driven away. The first settlement of Brunswick County had failed. It was not yet time.

In 1663 another group of colonists from Barbadoes purchased lands from the Indian Chief (Wat Coosa), although they abandoned it a few years later. Necoes and other Indian villages continued to exist on the lower part of the river. The village of Necoes was about 20 miles from the mouth of the Cape Fear, probably in Brunswick County.

1700

In 1709, English explorer John Lawson visited the Hatteras Indians, descendents of the Croatan tribe. He wrote that "their ancestors were white people and could talk in a book as we do, the truth of which is confirmed by gray eyes being found infrequently among these Indians and no others." Others surmise that a settlement in southeastern North Carolina near the Pembroke Indians integrated the colonists.

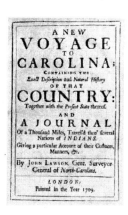

John Lawson wrote the book A New Voyage to Carolina. In it he describes how he first traveled to North Carolina about 1700 and recorded his observations. However, John Lawson was captured by the Tuscarora Indians in the Neuse River area and killed after being tortured, in September of 1711. This fate befell a man who only a few years earlier had written admiringly of the Native Americans, the Indian. They also captured Christopher Von Graffenreid but he was ultimately not killed and lived to record the events in his drawings. John Lawson demonstrated his artistic abilities in the following drawing depicting the animals he saw in the new world.

The Death of John Lawson - Drawing by Christoph Von Graffenried

By 1715 statistics documented only about 206 Cape Fear Indians in five towns along the river. Within a few years the Cape Fear Indians fled the area, never to return. The terror by Indians was replaced by the terror of pirates on the sea.

The Pembrokes (another Indian tribe) spoke pure Anglo-Saxon English and bore the last names of the colonists. Their features were fair eyes, light hair and an Anglo bone structure. The fate of the Lost Colony was still unknown when the *privateers* emerged.

By 1711-12, a few Cape Fear Indians were known to have accompanied Capt. Barnwell on his expedition and were active as scouts who guarded the region around Port Royal. After the Yahasee Wars, they were relocated to South Carolina and settled around Charleston. By the latter part of the 18th century, some of this tribe remained. The Pedee lived in the parishes of St. Stephens and St. Johns under a chief called King John. By 1808, only a half-breed woman remained of these two tribes. Others had been relocated to Catawba.

In 1719, Governor Col. Johnson listed the Indian tribes in Carolina *in the year 1715*, where the population was given as 206 for five total tribes.

By 1751, the South Carolina government described the Iroquois Indians as *peaceful*. It is unknown if the Cape Fear Indians are the same or related to the South Carolina Iroquois tribe, although early references associate them with the Siouan tribes. They may also have been a part of the Waccamaw tribe since the Cape Fear River is so near the Waccamaw River. The Waccamaw Indians ranged across the head of the Waccamaw River. Other possibilities include the Catawba tribes.

A Physical Description

The Indians were physically described by John Lawson, an early explorer, as: "The Indians of North Carolina are a well shaped, clean-made people, of different statures, as the Europeans are, yet chiefly inclined to be tall. They are a straight people, and never bend forward or stoop in the shoulders, unless much overpowered by old age. Their limbs are exceeding well shaped. As for their legs and feet, they are generally the handsomest in the world. Their bodies are a little flat, which is occasioned by being laced hard down to a board in their infancy. Their eyes are black, or of a dark hazel; the white is marbled with red streaks. Their colour is of a tawny, which would not be so dark did they not dawb themselves with bear's oil, and a colour (sic) burnt cork. They are never bald on their heads. Their eyes are commonly full and manly, and their gate sedate and majestic. Their teeth are yellow with smoking (sic), which both men and women are much addicted to. They have no hairs on their faces (except some few) and those but little. They are continually plucking it away from their faces by the roots. They let their nails grow very long, which they reckon, is the use nails are designed for."

Captain William Hilton, during his visit to the Cape Fear in 1662, described the Cape Fear Indians as: "very poor and silly creatures, divers of ym (?) are very aged; but they are not numerous: for in all our various travels for 3 weeks and more, we saw not 100 in all, they were very courteous to us,

12

and afraid of us, but they are very thievish." (Hilton 1662; quoted in Lee 1965:70).

Indian Culture

The Cape Fear Indians lived an existence that combined hunting, fishing and farming. They lived in farm communities in scattered locations. The towns had communal fields that the men planted and the women tended. Their homes were a dome shaped cabin or wigwam, made of a pole frame and covered with bark. The ground was the floor. A hole in the roof permitted smoke from a fire to escape. Some of these homes were located on the south side of the mouth of Town Creek and another known on Smith Island.

The natives grew corn and other vegetables; gathered fruits, nuts, herbs, roots, etc. Summer was for growing. Winter was for hunting.

The Siouan Indians believed in "one supreme God", who had several sub-deities under Him. They believed in Heaven that was an eternal spring and happy hunting ground of plentiful game and food. It was also a place "where women were bright as stars." "In hell, food was not so plentiful, and women were ill-tempered, ugly and had claws like a panther." They believed that if sent to hell, after a period equivalent to the degree of sin and guilt on earth, they were returned to the land to live again, a second chance, a reincarnation of sorts.

Indians had a strict moral code. Lying, cheating and stealing were not acceptable behaviors. Their ill treatment (and immorality) by the settlers led to an eventual desire for revenge. They begin to abuse shipwrecked sailors in a barbarous manner. Many Indians were killed in these attacks and others carried away into slavery by the whites.

y the year 1808, only about 30 Indians were known to be in the Cape Fear area.

Indian Burial Grounds

Of special interest is the location of southeastern North Carolina Indian burial grounds. Several burial grounds are known to exist in the Brunswick County/southeastern Carolina areas, although many have been rampaged and destroyed by vandals over the years. Some of these burial grounds were documented in the Southern Indian Studies project in the early 1960's before the majority of the vandalism occurred and population numbers grew.

Stanley South – Archaeologist

In 1960, Stanley South surveyed several sites in Brunswick and New Hanover Counties in North Carolina, and Horry County in South Carolina. He was interested in the types of pottery and composition identifying three basic series of potteries: Cape Fear, New Hanover, and Oak Island, each comprised of it's own ingredients. Cape Fear was primarily sand temper. Hanover contained crushed sherds, and Oak Island was comprised of shell. Time periods of excavated areas can be established using the composition of the pottery sherds. Excavations of this time period (the 1960's) identified over 300 historical sites ranging from the early Archaic to the Historic period. Stanley South also identified the McFayden Mound in Brunswick County.

The McFayden Mound

In October 1966, Southern Indian Studies, Vol. XVIII, published a study, which described extensive exploratory excavation of the McFayden Mound near Hood Creek and Hooper's Town in Brunswick County. (The Hooper family owned a plantation in this region at one time.) Stanley South, archaeologist at Brunswick Town State Historic Site, wrote a summary after a limited excavation led by him with members of the Lower Cape Fear Chapter of the Archaeological Society

14

of North Carolina, on February 4-5, 1962. They report was pared with the McLean Mound Site report (in the Fayetteville area) to describe their findings. His report stated: "The McFayden mound was pointed out to the Lower Cape Fear Archaeological Society by one of its members, R. V. Asbury, Jr., who secured permission from the owner, Mr. McFayden, for the society to explore the mound as a project." "The mound had been examined previously by Mr. South and Mr. Asbury who excavated a five-foot square, finding a pit with a cremated burial. The mound is located on a natural sand ridge, and can be seen only as a small rise above the surrounding area. The position of the mound can be seen, however, by the presence of a group (of) holes dug over a forty-foot area, around which quantities of human bones can be seen. Only two or three sherds have been found among these bones on the surface."

He describes the human remains located with a detailed description of the site. "The mass of broken bones of Feature 1 were cleaned and found to be fragments of a secondary burial or burials containing parts of two skulls. The jawbones were located several inches away from the skulls, and most bones appeared to have been broken before they were placed in the position in which they were found. Scattered among the bones were a number of flat, shaped shell beads. No articulation of any bones could be discerned. A dark outline could be seen around the bones measuring three feet in diameter. Near the northern edge of this pit, two objects of interest were found. One of these was a fragment of a chlorite schist pipe stem with incised diamonds filled in with parallel lines as a decoration. The other interesting object was a chlorite schist snake head effigy."

South stated that, "This feature was a concentration of burned bone fragments at the north edge of the square. A definite outline of the pit could not be determined, but from the concentration of burned bone fragments, the feature could be plotted. The area was sifted and two triangular projectile

15

points and a fragment were recovered. A total of six sherds have been found at the McFayden Mound. These are sand tempered, thin sherds with a fabric-impressed exterior surface finish, and have been described and named Cape Fear Fabric."

This mound is about forty feet across and has been greatly disturbed by the activity of relic hunters. In most instances the groups of bones were placed on a slight rise in the ground, some placed in a pile and covered with sand. In other places the bones were slightly charred. Piles included the bones, as well as teeth, and had obviously been gathered and placed. Most likely the bones were gathered at various times. The supposed village was probably located in the bottomlands, nearer the streams.

Mr. Stanley South, the original archaeologist who documented the McFayden Mound, described it as located on the peak of a natural hill, rising approximately two feet above the natural level of the ground. The northern five feet of the excavated area is on the outer edge of the mound area, indicating that the mound itself apparently follows the 99.6 contour, generally. The area to the south of the excavated square is badly pitted with deep holes made by relic hunters, so digging here would not be advisable." Mr. South identified three features of this mound, which was composed of concentrations of bones representing secondary burials found at a depth of one foot beneath the surface. The profile revealed a top layer of humus with a layer of gray sand beneath to a depth of half a foot. Beneath this was a six-inch thick layer of white fill sand, and under this light yellow-brown sand were bone fragments.

Hewlett Creek Indian Mounds

Additional mounds are (or were) located on both sides of Hewlett Creek near its mouth, according to James Sprunt in his *Chronicles.* "Numerous signs of Indian occupancy on the north side and rear of the old McKoy houses show traces of an extensive camp and many objects of Indian origin are said to have been found here in past years." Several Indian mounds are described in the Wilmington/Cape Fear area circa 1916. Among them are:

1. "A level area, several acres at the end of Myrtle Sound, is an Indian settlement with pottery fragments plentiful between oyster and clamshells, which are scattered over the surface."

2. "A large shell heap in which pottery fragments occur is several miles northward, on the left band of Barren Inlet Creek, about ½ mile from the sound. There are signs of a large settlement, possibly 4-5 acres, strewn with Indian pottery."

3. "Three miles north of Fort Fisher, less than 100 yards from the beach, are three small mounds about 30 inches high and about 20 feet in diameter."

4. "Sugar Loaf, less than one mile from the previous mounds, in a northwesterly direction, and contains three more small mounds, probably the last Indian settlement in the area." This is the location where the Coree Indians once camped and made forays upon the plantations of Orton and Kendal and who were destroyed by Roger Moore. (1-4, James Sprunt)

Nathan Henry, archaeologist, describes the current status of these mounds.... Near Sugarloaf, as well as all along the Cape Fear River and sound side of New Hanover, there are numerous remnants of shell middens--simply the refuse left by Indians utilizing shellfish resources. These would not be burial mounds per se though occasionally human burials are found within the middens. Any high ground overlooking the sound or river with a nearby fresh water source would have been occupied temporarily at some time--usually many times." So most likely the avid history buff can still see remains of our ancient neighbors.

Bladen County Mounds

In the Weekly Star, Wilmington, NC edition of 26 October 1883, it reports state that several Indian mounds had been identified in nearby Bladen County that may be further explored. These mounds were described as very similar to the *McFayden Mound*, low (about three feet high) and in sandy areas, covered lightly with bones were mounded in one area. Like the McFayden Mounds, they contained lightly charred bones, possibly cremations. Shell beads, 10-12 mm in length were recovered at this site. At least 21 skeletons were identified in a six by six foot square mound. In other burial mounds, only one individual occupied the same size space.

New Hanover County Indian Burial Site

Archaeologists documented the *Cold Morning Indian Burial* site in New Hanover County, NC about 1980. Salvage excavations were carried out. It was dated as a late Woodland occupation with skeletal remains located. Sixteen individuals were removed from this site. These were deemed as aboriginal inhabitants of the southeastern North Carolina coastal region, i.e. Indian burials. In addition to the ossuary, excavations uncovered 823 potsherds, two projective points (arrowheads), 29 flakes, and a few historic period artifacts. Sadly, this site has not been preserved. (Flakes: Stone Age hand tools, usually flint, shaped by flaking off small particles, or by breaking off a large flake which was then used as the tool.)

The Late Woodland period is estimated to be about 1,425 to 1,000 years ago. According to North Carolina archaeologist, Nathan C. Henry, "In southeastern North Carolina the Late Woodland Cultural Tradition is considered to have continued until the Contact Period. The Mississippian Cultural Tradition, elsewhere considered subsequent to Late Woodland, is evident in places like the *Town Creek Indian Mounds*. It never extended much further east than the Yadkin Valley or further north than the Narrows at Badin Lake. Mississippian mounds, though commonly containing human burials, were typically pyramidal in shape, reminiscent of Aztec/Mayan temple pyramids but made from earth instead of stone." "Ossuaries typically contain intact burials. The Mississippian Cultural Tradition was a short-lived phase in NC. The people, probably ancestors of the Creek Nation, were invaders who were disposed by the Siouan residents of the Upper Yadkin shortly before European Contact."

In addition, Mr. Henry says that "Coastal ossuaries in North Carolina commonly contain disarticulated individuals possibly indicating their initial interment in a charnel house that was later burned and the remains reburied. John White documented this practice by the Algonquian Indians of northeast North Carolina. Late Woodland ossuaries in southeastern North Carolina seem to follow this pattern."

Late Woodland settlements, tended to be small as compared with Middle Woodland period settlements. (Remember we are referring to Indian settlements.) Very few outstanding works of prehistoric art or architecture is known from this era.

Bow-and-arrow technology allowed increased hunting skill during this period. This replaced the more archaic spear and atlatl system (type of spear) for hunting game. Also at this time, new varieties of maize, beans and squash were introduced since game was easier to acquire in larger quantities. The populations increased and became more dependent upon agricultural production.

Henry described the Woodland Period, "The bow and arrow was probably invented at the beginning of the Woodland Period. Bow and arrows, the invention of ceramic pottery, and beginning agriculture practices mark the transition from the Archaic Period to the Woodland Period (about 3000 years ago). I know of no evidence to support a reduction in the group size from the mid-Woodland to the Late Woodland. In contrast, the increased usage of agriculture allowed for more dense populations within a given area, at least during the harvest time. Keep in mind, Indian groups were very fluid, linked by language and family, and their size and location dictated by resource availability. Here in the east, organized systems for food storage and allocation simply did not exist. Mobility was key for survival. Settlement, at least in the European sense, did not exist."

During the Late Woodland era (about 1,400 to 900 years ago), in the Carolinas, sand burial mounds were still used. They are differentiated from the early Middle Woodland periods based upon the tempering and surface treatment and pottery styles. Archaeologist Nathan Henry describes a simplified chronology of pottery types or "series" in southeastern North Carolina.

1. Thoms Creek and New River series, sand/quartz temper, Early Woodland

2. Hamps Landing series, limestone tempered, Early-Mid Woodland

3. Hanover series, clay tempered, Mid-Late Woodland

4. Cape Fear series, sand tempered, Late Woodland

5. White Oak series, shell tempered, Late Woodland (no further south than Pender/ New Hanover line).

(Many longtime Brunswick County residents relate stories about grandfathers and great-grandfathers finding sherds of pottery while plowing the fields during the colonial and mid 1800 eras. Families with these historic remnants are encouraged to preserve these artifacts through proper storage and display. Contact your local historical society or museum for details on proper handling.)

Indian Attacks

During the Yamassee War, Indians attacked Indians in the Cape Fear region, and also attacked the militia led by Col. Maurice Moore. Captives taken by Col. Moore marked the exodus by other local Indians. Settlers felt the wrath of the Indians in attacks by the Tuscarora, until they (the Indians) fled to more southerly settlements. Meredith, 1730, stated that "there is not an Indian to be seen in this place; the Senekas--- with their Tributaries, the Susquehannah, and Tuskarora Indians having almost destroyed those called Cape Fear Indians, and the small remains of them abide among the thickest of the South Carolina inhabitants, not daring to appear near the out settlements, for the very name of a Seneka is terrible to them."

Other accounts describe Col. Moore and Col. Barnwell from Charles Towne, SC, enlisting the aid of the Yamasee to defeat the Tuscarora and eventually to end the Tuscarora War (1711-1714). Two separate marches took him through the Cape Fear area and it is thought that the idea to settle in the region was born during these marches. The first permanent settlement came in 1725 by Maurice Moore in Brunswick Town. (See Section Two for more details about this settlement.)

It is not known exactly what happened to the Cape Fear Indians. There were still some around after the permanent English settlement at Brunswick Town. We do know that Col Moore's brother, Roger, mounted an attack on a group of Indians at Sugarloaf and massacred all of them. Roger Moore had built the Orton Plantation and Indians were thought to have burned the first Orton Plantation house, hence his vengeance battle.

Indian Legends and Relics

Rumor and legend has it that there are remnants of an old Indian burial ground, and/or Indian Village near the Gore Creek area in Brunswick County. Local residents there recall elderly parents, now deceased (in 2007), as they talked of the locals looting some of the relics from that area many years ago. It is estimated that those remains were discovered about one hundred years ago, during hunting trips, and have since deteriorated to an undetectable state. Living descendents of those hunters are uncertain of the exact location and speculate that any remaining evidence of the grounds may have been obliterated during logging operations throughout the years. One individual recalls a grandfather describing the remains of teepee poles, indicating a village site. This may have been the home of the nearby Waccamaw Indians. Suspected locations are noted between Gore Lake and the Waccamaw River. Sources of this information include Joyce Jacobs, and Ms. Esther, presently eighty-years young as she discussed her father's descriptions of the teepee. Miss Esther recalls seeing those Indian relics as a small child. Another cousin remembers when "the bays were just grass and there were waters called 'Indian Grave Lakes' which are no longer present. Georgia Pacific owns most of the bay area where that was...and it has long ago been ditched, burned, chopped and set in trees." That same area is the final resting place of a white man; he drowned and was quickly buried with little fanfare. An accident?

Another Indian burial ground is reportedly located west of the Gause Landing Road area, off highway 179 in the Ocean Isle Beach area. As a young woman, Mrs. Mary Piggot, now 80 years old, recalls visiting the site with her husband. Sixty-two years ago, about 1946, this site was only known through its wooden stakes, barely recognizable and through cultural lore known to have been an Indian burial ground. Although Mrs. Piggot now states she is unsure whether she "dreamed this or not", one can only imagine a young girl and her husband out for a leisurely walk, visiting local landscapes like this burial ground. Her memory is clear about her survival during Hurricane Hazel and numerous other storms as they passed though hurricane alley, southeastern North Carolina.

Two additional Indian burial locations are identified as being in the Silver Hill area, off Holden Beach Road, where reportedly Chicora Indians had a burial mound, long since destroyed by vandals. In recent times, as late as twenty years ago, vandals destroyed what was left of this sacred ground. The Old Hewett Farm, off Highway 130, midway between Shallotte and Holden Beach, holds the remains of pottery sherds, attributed to Indians of the area. As late as the late 1900's, sherds were recovered lying atop the ground. A burial ground? Perhaps. And it is likely an Indian occupation.

An Indian burial ground is reported to be located just off highway 211 just past the Lockwood Folly River Bridge. Although unidentified and not yet located, this is a probably location, on the river, for former Indian villages and burial grounds. More research is needed in order to locate this site.

Not far from this Holden Beach area, Woody Fulford talks of a time when his father, Isaiah Fulford (born in 1906 and died in 2001 at the age of 94 years young), told him tales of finding Indian arrowheads and Indian pottery sherds on their family land. On what was to become Tuscarora Lane and Cherokee Road, near the current causeway of Holden Beach, Isaih was laid near a palm tree while his father, Dave Fulford (who married Mary Hewett) plowed the fields to ready them for planting. Arrowheads and pottery pieces were uncovered and "thought" to be from a former Indian settlement at that very location. Woody and his father, Isaih, decided to call the area Tuscarora. Although Woody readily admits that they weren't sure of the specific tribe of the former Indian residents, this is the designation given to that historic location.

Dave and Mary Hewett Fulford subsequently had thirteen children, not uncommon for an era when plenty of farm hands were needed in order to survive. Three of those children remain in the Holden Beach area today (2007); Aunt Lydia Ann Fulford Hewett, Aunt Bessie Fulford Robinson, and Aunt Della Fulford Pickett living in the old Cotton Patch area, now known as Shallotte Point. All three children are now over 90 years old.

Indian relics have been found throughout Brunswick County. A polished stone, fully grooved, Indian ax was reportedly found at Long Beach and is on display at the NC Museum of History. Ash residents report various areas where numerous arrowhead points have been located during farming operations. This and many similar tales attest to the historic legacy of the Indians in southeastern North Carolina, and especially Brunswick County.

While multiple burial locations are noted, most seem to appear to be the same type of structures, little more than three feet high and circular from 20 to 40 feet in diameter. It appears that the bodies were placed on the ground and covered lightly with surrounding sand and dirt, with no additional items placed with the body. It is also reported that in many cases, charcoal has been found at the mounds. Some bones appeared to have been burned. In many cases the skeletons were found very near and often touching each other, some even on top of each other. (Descriptions of Duplin County Indian Mounds.) God rest their souls.

Indian Trails

The Indian Trail Tree in Keziah Memorial Park, in Southport, is estimated to be over 800 years old and was used by the Cape Fear area Indians. Its rich history is a delight for all visitors who can walk on the same ground as our Indian predecessors. While many stories relate the historic remains from cultures long past across Brunswick County, little remains to substantiate those who lived before us in southeastern North Carolina. Along with those few relics, the coastal folklore and legends may be all that can document the earliest Brunswick County residents, the American Indian.

Indian Pottery in Sunset Harbor

The following piece of historic Indian Pottery was found at the present location of the Sunset Harbor Fishing Club when the building was built and foundations dug. Additional pieces are also known to exist and date from 400 B. C. to 1000 A. D. "This is an example of fabric-impressed Hanover Series, mid to late Woodland Period pottery. Hanover series pottery is fairly easy to identify because of the temper, which is made of crushed, fired clay. If you look closely you will see the fragments in the paste. Hanover series pottery is typically fabric impressed over the entire outer surface and a lot of times on the interior, just around the rim. This piece probably came from near the rim. Less eroded pieces appear to have a sort of slip on the interior surface--like the makers took mud slurry and washed it around in the vessel prior to firing. Hanover Series is a fairly common type of prehistoric ceramic in coastal North Carolina, its spatial distribution extending from the Neuse River into South Carolina. At this time it is questionable as to whether the type (representing a cultural group) existed as late as European contact." (Nathan Henry, Assistant State Archaeologist and Conservator, Underwater Archaeology Branch NC Office of State Archaeology). This means over 400 years before Christopher Columbus even set foot on our great American land, an Indian fashioned and used this remnant. Amazing.....

Indian Pottery, C. 400 B. C. – 1000 A. D.

Chapter 2

Pre Colonial Exploration And Early Settlements

Over 150 years after Vasquex de Ayllon first explored New Hanover County (in 1526), Captain Hilton and his colonists, escaping the cold weather of the northern Massachusetts Bay areas, named the "Cape Fear" and settled there. They reportedly left abruptly, leaving a message attached to a post at the point of the cape warning others to stay away. No one is sure what the "fear" was or why they left. In 1664 another group of settlers came to the area but this settlement was doomed to failure also and by 1667, that settlement was abandoned. "Hilton, himself, never "settled" in the Cape Fear. Hilton was contracted by the Massachusetts Bay Company to explore the region in order to find a suitable settlement location. After the Massachusetts Bay colony departed from the area, Hilton was contracted by a group of Barbadians, for the same purpose, whose settlement centered at the mouth of Town Creek (Old Town). Hilton made a more complete survey of the Charles River and indeed named many of the places along the river that still bear his names." (Nathan Henry)

Note: During the Cape Fear visit of Vasquex de Ayllon, a ship was wrecked and the group paused long enough to build another vessel…. perhaps the first one built in the new world.

They eventually settled about 100 miles south, but ended the settlement due to cold, disease and hunger during the first winter, about 1526.)

By 1665, the Old Town Colony was established in Brunswick County on the south side of the river. The colonists bought land from the friendly Indians. Captain William Hilton visited this colony in 1663. However, they, too, soon abandoned this location.

The Original Colonies in 1524

North Carolina was one of the original 13 colonies. Settlers were busy establishing new homes just 34 years after Columbus discovered America, each facing new challenges, fears, and adventures. However, their settlement was a result of many unsuccessful ventures by pioneers from several countries. Among those investigating the new world were French, English, Italian and Spanish explorers.

The first European to land on Brunswick County soil was an Italian in 1524. Giovanni Verrazano was sailing for the King of France and landed in what would become southern New Hanover and northern Brunswick County. The Indians referred to this land as "Chicora". Explorers later named it Brunswick County.

Giovanni Verrazano

Verrazano described the area as "open country rising in height above the sandy shore with many fair fields and plains, full of might great woods, some very thick, and some thin, replenished with diverse sorts of trees, as pleasant and delectable to behold, as is possible to imagine." He saw the beaches, higher country and fields where he encountered the Indians who were somewhat larger than the Europeans; clothed in animal skins and feathers.

He was said to have named the present Cape Fear River the Rio Jordan, but did not settle in the area. Instead he took a brief look and continued traveling into South Carolina. Shore expeditions encountered friendly natives but northern winds made mooring unsafe so the crews sailed further south.

Map drawn by Juan Vespucci

In 1526, Juan Vespucci, a nephew of Amerigo Vespucci, sailed into the Cape Fear and was also said to have named the river the Rio Jordan. It is unclear if he or Giovanno gave this title to the Cape Fear River but maps attested to the same location and river. By this time about six hundred settlers arrived from the Dominican Republic and faced many tribulations as they began their new lives. By October of that year, over 300 had died. Other colonists remained only a few months longer and then moved to Winyaw Bay, South Carolina.

Juan Vespucci drew several maps of the world and America. He left his legacy through his exploratory adventures.

By 1561, King Phillip II of Spain declared no further plans to colonize the Cape Fear, or "Florida" as the territory (the entire east coast) was then known. Their spirits remain to remind us of their adventures as they battled pestilence, disease and basic survival. Their first attempts at colonization have not been forgotten.

The Lost Colony & Other Early Colonists

Sent by Walter Raleigh in 1584, explorers Philip Amadas and Arthur Barlowe visited Roanoke Island. Barlowe wrote inviting reports about the area which sparked the interest of the citizens of London. The following year,

Raleigh sent a party of 100 soldiers, miners and scientists to Roanoke Island.

Sir Walter Raleigh   *Christopher Columbus*

About 1585, the English attempted their first colony on Roanoke Island, north of Brunswick County in northern North Carolina but it failed also. Ralph Lane brought the first group to Roanoke but arrived too late for the seasonal planting, and supplies were dwindling rapidly. He alienated the local Indians and ultimately murdered their Chief Wingina. This did not set a peaceful precedent for further development in the area.

In 1586 Sir Francis Drake stopped at Roanoke. Lane and his men had abandoned the settlement and left behind a fort, although it has never been located. Ironically, less than a week later two supply ships from England arrived. They found the island deserted except for the fifteen men that the second ship had left to man the fort. These ships returned to England.

31

Raleigh then recruited 117 men, women and children to form a more permanent settlement and appointed John White governor of the new "Cittie of Raleigh". They arrived on Roanoke Island in July of 1587 and soon learned that the Indians had murdered the fifteen men who preceded them.

On the 18th of August 1587, Eleanor Dare gave birth to the first child born in American, Virginia Dare. Ten days later John White left with Ferndades for England to seek more supplies. It was the last time White would see his own family. On August 18, 1590 when he returned, he found the settlement deserted and plundered. On one of the palisades he found the word "Croatoan" carved into the surface and the letters CRO carved into a nearby tree.

White had arranged a signal with the colonists. Any carvings would signify the place where the settlers would go should they be forced to leave the area. If they were to leave under duress, they were to carve a Maltese cross above their destination. No such cross was found. He hoped the colonists and his family would be at Croatoan, the home of Chief Manteo's tribe, south of the present-day Hatteras Island. However, a large hurricane hit the area, damaging his ships and forcing him back to England before he could locate the group. He was never able to return to America again. The 117 pioneers of Roanoke Island had vanished.

Recently, scholars have discovered records in the Spanish and British archives that document White's departure from Roanoke in 1587. After that time the colonists split into two factions, the largest segment heading for the Chesapeake Bay area, with maps provided by White himself.

Spanish archives document the colonists "gone" by 1588 when a "raiding party" found the settlement deserted. Some assume they were assimilated into the Croatoan tribe.

When John Smith and the Jamestown colonists arrived in 1607, Smith searched for the colonists who had previously settled at Roanoke but his efforts proved futile.

The local hostile Indian Chief Powhatan claimed the colonists had lived among them for a time and most were murdered. He sported several weapons to prove his words.

By 1612, the Jamestown leaders had searched the area several times following up on reports hoping that at least some Roanoke colonists remained in the area. None were found.

In June 2007, the Houston Chronicle reported that researchers believe that they may be able to use DNA to discover the fate of the individuals of the Lost Colony. They plan to use genealogy, deeds, and historical narratives to trace the roots of 168 surnames and Indian descendents in hopes of determining the fate of the colonists.

The mysterious fate of Roanoke is unknown. It is but one of the towns established and faded from North Carolina history. However, rumors abound regarding the Green Swamp residents of Brunswick County, the uncharacteristic English accent of some coastal residents and their links to the Roanoke Island settlers. Within the Lost Colony records is a Thomas Hewett, a common surname of local Brunswick County residents. The stories of *Roe Noakers* and the heavy British accent is still related in some areas of the county, especially in the Green Swamp communities. Could part of the colony have moved southward into the coastal areas of Brunswick County and the Cape Fear? Local residents think so.

The Roe Noakers

Close to where President Cleveland stopped in a train trip through the northern part of Brunswick County, just a few miles away, is the Green Swamp. Here, amid a unique settlement, usually pronounced "Battle Rial", or "batterial" was *Battle Royal*. About 1890 this was a great and deep-forested area, with a little clearing where the *Over Creek People* lived. Young boys and girls acted old and looked old. This settlement was believed to have been in existence long before Brunswick County or North Carolina even existed.

There was said to be a heavy Elizabethan influence in their speech and their background was not a matter of the written record. A Battle Rial native himself described his people's history, "that generation after generation of his family had passed down the word that they were **Roe Noakers**, from an island in the sea." This section of Brunswick County has become known as Malmo, a few miles east of Maco. Were these the descendents of the "lost colony", off Roanoke Island?

The complete list of surnames of the 1587 Colonists includes:

Men

John White (Governor)
Ananias Dare (Assistant)
(Assistant)
Thomas Stevens (Assistant)
Dyonis Harvie (Assistant)
George Howe (Assistant)
Thomas Warner
John Jones
Ambrose Viccars
Thomas Topan
Richard Berrye
John Hemmington
Edward Powell
James Hynde
William Browne
Thomas Smith
Thomas Harris
John Earnest
John Starte
William Lucas
John Wright
Morris Allen
Richard Arthur
William Clement
Hugh Tayler
Lewes Wotton
Henry Browne
Richard Tomkins
Charles Florrie

Roger Bailie (Assistant)
Christopher Cooper

John Sampson (Assistant)
Roger Prat (Assistant)
Nicholas Johnson
Anthony Cage
John Tydway
Edmond English
Henry Berrye
John Spendlove
Thomas Butler
John Burden
Thomas Ellis
Michael Myllet
Richard Kemme
Richard Taverner
Henry Johnson
Richard Darige
Arnold Archard
William Dutton
William Waters
John Chapman
Robert Little
Richard Wildye
Michael Bishop
Henry Rufoote
Henry Dorrell
Henry Mylton

Henry Payne
William Nicholes
John Borden
William Willes
Cutbert White
Clement Tayler
John Cotsmur
Thomas Colman
Marke Bennet
John Stilman
Peter Little
Brian Wyles
Hugh Pattenson
John Farre
Griffen Jones
James Lasie
Thomas Hewet

Thomas Harris
Thomas Phevens
Thomas Scot
John Brooke
John Bright
William Sole
Humfrey Newton
Thomas Gramme
John Gibbes
Robert Wilkinson
John Wyles
George Martyn
Martyn Sutton
John Bridger
Richard Shaberdge
John Cheven
William Berde

Women
Elyoner Dare
Agnes Wood
Joyce Archard
Elizabaeth Glane
Audry Tappan
Emme Merrimoth
Margaret Lawrence
Jane Mannering
Elizabeth Viccars

Margery Harvie
Wenefrid Powell
Jane Jones
Jane Pierce
Alis Chapman
------ Colman
Joan Warren
Rose Payne

Children
John Sampson
Ambrose Viccars
Thomas Humfrey
George Howe
William Wythers

Robert Ellis
Thamas Archard
Thomas Smart
John Prat

Born in Virginia
Virginia Dare

---- Harvye

Brunswick County natives will recognize several of these surnames as very prominent in local history as well as residents of Robeson County. Brunswick and Robeson County may indeed share the legacy for the descendents of the Lost Colony.

The National Park Service has also created a list of early settlers and ship crewmen. They list the reconnaissance crews, sailors and settlers with known participation dates.

The 1584 Reconnaissance

Master Philip Amadas, Captain Captain

William Greeneville

James Browewich

Benjamin Wood

Nicholas Petman

Granganimeo, King's brother

Manteo

Master Arthur Barlowe,

John Wood

Henrie Greene

Simon Ferdinando

John Hewes

Wingina, King

Wanchese

The 1585-6 Colonists

(old spellings) Master Ralfe Lane
Master Philip Amades, Admiral of the country

Master Thomas Hariot

Master Edward Stafford

Master Maruyn

Captain Vaughan

Master Prideox

Rise Courtenay

Thomas Foxe

Darby Glande

Iohn Gostigo

Edward Ketcheman

Thomas Rottenbury

Iohn Harris

Mathewe Lyne

Thomas Wisse

William Backhouse

Henry Potkin

Ioseph Borges

Master Acton

Thomas Luddington

Master Gardyner

Master Kendall

Robert Holecroft

Master Hugh Rogers

Edward Nugen

Edward Kelle

Erasmus Clefs

Iohn Linsey

Roger Deane

Frauncis Norris

Edward Kettell

Robert Biscombe

William White

Dennis Barnes

Doughan Gannes
(Joachi Gan)

Randall Latham

Walter Myll

Steuen Pomarie

Iohn Brocke

Iames Stevenson

Thomas Hulme

Richard Gilbert

Charles Stevenson

Bennet Harrye

Christopher Lowde
Iames Mason
Richard Ireland
William Philippes
Master Anthony Russe
Master Michel Polyson
Thomas Parre
Geffery Churchman
Iohn Taylor
Thomas Phillippes
Iames Skinner
John Chaundeler
Richard Poore
Marmaduke Constable
William Wasse
Daniel
Richard Humfrey
Gabriell North
Richard Sare
Smolkin
Robert
Roger Large
Frauncis Whitton
William Millard
Edwarde Seklemore
Christopher Marshall
Nicholas Swabber
Syluester Beching
Haunce Walters
Thomas Skeuelabs

Ieremie Man
Dauvid Salter
Thomas Bookener
Master Snelling
Master Allyne
Iohn Cage
William Randes
William Farthowe
Philppe Robyns
Valentine Beale
George Eseuen
Philip Blunt
Robert Yong
Thomas Hesket
Iohn Feuer
Thomas Taylor
Iohn Wright
Bennet Chappell
Iames Lasie
Thomas Smart
Iohn Evans
Humfrey Garden
Rowland Griffyn
Iohn Twyt (John White?)
Iohn Anwike
Dauid Williams
Edward Chipping
Vincent Cheyne
Edward Barecombe
William Walters

Alphabetized list of all personnel 1584-1590

Includes those on ship crews and organizers in Europe. **The names of colonists are in bold letters.**

> **Acton, Master [John]**, 1585-1586
> **Allen, (Allyne), Master [Thomas?]**, 1585-1586
> **Allen, Morris**, 1587
> **Amadas, Master Philip (Captain)**, 1584, 1585-1586
> Annes, [?], 1586

Anwike, John, 1586-1586
Archard, Arnold, 1587
Archard, Joyce, 1587
Archard, Thomas (boy), 1587
Ardle, [?], 1586
Arthur, Richard, 1587
Arundell, John, 1585
Atkinson, Master, 1585
Aubry, Captain, 1585
Backhouse, William, 1585-1586
Baily, Roger, 1587, 1589
Baily, Captain Walter, 1586
Barecombe, Edward, 1585-1586
Barlowe, Master Arthur (Captain), 1584, 1585
Barnes, Dennis, 1585-1586
Barton, Captain George, 1586
Bayly, Thomas, 1586
Bayly, Walter, 1589
Beale, Valentine, 1585-1586
Beching, Sylvester, 1585-1586
Bedford, John, 1590
Bennet, Marke, 1587
Berde (Baird?), William, 1587
Berrye, Henry, 1590
Berrye, Richard, 1587
Bevis, Thomas, 1590Biscombe, Robert, 1585-1586
Bishop, Michaek, 1587
Bitfield, Captain, 1586
Blunt, Philip, 1585-1586
Boazio, Baptista 1586
Boniten, (Bonython?) Captain 1585
Bookener, (Buckner?) Thomas 1585-1586
Borden, John 1587
Borges, Joseph 1585-1586
Bragge, Robert [1585?]
Bremige, (Browewich or Bromwich?) Master (James?) 1585
Bridger, John 1587
Bright, John 1587
Brocke, John 1585-1586
Brooke, Francis 1585
Brooke, John 1587
Bromwich, See also Bremige.
Browewich, James 1584. See also Bremige.
Browne, Henry 1587
Browne, Henry (1585?)

Browne, William 1587
Burden, John 1587
Burke, [?] 1586
Butler, Richard (1584-1585?)
Butler, Thomas 1587
Cage, Anthony 1587
Cage, John 1585-1586
Careless, (Wright) Captain Edward 1586. See also Wright.
Carleill, Captain Christopher 1586
Cates, Lt. Thomas 1586
Cavendish, Thomas 1585
Cely, Captain Thomas 1586
Chamberlain, [?] 1586
Chandeler, John 1585-1586
Chapman, (adult male) 1585-1586
Chapman, Alis 1587
Chapman, John 1587
Chappell, Bennett 1585-1586
Cheven, (Cheyne?) John 1587
Cheyne, Vincent 1585-1586
Chipping, Edward 1585-1586
Churchman, Geffery 1585-1586
Clarke, John 1585
Clefs, Erasmus 1585-1586
Clement, William 1587
Cocke, Abraham 1590
Coffar, (Coffin?) (adult male) 1586
Coleman, Robert 1590
Colman, (adult female) 1587
Colman, Thomas 1587
Constable, Marmaduke 1585-1586
Cooper, Christopher 1587 1589
Cotsmur, John 1587
Courtney, Rise 1585-1586
Croftes, Lt. [?] 1586
Crosse, Captain Robert 1586
[?] Daniel, 1585-1586. See also Hochstetter.
Dare, Ananias 1587 1589
Dare, Elinor 1587
Dare, Virginia (child born on Roanoke Island) 1587
Darige, Richard 1587
Davell, William 1590
Deane, Roger 1585-1586
Diaz ,Franco (or Pimienta) Pedro 1586
Dimmocke, Humfrey 1589

Dorrell, Henry 1587
Drake, Sir Francis 1586
Drake, Captain Thomas 1586
Dutton, William 1587
Earnest, John 1587
Ellis, Robert (boy) 1587
Ellis, Thomas 1587
English, Edmond 1587
Erisey, Captain James 1586
Eseven, George 1585-1586
Evans, John 1585-1586
Facy, Arthur (Captain) 1586 1588
Facy, John 1586 1590
Farre, John 1587
Farthowe, William 1585-1586
Fenner, Captain Thomas 1586
Fernandez, Simon 1584 1585 1587
Fever, John 1585-1586
Fleetwood, Henry 1589
Florrie, Charles 1587
Foxe, Thomas 1585-1586
Frobisher, Captain Martin 1586
Fullwood, William 1587
Gamage, William 1589
Ganz, Joachim 1585-1586. See also Yougham.
Garden, Humfrey 1585-1586
Gardiner, Master 1585-1586

Gates, Sir Thomas 1585
George, William 1589
Gerrard, John 1589
Gibbes, John 1587
Gilbert, Richard 1585-1586
Gilman, Captain Edward 1586
Glande, Darby 1585-1586
Glane, Elizabeth 1587
Gorges, Edward 1585 1586
Goring, Captain John 1586
Gostigo, John 1585-1586
Gramme, Thomas 1587
Grant, John 1586
Greene, Henrie 1584
Grenville, Sir Richard 1585 1586
Grenville, William 1584
Griffyn, Rowland 1585-1586

40

Hakluyt, Richard 1587 1589
Hampton,John 1586
Hance, (adult male surgeon?) 1590. See also Walters Haunce.
Harden, Thomas 1590
Harding, Hugh 1589
Harding, Thomas 1589
Harrie, Bennet 1585-1586
Harriot, Thomas 1585-1586
Harris, Gabriel 1589
Harris, John 1585-1586
Harris, Thomas 1587 (name appears twice)
Harvye, [?] (child born on Roanoke Island) 1587
Harvye, Dionyse 1587 1589
Harvye, Margery 1587
Harvie, Master Thomas 1585-1586
Hawkins, Captain Richard 1586
Hawkins, Captain William Jr. 1586
Hemmington, John 1587
Henley, [?] 1586
Herne, Griffith 1586
Hesket, Thomas 1585-1586
Hewes, John 1584
Hewet, Thomas 1587
Hochsetter?, Daniel 1585-1586
Holecroft, Robert 1585-1586
Hoode, Thomas 1589
Howe, George 1587
Howe, George (boy) 1587
Hulme, Thomas 1585-1586
Humfrey, Richard 1585-1586
Humfrey, Thomas (boy) 1587
Hutton, Robert 1590
Hynde, James 1587
Ireland, Richard 1585-1586
Irish, Captain William 1587 [1590?]
Johnson, Henry 1587
Johnson, Nicholas 1587
Jonas, [?] 1586
Jones, Griffen 1587
Jones, Jane 1587
Jones, John 1587
Kelborne, Edward 1590
Kelley, Edward 1585-1586
Kelley, Edward 1590
Kemme, Richard 1587

Kendall,Abraham 1586
Kendall, Master 1585-1586
Ketcheman, Edward 1585-1586
Ketill, Lt. [?] 1586
Kettell, Edward 1585-1586
Knollys, Captain Francis 1586
Lacy, James 1585-1586
Lacy, James 1587
Lane, Ralfe 1585-1586
Lane, Captain William 1586
Large, Roger 1585-1586
Large, Roger 1587
Latham, Randall 1585-1586
Laurentson, Martin 1585
Lawrence, Margaret 1587
Linsey, John 1585-1586
Little, Peter 1587
Little, Robert 1587
Longe, [?] 1586
Lowde, Christopher 1585-1586
Lucas, William 1587
Luddington, Thomas 1585-1586
Lyne, Mathewe 1585-1586
Macklyn, Robert 1589
Man, Jeremie 1585-1586
Mannering, Jane 1587
Marchant, Captain John 1586
Marler, Walter 1589
Marshall, Christopher 1585-1586
Martin, Captain John 1586
Martin, Thomas 1589
Martyn, George 1587
Marvyn, Master 1585-1586
Mason, James 1585-1586
Masters, Robert 1585
Matthew, John 1587
Mayne, Randall 1585-1586
Merrimoth, Emme 1587
Mill, Walter 1585-1586
Millard, William 1585-1586
Millett, Henry 1590
Morgan, Captain Mathew 1586
Myllet, Michael 1587
Mylton, Henry 1587
Nevil, Edmund 1589

Newsome, John 1586
Newton, Humfrey 1587
Nicholes, William 1587
Nicholls, Philip 1586
Nichols, John 1587
Nichols, John 1589
Norris, Frauncis 1585-1586
North, Gabriell 1585-1586
Nugent, Edward 1585-1586
Parre, Thomas 1585-1586
Pattenson, Hugh 1587
Payne, Henry 1587
Payne, Rose 1587
Petman, Nicholas 1584
Pew, Captain Robert 1586
Phevens, Thomas 1587
Philips, Thomas 1585-1586
Philips, William 1585-1586
Pierce, Jane 1587
Plat, James 1587
Platt, Captain Anthony 1586
Polison, Michael 1585-1586
Pomarie, Steven 1585-1586
Poore, Richard 1585-1586
Potkin, Henry 1585-1586
Powell, Edward 1586
Powell, Edward 1587
Powell, Wenefrid 1587
Prat, John (boy) 1587
Prat, Roger 1587 1589
Prideauz, Master [Richard?] 1585-1586
Ralegh, Sir Walter 1584 1585 1586 1587 1588 1589 1590
Randes, William 1585-1586
Raymond, Captain George 1585
Rivers, Captain John 1586
[?], Robert 1585-1586
Robyns, Philppe 1585-1586
Rogers, Master Hugh 1585-1586
Rottenbury, Thomas 1585-1586
Rowse, Master Anthony 1585-1586
Rufoote, Henry 1587
Russell, Master [Gregory or Rowland?] 1585
Salter, David 1585-1586
Sampson, John 1587 1589
Sampson, John (boy) 1587

Sampson, Captain John 1586
Sanderson, William 1589 1590
Sare, Richard 1585-1586
Scot, Thomas 1587
Seklemore, Edwarde 1585-1586
Shaberdge, Richard 1587
Skevetabs, Thomas 1585-1586
Skinner, James 1585-1586
Skinner, Ralph 1590
Smart, Thomas 1585-1586
Smart, Thomas (boy) 1587
Smith, Thomas 1587 (name appears twice)
Smolkin, [?] 1585-1586
Smythe, Thomas 1589
Snelling, Master 1585-1586
Sole, William 1587
Sparrow, Philip 1586
Spendlove, John 1587
Spicer, Edward 1590
Stafford, Edward 1585-1586 1587
Stanton, Richard 1586
Starte, John 1587
Stevens, Thomas 1587 1589
Stevenson, Charles 1585-1586
Stevenson, James 1585-1586
Stilman, John 1587
Stone, William 1589
Stukely, John 1585
[Stuteville, Sir Martin] 1586
Sutton, Martyn 1587
Swabber, Nicholas 1585-1586
Swanne, Henry 1590
Tappan, Audry 1587. See also Topan.
Taverner, Richard 1587
Tayler, Clement 1587
Tayler, Hugh 1587
Taylor, John 1585-1586
Taylor, John 1590
Taylor, Thomas 1585-1586
Tenche, William 1585-1586
Thorowgood, [?] 1586
Tomkins, Richard 1587
Topan, Thomas 1587. See also Tappan.
Twyt, John 1585-1586 [Possibly John White?]
Tydway, John 1587

44

Vaughan, **Captain** 1585-1586

Vaughan, **Captain John** 1586

Viccars, **Ambrose** 1587

Viccars, **Ambrose (boy)** 1587

Viccars, **Elizabeth** 1587

Vincent, [Thomas?] 1585

Wade, Thomas 1589

Walden, Edmund 1589

Walsingham, Sir Francis 1585

Walters, Haunce 1585-1586. See also Hance.

Walters, William 1585-1586

Warner, Thomas 1587

Warren, Joan 1587

Wasse, William 1585-1586. See also Wisse.

Waters, William 1587

Whiddon, Jacob (1585?)

White, Cutbert 1587

White, John [1584?] 1585 1587 1588 1589 1590

White, William 1585-1586

Whitton, Frauncis 1585-1586

Whyte, Captain Henry 1586

Wildye, Richard 1587

Wilkinson, Robert 1587

Willes, William 1587

Wilson, Captain John 1586

Wisse, Thomas 1585-1586. See also Wasse.

Willett, Richard [1586?]

Williams, David 1585-1586

Willis, [?] 1586

Wood, Agnes 1587

Wood, Benjamin 1584

Wood, John 1584

Wooten, Lewes 1587

Wright, (Careless) Captain Edward 1586. See also Careless.

Wright, John 1585-1586

Wright, John 1587

Wright, Richard 1589

Wyles, Brian 1587

Wyles, John 1587

Wynter, Captain Edward 1586

Wythers, William (boy) 1587

Yougham, Master 1585-1586. See also Ganz.

Yong, Robert 1585-1586

INDIAN IN BODY PAINT (no. 52A, cf. pls. 83 (a), 123 (b))

John White was quite the artist and drew the *Indian in Body Paint* watercolor artwork in 1585. He was the grandfather of Virginia Dare, the first child born in the New World. Virginia would have celebrated her 420th birthday in 2007.

Naming The Cape Fear River

In 1606, maps of the area identified the Cape Fear River as "C of faire" and in 1624 on John Smith's map as "C:Feare." By 1651 it was called "Cape Feare." This map had an Indian Fort near the mouth of the river and the word "Secotan" near it. Was the name reminiscent of a "fear" of the cape, a fear of Indians, or the Fair Cape, beautiful but untamed?

By 1711, Christopher Gale, a N.C. Chief Justice, spelled the name "Fare", yet another spelling altogether. Our ancestors, were often prone to various spellings, as is attested in many Wills, land deeds, and other lawful documentations, to include census records. Varying maps and cartographers took great liberties to spell the river's name. However, in the earliest known documentation, June 1585, in a narrative of Sir Richard Greenville, he addresses the "Cape Fear".

Even earlier, the Cape Fear River was said to be known as the "Sapona" to the early Indians, and originally as the Charles River to Englishmen. More detailed information about the development of the Cape Fear River and its tributaries inland can be found in the James Sprunt book, Chronicles of the Cape Fear, 1660 – 1916, including the dredging history and development of channels.

James Sprunt elaborated his opinions on the origins of the name of the present Cape Fear River with many intelligent citizens of the early 1900's believing it was originally called Cape Fair…an indication of the "fair, attractive, and charming area". It has been thought that the river had never been called the Cape Fear until about 1750 and not officially until 1780. However, James Sprunt documents that the Cape Fair legends are, alas, unfounded, and the Cape Fear name most accurate. Hilton, in his early exploit reports spelled the name "Fair". However, three years later, under the watchful eye of the land proprietors, wrote "Fear" as the correct spelling.

Early Land Grants & Settlements Circa 1600

King Charles I of England granted the present-day North and South Carolina land grants about 1629. However, the original proprietors never settled "Carolana". The land was renamed Carolina by the Lords Proprietors who had been given the Heath Grant in 1663.

Later grantees attempted to settle the Cape Fear area about 1663 but returned to England, abandoning their settlements.

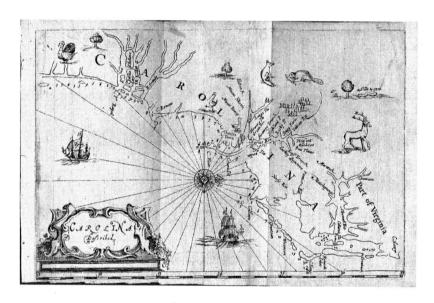

William Hilton, Anthony Long, Peter Fabian, and John Vassal brought settlers to the Brunswick area about 1663 and within two years had over 800 persons living in southeastern North Carolina. The center of that settlement was **Charles Town** and is now called **Town Creek**. He called the Cape Fear River "Charles River" and called the present Town Creek "Indian River". He reported about 100 Indians in the area mostly around Town Creek (Indian River) but increased this count on subsequent trips as he traveled further inland. He described them as thievish, poor and simple. Most of those

48

seen were aged. Hilton was dissatisfied with the land and left the area about four months later. Again the settlers became disillusioned with the harshness of the wilderness around Town Creek. The local Indians made life difficult for them. They packed up and left within a year. When the colonists left the area, the Indians on Smith Island (Bald Head Island) kept the colonists' cattle.

Around this same time period, the privateers began visiting the eastern coast of North Carolina.

Chapter 3

The Pirates

In English, the word piracy has many different meanings and its usage is still relatively new. Today, some uses of the word have no particular meaning at all. A meaning was first ascribed to the word piracy sometime before the XVII century. The word pirate, (peirato), was first used about 140 BC by the Roman historian Polybius. The Greek historian Plutarch, writing in 100 A.D., gave the oldest clear definition of piracy. He described pirates as those who attack without legal authority not only ships, but also maritime cities. Piracy was also described for the first time, in Homer's The Iliad and The Odyssey.

For a great many years there remained no unambiguous definition of piracy. Norse riders of the 9th and 11th century AD were not considered pirates but rather, were called "Danes" or "Vikings". Another popular meaning of the word in medieval England was "sea thieves". The meaning of the word pirate most closely tied to the contemporary interpretations was established in the XVIII century AD. This definition dubbed pirates "outlaws" whom even persons who were not soldiers, could kill. The first application of international law actually involved anti-pirate legislation. This was due to the fact that most pirate acts were committed outside the borders of any country." (So maintains Krzysztof Wilczyski who provides us with this historical perspective of the first pirates dating back over 3000 years

Privateers …..Pirateers of the Early 1700's

The War of the Spanish Succession (which began in 1702) was a struggle of the English against the French and the Spaniards, and affected America as well as Europe. The custom of the time was for countries to hire civilian ships and their crews as auxiliary ships for the navy. The commissions gave these "privateers" the rights to act on behalf of the navy whom they represented. This often led to their "right to steal", provided it was from the enemy.

This business attracted many who were pirates before the war and were now somewhat shielded by the law. After the end of the war in 1713, they returned to their old practices of robbing regardless of national flag. Soon the American seas were swarming with pirates.

Pirates are known to have traveled the Carolina coast and many reports of their escapes remain to attest to their activities. Among those known to have been in the southeastern North Carolina area is Captain William Kidd.

Winnabow Pirates - Captain William Kidd

The pirate, Captain William Kidd, was born about 1665, and is said to have buried a chest of treasure in the area of Winnabow. Other chests of his treasure were buried in Long Island, New York; areas that welcomed pirates about 1699. He also buried treasure on Gardiner's Island about this time. A boulder with a bronze tablet marks that spot.

In 1654, plantation owners tried to band together for protection against robbers and pirates like Captain Kidd. They were often not successful. Eventually the seas were made safer, although some say a few pirates still roam the seas today.

Kidd was eventually captured, put through the motions of a trial, and hanged in London in 1701. His alleged crime was hitting an unruly sailor over the head with a bucket, causing the sailor's death. He never cut a throat or made a victim walk a plank. His name has come down through the years as a symbol of piracy. Ironically, Captain Kidd had originally been employed to rid the seas of pirates. Kidd experienced a terrible death: the hangman's rope broke twice, the third time it held. Once he was dead: his body was dipped in tar and hung by chains along the Thames River. Kidd's body served as a warning to all would-be pirates for years to come. From Kidd's farewell speech he leaves his words:

"My name was Captain Kidd, when I sail'd, when I sail'd, and so wickedly I did, God's laws I did forbid, When I sail'd, when I sail'd. I roam'd from sound to sound, and many a ship I found, And then I sunk or burn'd, When I sail'd. I murder'd William Moore, and laid him in his gore, Not many leagues from shore, When I sail'd. Farewell to young and old, all jolly seamen bold. You're welcome to my gold, for I must die, I must die. Farewell to Lunnon town. The pretty girls all round, No pardon can be found, and I must die, I must die, Farewell, for I must die. Then to eternity, in hideous misery, I must lie, I must lie."

Piracy was at its height in 1696, when Captain William Kidd set out from London on the "Adventure Galley." Thirty years later the profession was beginning to wane but before that time the likes of Samuel Bellamy and others graced our coast.

Samuel Bellamy

According to Krzysztof Wilczynski, Captain Samuel Bellamy whose last name is quite common on the southeastern coast of North Carolina, and in particular, Brunswick County, sailed the North Carolina coastline. He was later called "Black Bellamy" and was known as one of the most active freebooters. (freebooters: n. A person who pillages and plunders, especially a pirate. Dutch vrijbuiter, from vrijbuit, plunder: vrij, free + buit, booty).   He came to the new world to seek his fortune and found a wealthy sponsor to finance a southern expedition to look for sunken Spanish treasures. He was not successful in that venture. Instead he served as an apprentice to Benjamin Hornigold and was elected as captain when Hornigold was deposed. Bellamy proved to be a quite successful pirate, known for his flowery orations. His business of piracy came to an end in April 1717, off Cape Cod when his fleet was hit by an intense storm. He capsized and it destroyed his ship the *"Whydah"*.   A more detailed account describes the incident.

"When the storm hit on April 26, 1717, the *Whydah* (WID-uh) was under the command of Capt. Bellamy, a former British sailor. Bellamy, known as Black Sam, and his crew looted more than 50 ships. Much of the loot—gold, silver, ivory, and jewelry—was stored on the *Whydah.* The powerful storm was too much for the crew. The *Whydah* ran into a sandbar off the coast of Cape Cod, Massachusetts. When a huge wave crashed over the ship, the mainmast snapped and the ship began to roll, its heavy cannons crashing through the decks. Breaking in half, the ship sank." The pilot swam to shore, one of two men who survived. Meanwhile, the pirates' treasures dropped to the ocean bottom.

Thomas Davis, one of the two surviving men aboard, lived on to pass down this account of the Cape Cod shipwreck and piracy legend.

Stede Bonnet

Nearby Southport became the home, albeit temporary, of one of the county's most famous pirates, Stede Bonnet. He came from an old and respected family and was previously a planter on Barbados. Bonnet sailed the Royal James through Virginia and Delaware and southward to the Cape Fear River. With no experience in sailing, he never quite learned how to become a pirate cutthroat until he met Blackbeard, a more experienced and dangerous man. That partnership was not very successful, especially for Bonnet, but at one point Bonnet convinced Blackbeard to allow him to command the ship the *Revenge*. Soon after, the two parted, and Bonnet left his ship for the town of Bath and surrendered himself as a reformed pirate to the Governor of North Carolina, Charles Eden. This act however did not subside Bonnet's desire for piracy, and he continued to scour the sea for vessels and treasure. He was reportedly seen on the Cape Fear River and Col. William Rhett was sent to seize him and his ships. A furious battle ensued. In the confusion all three vessels (two belonging to the Rhett party), ran aground. The pirates finally surrendered to Rhett. During this battle Rhett had twelve men killed and eighteen were wounded. Seven of the pirates were killed and five wounded, two mortally.

Stede Bonnet, the Gentleman Pirate, 1688-1718, was repairing his vessel in a nearby creek when he was captured. Bonnet's Creek was a haven for Stede Bonnet who operated in the area and was captured in the harbor during the 'Battle of the Sand Bar' in 1718. Prior to his capture, he buried three chests of treasure on the shoreline of an inlet close to the mouth of the Cape Fear River. The reported location is near the end of the peninsula. Folklore says the Cape Fear was a popular rendezvous for pirates and they came in large numbers, although Stede Bonnet was the only one known to use the Cape Fear River, in what is now Brunswick County.

About 1719, pirate Stede Bonnet established himself within the harbor of Charleston. Not long after, a notable battle took place near the present day Southport to end the reign of the pirates where hundreds of pirates were hanged in Charleston, South Carolina. It is said that some of Bonnet's men escaped this roundup in the Cape Fear and formed the first settlement of the Cape Fear area about 1725, joined by a group of Lumbee Indians. He was brought to trial under a Court of Vice-Admiralty in Charles Town (Charleston), South Carolina. Sir Nicholas Trott Esq., who at that time was the judge of the Vice-Admiralty Court, sentenced Bonnet to death on the gallows. Stede Bonnet was hung for piracy on December 10, 1718.

Flag of Stede Bonnet

Captain William Hewett

Captain Hewett was a member of Stede Bonnet's crew that sailed the Cape Fear/New Hanover/Brunswick seas. As a member of this crew, he later joined Blackbeard to terrorize other ships. He was eventually tried and hanged in Charleston, South Carolina in 1718 along with his fellow crewmembers and Stede himself.

It is interesting to note that he may have owned a plantation on the Charleston's Cooper River as some matching surnames appear in that area on local census records. The same surname also appears on the 1670 Census of Jamaica where a John Hewitt owned 800 acres. Were some of the descendents of the Hewett/Hewitt pirate family relocated to the Jamaica area with treasures untold and eventual heirs of many hundred acres of land? Legend does not provide us with the whole story. Only speculation remains.

Edward Teach - Blackbeard

Edward Teach, known as Blackbeard, perhaps the most famous pirate of all-time, is most at home in the Ocracoke Island area. However, locals around the Holden Beach area will whisper reminders of his visits to the Holden area from time to time. Throughout the past hundred years, he was "almost" spotted near the Lockwood Folly River mouth, searching for his missing head.

According to legend, a British sailor killed Blackbeard and cut off his head during a battle on another ship. He died at the naval Battle of Ocracoke (1718) from multiple gunshot and stab wounds, after which he was beheaded, his head put upon a bowsprit, and his skull ultimately turned into a drinking mug. From throughout the Carolina coast, the keen eye may be able to see the headless body of Blackbeard in the dark of the moon from the beaches of southeastern North Carolina.

The pirate, Edward Teach, known as Blackbeard, sailed in and out of the Cape Fear inlet often hiding around Topsail Island. Teach was captured and returned to Bath in 1718. Pirate Stede Bonnet was also captured in 1718 on the Cape Fear River and hanged in Charleston. At about the same time the land adjoining the Cape Fear River began to see development in the Wilmington area. New Hanover County history is said to begin with the end of the reign of terror by the pirates.

Jerry Hill described Blackbeard's (Edward Teach) last efforts to remain alive in the following expose: "In 1718 Alexander Spotswood, the Governor of Virginia Alexander, was under enormous pressure to remove pirates from his domain, so he offered rewards for their capture. Top of the wanted list was Blackbeard with £100 on his head. Spotswood was worried that pirates were increasingly harboring in the Pamlico Sound naturally protected by the barrier islands of the Outer Banks, and accessed by the Ocracoke Inlet. There was even talk of Buccaneers fortifying Ocracoke Island itself to make a more imposing base."

"Spotswood enlisted the help of two experienced buccaneer hunters: - Captains Maynard and Hyde. They were both keen to pursue Blackbeard but their ships were unsuitable for the shallow inlets around the Pamlico Sound. Spotswood funded two sloops for the navy men, these boats could safely move through the shallow water. Robert Maynard captained the first sloop the *Jane,* and took command of the expedition of 60 men; Captain Hyde assisted in the *Ranger.* The two sloops had no guns fitted so the pirate hunters had to rely on small arms, a distinct disadvantage against Blackbeard's' *Adventure* carrying 10 guns."

Edward Teach – Blackbeard

"Once Blackbeard's whereabouts was known, the party set sail and arrived at the Ocracoke Inlet on the evening of 21st October 1718. A local pilot guided the sloops through the sandbars and shoals protecting the anchorage, and the *Adventure* was sighted late in the evening. It was decided that a morning attack would take advantage of the after effects of the night's revelry on board the pirate vessel. Blackbeard, unaware of the impending fight, only had a crew of 19 on board and spent the evening drinking heavily with some of his men." "In the morning Maynard and Hyde cautiously moved into the Sound following a small boat taking depth soundings. An observant lookout quickly raised the alarm, and a volley of shot peppered the expedition's boats as the *Adventure* slipped anchor. Maynard and Hyde were soon in hot pursuit but in the rush both their sloops ran aground. The three vessels were close enough for a shouted exchange to take place, and Blackbeard mocked Maynard and his men making it clear that he would be taking no prisoners."

"As the tide rose the two sloops were freed; the wind was so slack that they had to resort to oars. The *Adventure* fired a murderous close range broadside of shot mixed with nails decimating the party and the *Ranger* was put out of the fight losing 5 crew and Captain Hyde."

"Maynard attacked; a volley of shot crippled the *Adventure* by bringing down sails and masts. Maynard had craftily hidden most of his men below decks, so as the two boats ran together Blackbeard boarded with 10 of his pirates thinking his earlier fire wiped out the crews. A life and death struggle ensued as the hidden crew streamed up through the hatches hacking at Blackbeard's men and knocking them down in their wake. Maynard and Blackbeard were soon involved in a desperate struggle. Maynard, wounded by Blackbeard's cutlass, fired his pistol at the Pirate at point blank range. Although wounded Blackbeard continued to fight, and was attacked by several of the sailors who slashed at his face and hands. A Highlander from the *Jane* joined the fight and set about Blackbeard with his broadsword. The first blow cut Blackbeard's neck, and he cried out "Well done lad" the second mighty blow took off the Pirate's head." "The crew of the *Adventure* continued to fight for their lives but the *Ranger* finally rallied and got back into the battle. Despite the desperate fight of the pirates the battle was soon over and a number of prisoners taken, the *Adventure* was secured with its decks running in blood."

"The battle could have had a different ending. Blackbeard had ordered one of his crew to blow up the powder magazine if the boat was taken, and fortunately for the survivors one of his less determined shipmates stopped him. The battle was over. It was rumored that Blackbeard's headless body ran amok and jumped into the water swimming around the ship. Whatever the truth of these tales Maynard sailed home with Blackbeard's head on a pole."

Blackbeard's Final Demise

Blackbeard's Flag

The death of Blackbeard and the trial of the remaining crew was seen as the beginning of the end of the years of buccaneering glory, and a big coup in the war against piracy." (Jerry Hill, Blackbeard's Last Stand, Cordingly, David "Life among the Pirates" 1995. Exquemelin. A.O."The Buccaneers of America", 1923. Ocracoke Island Web Site www.ocracokeisland.com.)

Throughout the 21st century, modern explorers have continued to search for sunken pirate ships, particularly Blackbeard's, *Queen Anne Revenge*. In October of 2007, archaeologists recovered a 2,500-pound cannon from the ship. The *Queen Anne's Revenge* was believed to have sunk in the Beaufort Inlet about 1719 when it ran aground. The treasure below attests to the presence of pirates off the shores of the Carolina's and continued efforts at recovery of items from this flagship of Blackbeard are expected to result in Pewter platters, ornamental brass items, shards of ceramics and glass, a small rail cannon, and considerable amounts of lead shot and gold dust. Archaeologists expect to eventually recover over 1,000 items, and perhaps eventually, over tens of thousands of individual artifacts.

Bronze bell recovered from the Queen Anne's Revenge, Blackbeard's ship.

Jacob & Ann Johnson

Another set of Brunswick County pirates known to have been in the area about ten years later was Jacob Johnson and his wife, Ann, circa 1724. They were caught and charged with having "feloniously stolen divers goods and wares and merchandise belonging to Peter Pedro of Cape Fear, who was recently murdered." (The History of Brunswick County, NC by Lawrence Lee.) Interestingly, there were no land grants to a Peter Pedro at that time. There was a stream on the west side of the river known as Perdreau's Creek. It later became Orton Creek.

Fort Caswell Pirate - Mary Anne Blythe

Mary Anne Blythe, a female buccaneer, supposedly buried her pirate treasure in the area of old Fort Caswell, at the mouth of the Cape Fear River. It has yet to be discovered. Another cache is reportedly on Plum Point in Beaufort County, a chest full of jewels. A chest of pirate treasure was removed from the ground at Plum Point in 1928. It was attributed to her. Is there more? She is but one of a known women pirates as tough and vicious as their male counterparts.

Pirates continued to plague the coast in the early 1700's, just prior to the development of Wilmington and the Lower Cape Fear. Among those known to have been in the southeastern coastal area are:

Anne Bonny

Anne Bonny, born in Ireland, dressed as a boy, pretending to be a son to her father's friends. Her father was a successful lawyer and merchant and bought a plantation in the new land. Upon her mother's death, Anne took over the duties as her father's housekeeper. Anne grew into a hardy girl with a fierce and courageous temper. She was said to have murdered a serving girl with a knife during one of her fits of rage. She was also said to have thrashed a young man with a knife that made unwanted advances toward her. He was badly injured. She eventually married James Bonny whom her father described as "not worth a groat". Later she left him to be with Jack Rackham and the two took to the sea, Anne disguised in men's clothing. She had one child by him, in Cuba, and then rejoined him at sea.

Jack Rackham

John Rackham, "Calico Jack", acquired his ship, the *Treasure*, through neglect by the former commander. Mary Read and Anne Bonney, the best-known female pirates, sailed with him on this ship. The two "ladies" eventually took control of his ship. The ship was captured in November of 1720 and nearly it's entire crew, including Rackham, were sentenced to hang.

Mary Read

Mary Read was a fierce pirate and would attempt any hazardous task. She cursed and swore with the best of the men and tolerated murder. She dressed as the male pirates, in men's jackets, trousers and a handkerchief tied around her head. She was captured by Captain Burnet, tried and imprisoned but released when she claimed she was expecting a baby. Shortly thereafter she disappeared, never to be seen again. Anne claimed the same and was also released to disappear into the world.

Before she died Mary made a last statement. She was heard proclaiming, "As to hanging, it is no great hardship. For were it not for that, every cowardly fellow would turn pirate and so unfit the sea, that men of courage must starve."

For Mary Read, who had always been a woman in a man's world, in the end it all came down to courage."

Mary Read

Pirate Treasures

With all the talk of pirates in and around Brunswick County, one has to ponder how treasure got into a particular Southport home chimney.

"On July 31, 1907, as reported in a local newspaper, Mr. Thomas Swain of Wilmington will accompany his mother to the old family home near Southport to investigate the interesting rumor that workers removing the chimney from an old house on the estate found a large sum of money just under the hearth. There have been rumors for years that the house contained hidden treasure. But nothing had been discovered until now when dismantling of the house, which is in the line of the new railroad in the county. One rumor suggested there was upward of a hundred thousand dollars in gold." A long forgotten pirate treasure? This mystery may never be solved.

Holden Beach has been a mecca for finding historic English coins. In 1980, 80 coins were recovered within a 50-yard area on the coast of Holden Beach. Were these remnants of a treasure formerly aboard the shipwrecks off the shores of Brunswick County? Pirate treasure? Or relics washed ashore from far away lands? During the Civil War, five blockade-runners sank in the area of Lockwood Folly Inlet with an unknown quantity of treasure on board. It has never been recovered.

Modern Pirates

Although some claim that modern descendents of the aforementioned pirates are still among the citizens of Brunswick County, make no mistake that every young boy wants to dress as a pirate on that once a year Halloween Trick or Treat night.

Captain Isaih D. Fisher, son of Jonathan and Jennifer Fisher.
Grandson of the Author. October 2007.

Chapter 4

Colonial Settlements

1700's

Indian Murders

From 1667 to 1725, few Englishmen ventured into Brunswick or New Hanover County but about 1713 Thomas James was one who was granted 1000 acres on the west side of the Cape Fear River. Sadly, an expedition led by Maurice Moore in 1715 found him dead. The local Indians had murdered his entire family, including Thomas.

One earlier land grant of about 48,000 acres was given to Thomas Smith in 1691. This land was in the Calabash area. Despite the Thomas James tragedy, development continued in Brunswick County and merchant activities began to occur between 1700 and 1725.

Land Grants

By 1710 North and South Carolina were established. In 1712, on January 12th, the governor established the boundaries separating North and South Carolina. By 1725 Governor George Burrington began to distribute land along the Cape Fear for colonization and many of the new settlers came from South Carolina because of the lower tax rates in North Carolina. Brunswick Town was about to be formed.

Calabash

The area was originally considered part of Little River and was a part of South Carolina until 1735. Early settlers arrived in Calabash from New England and Charleston. Among them were Nicholas Frink and his grandson, Samuel Frink, who arrived about 1735 and became plantation owners. (The Will of Samuel Frink is included in Chapter 6. He is buried in the Frink-Long Cemetery.)

Brunswick Town Formed

Brunswick Town was formed continued to develop. By 1725 it was officially *named* Brunswick Town. Maurice Moore founded the town of Brunswick and it later became the county seat. New Hanover County was not officially formed until after 1729.

Over 60 building foundations have been identified in the once busy colonial seaport town of Brunswick, located about 19 miles south of Wilmington on the west side of the Cape Fear River. It was a bustling shipping area for exporting tar, pitch, and turpentine. These products were referred to as "sticky gold" and essential for building and maintaining the great wooden sailing ships of the Royal Navy and the merchant fleet sailing between Europe, the American colonies and the islands of the Caribbean.

Col. Maurice Moore was born before 1686 in Charleston, South Carolina and died on 17 May 1743 in Edenton, NC. He married c. 1712 [1st] Elizabeth Lillington [Swann], b. 1678 d: 1725, and had several daughters. He then married Mary Porter and had several more children. He was a Major in the British Army when he was first sent to North Carolina to aid his brother, Col. James Moore in a war against Indians. Maurice remained in North Carolina and became the largest landowner in New Hanover County. He had patents for 25,000 acres of land, most of it in the Rocky Point area.

Maurice and his brothers, Roger and Nathaniel, who both owned thousands of acres of land there, opposed the Governor of North Carolina on many issues. Because of their power and influence these Moore men became known as "The Family." The town of Brunswick was subsequently burned to the ground during the Revolutionary War.

Col. Moore's main home was at Rocky Point. He died suddenly on May 17, 1743 in the garden of his sister-in-law, Mary Vail's home. However, his influence on the development of Brunswick Town and Orton Plantation in Brunswick County remains his legacy for southeastern North Carolina.

Archeological Remains of Brunswick Town
All photographs of Brunswick Town by John Muus

Orton Plantation

By 1725, Maurice Moore received land grants and he developed the Orton Plantation on more than 10,000 acres. (He also began to develop Brunswick Town about the same time, in 1725.)

Orton Plantation was first owned by Colonel Maurice Moore and then sold to his brother, Roger, who developed it into a colonial rice plantation. Roger Moore built the first home on the plantation. Indians destroyed that home. Roger, in turn, destroyed the Indian tribe and rebuilt his home again about 1735. The plantation was put up for auction (all 4975 acres) in 1824, when the present owner, Benjamin Smith had financial misfortunes. (Note: Benjamin Smith later became Governor of North Carolina.) Dr. Frederick Jones Hill became the owner in 1826 and about 1840 added another floor and attic. James Sprunt later purchased the plantation. In 1910 Mrs. Sprunt added wings to the house and began to design and plant the gardens.

The arch formed by majestic oak trees lead into the Orton Plantation. The Orton Plantation rice fields are now home to alligators and many unusual species of birds. It remains as beautiful today as it was in 1725 nestled along the coastal shores of Brunswick County.

(Orton Plantation Photography by John Muuss)

The Entrance to the Orton Plantation

After Moore's death, it was revealed that within "100 paces of the great house" he had buried a fortune in treasure, valued at 75,000 pounds sterling at the time. No trace of the hoard has ever been found.

The beautiful Orton Plantation Chapel is the perfect location for southern weddings.

Orton Plantation Chapel

By 1730 a few Quakers had settled the area but little is known about them. Around 1731 a few wealthy families began to enter the Cape Fear region. The Moores–Maurice, Roger and Nathaniel, Edward Mosely, John Baptista Ashe, Samuel and John Swann, Thomas Jones, Edward Smith, Mosely Vail, Eleazer Allen, John Porter, and John Grange collectively owned about 115,000 acres.

In 1731, Brunswick County was flourishing, and 42 vessels carrying cargo sail from the port in one year. Among their names were the *Orton,* the *Wilmington,* and the *Rake's Delight.* Cargo included Negroes, salt, lumber, tar, indigo, rice, corn, wheat, tobacco, and rum.

By April of 1733, James Wimble, John Watson, Joshua Grainger and Michael Higgins began a new settlement on the "other" side of the Cape Fear River. It's name changed several times from New Carthage, New Liverpool, New Town (Newton) and eventually incorporated as Wilmington in 1740. Wilmington was named for Spencer Compton, Earl of Wilmington, who later became prime minister of England.

Bald Head Island Established

In May of 1713, Barren Island (sometimes called Smith Island and now Bald Head Island) was granted to Thomas Smith. It presently consists of fourteen miles of ocean front beach and is accessible only by ferryboat. Cars are not allowed on the island and the mode of transportation includes golf carts with a maximum speed limit of 18 mph. There are 10,000 acres of protected salt marsh and tidal creeks, and a vast maritime forest preserve. The island itself is about 1700 acres.

Bald Head Island contains extensive maritime agriculture and eight rare animals including the loggerhead and sea green turtle.

Since 1913, ownership, development and the stewardship of the island had been entrusted to Bald Head Island Limited, owned by the George P. Mitchell Family. The natural environment is protected by the Bald Head Island Conservancy. Other sections of the island are owned by the North Carolina Coastal Management and the North Carolina Division of Parks and Recreation.

The Bald Head Lighthouse, affectionately called "Old Baldy", was first lit in 1817. It was deactivated in 1930 and is not currently operational. It's octagonal shape towers over 90 feet high and when operational shown for 18 miles. Constructed in 1794, the original tower at this site was lost to erosion in 1813.

It was this lighthouse that the Confederate forces disabled in January of 1865, prior to losing control of the Cape Fear River in the battle at Fort Fisher. In the early 1900's, the lights were downgraded to a low-intensity, steady light, and were finally discontinued in 1935. From 1941 to 1958, Old Baldy produced a radio beacon to direct ships into the Cape Fear River Channel in times of fog and bad weather. Today, it emits a long steady beam as a restored historical site on Bald Head Island.

Although no additional "lights" have been reported (those unearthly type)…strange noises have been known to emit from the ladders inside of the Bald Head Lighthouse…presumably some previously lighthouse tenders as they continually climb the steps to the top.

Bald Head Lighthouse   *Photography by John Muuss*

Bald Head Island is visible from the shoreline of Southport and also the home of the former Theodosia Burr.

Theodosia Burr

Theodosia's Bed and Breakfast was home to Theodosia, the daughter of American's most famous duelist,

Aaron Burr. Ms. Theodosia disappeared off the coast of North Carolina about 1812 in an unfortunate accident. Her spirit is said to continue to visit the inn and continues to call Bald Head Island home.

The disappearance of a very remarkable and beautiful woman continues to baffle historians. She was the daughter of the Vice President of the U. S. and a formidable belle of the elite society. Was she shipwrecked? Kidnapped by pirates? She was last seen when she boarded the boat *Patriot*, in Georgetown, South Carolina, set for New York. She planned to meet with her father, who had recently returned from Europe, after being ostracized for killing the Secretary of the Treasury, Alexander Hamilton in a duel. Theodosia was a daughter of wisdom, but her father neglected her spiritual or emotional development as he so carefully laid out her educational training. Her mother supplied her spiritual training. (Photo of Aaron Burr).

Although the *Patriot* was considered a very fast boat, expecting to complete the trip to New York in six days, Theodosia never arrived. What is known is that as soon as the *Patriot* left Georgetown, an extremely violent storm occurred, perhaps off the northern coast of North Carolina, around Cape Hatteras. Others attribute her death to pirates who left deathbed confessions of her unfortunate fate. One Frank Burdick claimed to be among the persons on the pirate ship, which abducted the beautiful Theodosia. According to his testimony, Theodosia was given a choice...death or consortium with the pirate Captain. Just as she walked off the plank, she turned to her captors and said, "Justice is mine, sayeth the Lord, I will repay." One pirate chief, Dominique You, even pronounced the date, January 3, 1813. He describes finding the disabled ship off the coast of Hatteras. He describes her as walking the plank and "descending into the sea with graceful composure."

However, some say a nameless grave in Alexandria, Virginia is said to hold the body of Theodosia, a survivor of the shipwreck off the coast of North Carolina. Her true fate may never be known.

Bald Head and other smaller islands flank the coast of Brunswick County. Among them are Battery Island, Bluff Island, East Beach.

Russellborough Home - 1751

One of the most historic homes in Brunswick County was the Russellborough, just north of Brunswick Town. Captain John Russell, an officer on the H. M. Sloop Scorpion, acquired it in 1751. It was owned by Governor Arthur Dobbs, William Tryon, and Captain Russell. Excavated ruins are all that remain of this home. It was described, at the time of Cpt. Russell's purchase as:
"This house has so many assistances (and) is of an oblong square built of wood. It measures on the out side faces forty-five feet by thirty-five feet and is divided into two stores, exclusive of the cellars. The parlor is about five feet above the surface of the earth. Each story has four rooms and three light closets. The Parlour below and the drawing room are 20 X 15 feet each; ceilings are low. There is a Piaza Run Round the house both stories of ten feet wide with a balustrade of four feet high, which is a great security for my little girl. There is a good stable and coach houses and some other out houses. If I continue in this house, which will depend on Capt. Dobbs' (son of the governor) resolution in the manner he disposes of his effects here, I shall and must build a good kitchen, which I can do for forty pounds sterling of 30 ft X 40 ft."

The Little Charlotte River and Shallotte

By 1734, the Little Charlotte River had been named. This later became known as the "Shallotte River" leading into the town of Shallotte. Prior settlement of the area dated back to around 1750 with an earlier reference to the river and the town as early as 1734. According to some accounts, the town received its name from a traveler who crossed the river by ferry and referred to the river as the "Charlotte" River. The Charlotte River later took on the name of the Shallotte River.

A post office was established there in 1837 but the town did not incorporate until March 6, 1899. Early residents relied on agriculture, fishing and a river full of flatboats, rafts and other small crafts. They transported goods throughout the county. It has grown to become a focal point of the southern part of Brunswick County.

Sunnyside School

The Town was later called Shallotte and presently consists of about 1600 residents. The Leonard School was the first school built in Shallotte about April 1891. A new school, funded in 1915, was called Sunnyside School. It contained

80-90 students and two teachers. Shallotte High School was built in 1927 to replace the one room schoolhouse that currently sits on the grounds of Shallotte Middle School on Village Road in Shallotte.

A 1734 Tour of the Cape Fear Area

A visit to the Cape Fear in 1734, (visitor unknown) as related in the Georgia Historical Papers, Vol. 2, page 54, (as referenced by James Sprunt) is described below:

(Note: The original version of this tour of the Cape Fear area was taken from A new voyage to Georgia. By a young gentleman. Giving an account of his trip to South Carolina, and part of North Carolina. To which is added, A curious account of the Indians, By an honorable person. And a poem to James Oglethorpe, Esq., on his arrival from Georgia. London. Printed by J. Wilford, 1735." This is the title of the second edition.)

"My first night, I reached Mr. More's in Goose Creek. The next morning...we reached Little Charlotta about dinnertime, which is about 15 miles from Ashs, or Little River; we dined there and in the afternoon crossed the ferry, where we intended to sleep that night. We reached there about eight one night after having crossed the ferry. It (Lockwoods Folly) is so named, after one Lockwood, a barbarian, who attempted to settle it some time ago, but by his cruel behavior to the Indians, they drove him from thence, and it has not been settled above ten years." (Note: the addition of the violence which Mr. Lockwood apparently brought upon himself, not often included in the historical accounts of the name of Lockwood's Folly area.)

"We left Lockwood's Folly about eight the next morning. And by two reached the town of Brunswick which is the chief town in Cape Fear; but with no more than two of the same horses which came with us out of South Carolina. Mr. Roger More, hearing that we were come, was so kind as to send fresh horses for us to come up to his house, which we did, and were kindly received by him; he being the chief gentlemen in all Cape Fear. His house is built of brick and extremely pleasantly situated, about two miles from the town, and about a half of a mile from the river; although there is a creek comes close up to the door, between two beautiful meadows about three miles length. He has a prospect of the town of Brunswick, and of another beautiful brick house, a building about half a mile from him, belonging to Eleazar Allen, Esq., late speaker to the Commons House of Assembly, in the province of South Carolina. There were several vessels lying about the town of Brunswick, but I shall forebear giving a description of that place; yet on the 20th of June we left Roger More's, accompanied by his brother, Nathaniel More, Esq., to a plantation of his up the northwest branch of the Cape Fear River. The river is wonderfully pleasant being next to the Savannah, the finest on all (of) the continent.

We reached the forks, as they call it, that same night, where the river divides into very beautiful branches, called the Northeast and the Northwest, passing by several pretty plantations on both sides. We lodged that night at one Jehu Davis', and the next morning proceeded up the Northwest branch; when we got about two miles from thence, we came to a beautiful plantation belonging to Captain Gabriel, who is a great merchant there, where were two ships, two sloops, and a brigantine, loaded with lumber for the West Indies: it is about twenty-two miles from the bar; when we came about four miles higher up, we saw an opening on the northeast side of us, which is called Black River, on which there is a great deal of meadow land, but there is not anyone settled on it

The next night we came to another plantation belonging to Mr. Roger More, called the Blue Banks, where he is a-going to build another very large brick house. This bluff is at least a hundred feet high, and has a beautiful prospect over a fine large meadow, on the opposite side of the river; the houses are all built on the southwest side of the river; it being for the most part high champaign land: the other side is very much subject to overflow; but I cannot learn they have lost but one crop. " The writer went on to describe the abundant crops of corn and affluence he saw in his trip through Brunswick County and his desire to continue his touring of the southeastern Brunswick land up to the Waccamaw Lake. He did return some time later, with a Negro and Mr. Roger More who rode horseback the twenty miles toward Lake Waccamaw. He described the largest "musquetoes" he has ever seen in his life, which "fetched blood through our buckskin gloves, coats and jackets." After riding through the "swamps", they came upon a " great herd of deer", the largest and fatest spotted. Needless to say, these became dinner. They rode another two miles and came upon a she-bear and two cubs, which they shot. They slept in the rain, as well as they could that night, proceeding toward lake Waccamaw again the next morning. His view of the area was more positive the next morning, describing the hickory trees, oaks, and cypress swamps. He describes an old Indian field, which appears not to have been occupied for the past fifty years. Nor can any Cape Fear Indian account for this particular location. Wild turkeys, geese and ducks rounded out their feasts.

He continues describing Newton and Rocky Point, as the finest places along the Cape Fear. Further exploits surveyed into South Carolina, eventually returning to London in January of 1734.

(Traveler unknown)

Lockwood's Folly

Lockwood's Folly received it's name from a man named Lockwood, from Barbados, who established his land grant just south of the Cape Fear River branches into what is now Brunswick County. Lockwood was described as a barbarian, who attempted to settle this area but because of his cruel behavior to the Indians, they drove him from it. Although no specific deeds are known, they retaliated and he was not able to return to his land or home. The area was not settled again for at least ten more years. Hence, the area was named Lockwoods's Folly. This story was related as early as 1734 in a travelers log as he visited the plantations along the Cape Fear River.

In 1779 the county seat was authorized to relocate to the plantation of John Bell near Lockwood's Folly Bridge. In 1784 Walkersburg, named in honor of John Walker on whose land it was situated, was established. Provisions were made in the act for a courthouse and other public buildings to be established there. It was located near Deep Water Point. This act specified that the courts were to be held at the most convenient place until the courthouse was completed. It is doubtful that the act was put into effect because in 1808 an act was passed authorizing the removal of the courthouse from Lockwood's Folly to Smithville. Court was held at the courthouse from 1805-1858. The record does not indicate where the courthouse was. This town, established in 1792, was named in honor of Benjamin Smith, Governor of North Carolina, 1810-1811. In 1879 an effort to move the courthouse failed. In 1887 Smithville was changed to Southport. Southport served as the county seat until 1977 when the county seat was moved to Bolivia.

The County Courthouse was destroyed in 1865 from the civil war, and again there was a fire in the clerk's office in 1957. Some records were destroyed in the 1865 fire.

By 1735, surveyors begin defining the North and South Carolina borders. In 1735 the counties of New Hanover, Onslow and Bladen were created. By 1739, the town of Wilmington was incorporated by the General Assembly. This was the previously referred to village of Newton.

Navassa in 1736

In 1736, the Bluff Plantation was the site of an early ferry from Newton (New Town)...i.e. Wilmington, to Brunswick County. It is sometimes referred to as Gaboural's

82

Bluff or Maclaine's Bluff, for the owner, Archibald Maclaine. Its former location is now the town of Navassa located about five miles from Wilmington.

Early Wilmington Census Records Circa 1740's

The 1741 NC Census Record lists only one family in New Hanover County... Hugh Alexander. The next year more families appeared to be listed including: Benjamin Beveret, Timothy Bloodworth, Henry Bousher, Chambers Caine, Joseph Clark, Peter Clift, Thomas Corbett, Christopher Crofts, Thomas Cunningham, Jacob Hanshey, David Jamerson, Mary Littgow, ----- Mc Kain, Joseph Meredith, Grace Merrick, John Miller, Timothy Murphy, David Pursell, and John Warner. In the twenty years after its founding Wilmington which was declared an official port of entry, had a shipyard between Church and Castle Streets, a silversmith, a watchmaker, a meetinghouse and land was deeded for a church.

St. Philips Parish Created

In 1741, all lands west of the Cape Fear River were incorporated in the parish of St. Philips, although the townspeople of Brunswick Town continued to declare their independence.

Shipping, lumber, naval stores and rice were the main sources of income for the area.

Scots begin to Arrive

By 1747, many highlanders from Scotland began arriving in North Carolina, especially coming to the Cape Fear area after the failed revolt in their homeland. By 1773, over 4,000 Scots had arrived bringing their population to about 20,000.

Fort Johnson

Located near Southport, Fort Johnson was originally built as a defense against pirates in 1748. The Pilots who guided ships through the difficult shoals of the area also settled at Fort Johnson. This was to become the future site of Southport. It was burned by the Patriots to keep it from falling into the hands of the British in 1775.

The Boundary House in 1750

The "Boundary House", in the southern portion of Brunswick County, with the provinces line running down the middle, existed prior to 1750. It was built by twenty-four gentlemen, twelve from each province as a place of rendezvous for travelers. Another settler, Issac Marion, brother of Francis Marion, was serving a Justice of the Peace at the Boundary House, when a dispatch rider delivered the message of the "shots heard around the world".

The Altson family owned most of the Calabash area during the late 1700's.

Ash

The Ash community is located around the Whiteville Highway 130 in the vicinity of roads 1300 and 1325 intersections. It is primarily a rural and agricultural area.

Although little is known about the origins of the first settlers of the Ash community, there is one plantation recorded under the ownership of John Baptista Ashe is Brunswick County, around the Cape Fear Region. One has to wonder if this community was named for the famous Mr. Ashe.

John Baptista Ashe (1748 – 27 November 1802) was an American planter, soldier, and statesman from North Carolina. He was born in Rocky Point township of Pender

County, North Carolina in 1748, the son of Samuel Ashe. He was a Colonel in the Continental Army, served at Valley Forge, and fought in the Battle of Eutaw Springs.

Ashe was elected to the North Carolina House of Commons and served as Speaker of that body. He was a delegate to the Continental Congress in 1787. In 1789, Ashe was a delegate and Chairman of the Committee of the Whole of the state convention that ratified the U.S. Constitution. That same year, he served in the North Carolina Senate.

Ashe was elected to the First United States Congress and the Second United States Congress as an "Anti-Administration" (what became Anti-Federalist or Democratic-Republican) candidate, serving from 1790 to 1793.

In 1802, the North Carolina General Assembly elected Ashe Governor, but he died before he could take office. His namesake and nephew, John Baptista Ashe, served in Congress as a Representative from Tennessee.

Samuel Ashe (March 24, 1725 – February 13, 1813) was the Anti-Federalist governor of the U.S. State of North Carolina from 1795 to 1798.

Samuel Ashe was born in Beaufort, North Carolina. His father, John Baptista Ashe, had been Speaker of the North Carolina Colonial Assembly, or House of Burgesses. Ashe became an orphan at the age of 9. He married Mary Porter in 1748; they had three children, including John Baptista Ashe, who would serve in the Continental Congress. After Mary died, Ashe remarried, this time to Elizabeth Merrik.

Ashe studied law and was named Assistant Attorney for the Crown in the Wilmington district of the colony. He became involved in the revolutionary movement and served in the North Carolina Provincial Congress and as a member of the North Carolina militia. For a little more than one month in 1776, Ashe served as president of the Council of Safety, the state's executive authority. He was also appointed to the committee that drafted the first North Carolina Constitution. In

1776, he was elected to the new North Carolina Senate and was elected its first speaker. The following year, Ashe was appointed presiding judge of the state Superior Court; a post he held until 1795.

In 1795, the General Assembly elected him governor at the age of 70. He served three one-year terms, the maximum constitutional limit, before retiring in 1798. Ashe continued to remain active in politics after his term as governor, serving as a member of the Electoral College in 1804.

Ashe County and the cities of Asheville, North Carolina and Asheboro, North Carolina are named in his honor. In World War II the United States liberty ship SS Samuel Ashe was also named in his honor.

Ashe's grandson William Ashe was a Confederate soldier in the American Civil War; and a son of John B. and Eliza (Hay) Ashe. He was killed at Shiloh in 1862. William's brother, Samuel Swann Ashe, was also on the field at Shiloh.

One of the oldest cemeteries in the Ashe area is the McKeithan Cemetery, located off of Ash Little River Road, on Ash Long Road. It contains early 1800 burials from many McKeithan, Stanaland, Jenrette and Hugh family members. Early births to 1821 are noted. It is still being used today and kept in serene condition with a large statue of an angel at the entrance of this small but historic landmark.

Plantations

Some of those plantations known to be on the east side of the Cape Fear River were:

San Souci   Mr. Arthur Hill

Kendall   Mr. Owen Holmes

Aspern	Col. Maurice Moore
Clarendon	Mr. Joseph Watters
Buchoi	Judge Alfred Moore
Old Town	Mr. Tom Cowan
Belvedere	Mr. John Waddell
Orton	Mr. Roger Moore
Belfont	Mr. Hugh Waddell
The Oaks	Col. John Taylor
Hilton	Mr. Cornelius Harnutt
Greenfield	Mr. Tom McIlhenney
The Hermitage	Mr. Burgwyn
Cobham	Mr. June Davis
Lilliput	Dr. John Hill
Gander Hall	Mr. James McIlhenney

1760

In 1760, as King George III began his reign in England, North Carolina's Governor Dobbs ordered a celebration in his honor. This celebration occurred in Brunswick Town. About this time, Governor Dobbs, then about seventy-three years old, married a fifteen-year old girl, Justina Davis. There was an outrage in the political circles, but the girl and the Governor seemed happy and content. She tended to him after his stroke and was a great comfort to him until his death in 1765. Governor Dobbs was buried inside the unfinished St. Philip's Church (referred to as His Majesty's Church) in Brunswick Town in the then one-year old Brunswick County.

St. Philips Anglican Church

The extravagant St. Philips Anglican Church building dates back to 1762 although the parish itself was created in 1741. All that remains today are portions of its majestic walls (nearly three feet thick) and the nearby graveyard bearing the final resting place of many prominent citizens from the 18th century.

The communion plate, surplice and furniture for the communion table and pulpit, including a bible and common prayer books, were the gifts of King George II, "in order that the services may be performed with decency". In the frequent absence of the incumbent, services were regularly conducted by the Honorable William Hill, the licensed lay-reader, whose tomb under yonder tree is one of the few remaining of all those who were laid to rest in these consecrated grounds.

The minister of St. Philip's Church wrote this letter on June 15, 1762, giving an account of the situation at St. Philips church at that time.

Brunswick June 15, 1762

My parish of St. Philips runs from the mouth of Cape Fear River along the seaside about 40 miles to Little River which divides this from South Carolina; then about 45 miles along the south line then joining Bladen County; runs about 45 miles to the north west Branch of Cape fear River; then down said north west branch to the ferry opposite Wilmington, about twenty miles, and from the down to the river's mouth about thirty miles. Brunswick is situated on the West Bank of the River, about halfway between Wilmington and the river's mouth, where we have a fort. Wilmington stands on the East

88

Bank of the River, but I intend to send a map of my Parish, which will give a better idea of it than this description; we have about 800 taxables in this parish. Taxables here are males, white and black and mixed blood, from 12 years of age and upward, and female blacks or mixed blood from the same age. We have but few families in the Parish but of the best in the Province, viz His Excellency the Governor, his honor the President, some of the honorable the council, Col. Dry, the Collector, and about 20 other good families who have each of them great gangs of slaves. We have in all about 200 families; and are about to have our Parish made into a County. We have no dissenters of any sort excepting a few poor families of fishermen who came from Cape May at the mouth of the river Delaware and are settled by the seaside between the mouth of the river Lockwood's Folly and Shallot, they call themselves new light Anabaptists; but we hope this frolic will soon dwindle away and disappear among them as it has already done in many places in this and neighboring provinces. We have this spring repaired our old chapel at Brunswick in a decent manner and the timber for the roof of our new church is provided. I have but 15 actual communicants as yet, whereof 2 are black, but I hope the number will soon increase. I am with profoundest submission and their most devoted humble servant.

John McDowell

Interestingly, the poll taxes were not quite sufficient to pay for the construction of the church and it was finished with funds raised in two lotteries along with the sale of items saved from a destroyed Spanish ship. (Heartening Heritage on a Carolina Crescent by J. M. M. Holden, c.1989.) St. Philip's was almost complete by 1762 when struck by lightning, which destroyed the roof. The church elders then repaired the old small chapel and postponed work on the new brick structure.

The cemetery behind the St. Philips Church left a testament to the former members dating back to the early 1700's.

Today, the remains of St. Philip's Church are a
rectangular shell with 23-foot high walls that are three feet
deep. Several Colonial-era graves are evident with more
surfacing as time passes. There is little evidence to tell us the
remaining detailing of the church other than suggestions of
Georgian detailing. It had three entrances open to the west,
north and south. The body of North Carolina's first royal
governor (Arthur Dobbs) are said to be interred at St. Philip's
as he requested, however it has not been definitively

identified. Services are still held in the St. Philip's Church periodically.

The entire area of southeastern North Carolina is a relic hunter's paradise of treasure and rich with tales of the past, including ghosts. The excavated colonial town of Brunswick is among those sites and reportedly haunted by some of its former residents; ship builders, captains, pirates, businessmen, and their families.

During tours of Brunswick Town, visitors occasionally hear footsteps where "no one is there". Unexplained fire alarms cause speculation of "acts" by former residents. Music has been reported originating from the remnants of the old St. Philips Church. Could these be the voices of the former parishioners or stereos from across the bay? One can only imagine the colonists as they lifted their voices in glory at the magnificent St. Philips Anglican Church.

The Holden Beach history is described John Holden in his book entitled <u>The Beginning and Development of Holden Beach, 1756-2000</u>. In it, he details the settlement of Holden Beach by Benjamin Holden who arrived with his family in 1756.

Benjamin Holden selected five tracts of land, an island (Holden Beach), and four tracts of woodland adjacent to the island. Lockwood Folly River Inlet was the east boundary and Bacon Inlet the west boundary. The Atlantic Ocean bounded it by the south and the tidal creeks near the woods were the north boundary. Benjamin paid 50 shillings for the island and bought it for business purposes to establish a fishery. This land encompassed about 400 acres. (i.e. four, one hundred acre tracts plus an island). His home was located in the near vicinity of the Sea Aire Estates today. His three sons, Job, James and Amos served in the American Revolutionary War and are most likely buried in the Job Holden Cemetery.

In his will (dated 1778), Benjamin Holden divided the island into two pieces for his sons Amos and James. Job

92

Holden inherited his father's plantation where the family cemetery is located. Three generations of Holden's are buried there including Benjamin, his son, Job, and grandson, John Holden, Senior. (See pictures in Chapter 6.)

Although the island changed ownership several times, by the year 1905, two of Benjamin's great grandsons, George Washington Holden and John Holden, Jr., became the owners. By 1924 John Holden, Jr., had a subdivision plotted on the island and in 1925 realized a bridge was needed. With no power tools, the building process was a slow one but completed that same year (1925). The Holden Beach Hotel was soon opened the following year marking the beginning of tourism for Holden Beach. It was the first building of its kind on any of the Brunswick beaches. The old hotel was never very profitable during the "Great Depression" and church groups used it mainly for summer retreats and picnics.

The Intracoastal Waterway digging delayed the development of the island and caused damage to the natural resources in the area. In 1930 a government dredge passed through the Lockwood Folly Inlet and the Eastern Channel through Sunset Beach. The Galloway Flats were split and Sheep Island was created, the spoil of dredge deposits. The channel passed Brown's Landing enroute to the Shallotte River. The bridge built in 1925 was destroyed when the channel was dug through that area. The channel was completed in 1931.

About that time a ferry was built to provide the first public access to Holden's Beach. A special tool (about three feet long) called a "jack stick" was used to ferry the craft across the water. It was used as the operator placed it on the cable behind the front roller in the direction he wished to travel. As he applied his weight and strength, the ferry would move in that direction. The first ferry began operation in 1934 at the end of the present Old Ferry Road. Louis Robinson was the first operator at a wage of $40 per month. The oil lamps required by the Coast guard at night, were put on the fender of the ferry during night operations. The state paid an additional $6 per month to have the lamps filled each evening.

Mr. Robinson's sons did this job to earn extra spending money.

The ferry operated until 1954. The first bridge (turn-table type) opened on February 20th, 1954 and operated until June 6, 1986 when it was replaced by the current high-rise bridge spanning the inland waterway.

The Town of Holden Beach was finally incorporated on February 14, 1969.

Holden Beach Ferry Remains

New Hanover, Bladen, Columbus, & Brunswick Counties Formed

In 1764 Brunswick separated from New Hanover and in 1875 Pender County was formed. Land demarcations were being created and various communities emerging.

Officially created in 1764, from New Hanover and Bladen Counties, Brunswick County later released some of its land to Columbus County in 1808. The following tax list includes those Brunswick County residents, including those who may have lived in the northern end of the county, which

94

is now Columbus County. Brunswick Town was already established when the county was created and both are named for King George I, Duke of Brunswick and Lunenburg. Although Brunswick County endured, the town of Brunswick was abandoned about 1776 after a fire. Early residents of the Saint Philips Parish are listed in the 1769 Brunswick County Tax Lists, some of the very first settlers to establish the county of Brunswick.

The region of Brunswick was made famous during colonial times when gunshots were heard from the residence of General Robert Howe, one of Washington's lieutenants, during the Revolutionary War. A landing party under Lord Cornwallis destroyed General Howe's residence in May 1776, by order of Sir Henry Clinton. The Orton Plantation was the location for the first armed resistance to the stamp act. Just beyond this forested area is the Liberty Pond, an ever-changing lake of white spring water that mingled on its margin the blood of friend and foe, in 1776. This would have been Boiling Spring Lakes of today.

Early Brunswick County history is described by Colonel Waddel as "Memorable, for some of the most dramatic scenes in the early history of North Carolina as the region around Brunswick was- being the theatre of the first open armed resistance to the Stamp Act on the 28th of November, 1765, and not far from the spot where the first victory of the Revolution crowned the American arms at Moore's Creek bridge on the 27th February, 1776--its historic interest was perpetuated when, nearly a century afterwards, its tall pines trembled and its sand hills shook to the thunder of the most terrific artillery fire that has ever occurred since the invention of gunpowder, when Fort Fisher was captured in 1865. Since then it has again relapsed into its former state, and the bastions and traverses and parapets of the whilom Fort Anderson are now clad in the same exuberant robe of green with which generous nature in that clime covers every neglected spot. And so the old and the new ruin stand side by side in mute attestation of the utter emptiness of all human ambition, while the Atlantic breeze sings gently amid the sighing pines, and the vines cling more closely to the old church wall, and the lizard basks himself where the sunlight falls on a forgotten grave."

Just as Brunswick County officially became a recognized county, many residents were quite busy selling and buying land. An example of the transactions is found in the deed between Thomas Bell and Richard Melton, dated 8 November 1766. In the deed, Thomas Bell sells about 500 acres, more or less, to Richard Melton for the sum of thirty pounds. The parcel is described as beginning at the large cypress on the NE side of the branch of the Lockwood Folly River about three miles above the fork, then N 37, Et 70 chains, 71 links to a cypress in a swamp; then No 35 Wt 71 chains, 71 links to a stake, then S 55 Wt 70 chains, t0 links to a pine; then S 35 E 70 chains, 71 links to the first station. This land was originally acquired by Thomas Bell on the 18th of January 1738-9; surely one of the first settlers in this area. Just three years later, he is not listed on the 1769 Brunswick County Tax lists or on the 1772 Census. Thirty-four years had elapsed between when he acquired the land and he sold it. Would this have possibly been the land he acquired as a land grant from the King upon arriving in America as an adult colonist, at least twenty-one years of age? In that case, he may have been a minimum of fifty-five years old and died about that time period. If he was any older, perhaps fourty-one years old, his death age would be seventy-five years old. One can only surmise that he died within this three-year period, anywhere from 55 years old or older. Or moved to another area, less likely when one considers the mode of the time, although he may have traveled to live with one of his children who did not reside in the immediate area. However, when the census is looked at more closely, one finds several other Bell's listed, notably a James and John Bell in 1769...the list of Bell's growing with each subsequent census report. I wonder who Thomas Bell really was and what happened to him...does he rest beneath one of the many historical cemeteries in our county?

1769 Brunswick County Tax Lists

Note: Statistics include 1. Number of Chair Wheels (a two wheel one horse carriage), 2. Number of white men, 3. Number of Negro men, 4. Number of negro women, 5. Number of Negro boys.

Notice that the number of white women or Negro girls was not included in this tax roster. Following is the alphabetical list of taxables in the Saint Philips parish of Brunswick County in 1769. Many names are repeated in the 1772 North Carolina tax lists with a slightly different spelling. Since some residents were not formerly educated and often could not read or write, the census taker was forced to spell the name as closely to what the "source" reported at the time. Therefore, spellings of surnames and first names often varied in successive census records although they represented the same individual.

Adderson, Christopher	0-1-0-0-?
Adkins, Eleazer	0-1-0-0-0
Allen, Drury, Constable	0-1-4-2-0
Allen, Joel	0-1-0-1-1
Alston, Joseph	
by Josa. G. DuPree &	
Lewis DuPree	0-0-10-6-0
Alston, Peter	0-2-2-3-0
Anderson, John, Junr.	0-1-0-0-?
Baker, Edward	0-1-0-0-0
Balloone, Michail	0-1-4-3-0
Barnes, John	0-1-0-1-?
Bassford, James	0-1-2-0-0
Bell, James	0-3-0-2-0

Bell, John	0-3-0-0-0
Boone, Thomas	0-3-0-0-0
Brown, John	0-1-0-0-?
Buck, John	0-1-0-0-0
Burger, John	0-1-0-0-?
Cains, Christopher	0-1-0-0-0
Carter, Edward	0-1-0-1-0
Carter, Robert	0-1-0-0-0
Caulkins, Wm.	0-1-0-0-?
Church, Abner	0-1-0-0-?
Clemonds, Edward	0-1-0-2-?
Cobham, Thomas	2-1-16-13-0
Conner, Morris	0-1-0-0-0
Conningham, James	0-1-0-0-0
Corbett, James	0-1-0-1-0
Couples, Wm.	0-1-0-0-?
Cumbo, Stephen (Mollo.)	0-3-0-1-0
Dalyrumple, Martha	2-1-11-5-2
Daniell, George	0-1-4-4-0
Daniell, John	2-1-6-4-0
Daniell, Robert	2-2-9-19-0
Daniell, Wm.	0-1-3-6-0
Davis, Elizabeth	0-0-2-3-0
Davis, Jeane	0-0-1-3-1
Davis, John	0-1-11-16-0
Davis, Robert	2-2-15-?-?
Davis, Thomas	2-1-18-19-2
Davis, Wm.	0-1-10-10-0
Dick, Thomas	0-2-0-1-0
Doane, Hezekiah	0-2-4-1-0
Doaty, Benjamin	0-2-0-1-0
Dry, Wm.	0-2-54-63-11
Du Pree, James	0-2-0-1-0
Du Pree, Josa. Garn.	0-1-0-0-0
Du Pree, Lewis	0-1-0-0-0
Du Pree, Samuel	0-1-0-0-0
Dwight, Samuel	2-1-5-7-0

98

Eagan, Darby	0-1-3-5-1
Eagle, Richd. Estate	0-1-34-39-4
Earle, Joseph	0-1-0-0-0
Ellis, Robert	0-2-10-3-0
Faulkner, Wm.	0-1-0-0-0
Fergus, John	0-1-1-2-0
Frankum, Joshua	0-1-0-0-0
Gallaway, John	0-2-0-0-0
Gallaway, Thomas	0-1-0-1-0
Gallaway, Wm.	0-2-0-0-0
Gawse, Needham	0-1-3-2-0
Gawse, Wm.	0-1-3-4-0
Goldwin, Joseph	2-1-1-2-0
Grange, John	2-2-27-33-0
Gressett, George	0-1-4-0-0
Gressett, Wm.	0-3-2-4-0
Groves, Joseph	0-1-0-0-0
Hall, Thomas	0-0-0-0-0
Hart, Abigal	0-0-1-2-0
Hasell, James	2-2-18-10-0
Hassell, James Junr.	2-2-10-9-0
Hewett, Ebenezer	0-1-0-0-0
Hewett, Jacob	0-1-0-0-0
Hewett, Philip	0-1-0-0-0
Hewitt, Ebenezer, Junr.	0-1-0-0-0
Hewitt, Elisha	0-1-0-0-0
Hewitt, Randall	0-2-0-0-0
Hewitt, Randall, Jur.	0-1-0-0-0
Hewitt, Richard	0-1-0-0-0
Hickman, John	0-1-0-0-0
Hill, George	0-1-0-0-0
Hill, Wm.	2-1-2-5-0
Hillyard, Jesse	0-1-0-0-0
Holding, Benjamin	0-2-0-0-0
Holding, Joshua	0-1-0-0-0
Holmes, Edward	0-1-2-0-0
Howe, Robert	0-0-0-0-0
Humphreys, Wm.	0-1-0-0-0
Hunnicut, Meredith	0-1-0-0-0
Iunkeson (or Junkeson), Walter	0-2-0-0-?
Johnston, John	0-1-0-0-0
Jones, Philip	0-2-0-0-0
Keeter, Charles	0-1-0-0-0
Knowls, George	0-1-0-0-0

Lay, Enus	0-1-0-0-0
Lay, John	0-1-0-0-0
Leonard, Henry	0-2-0-0-0
Leonard, Jacob	0-1-0-0-0
Leonard, John	0-1-0-0-0
Lor, Wm.	0-1-8-7-0
Ludlam, Jermh.	0-1-0-0-0
Ludlum, Isaac	0-1-2-3-0
Lyles, Benjamin	0-1-0-0-0
Mackay, Arthur	0-1-1-0-0
Marion, Isaac	0-1-4-6-0
Marlow, James	0-1-0-0-0
Marlow, Will, Jur.	0-1-0-0-0
Marnan, Thomas	0-1-1-0-0
Mills, Edward	0-2-0-0-0
Mills, Wm.	0-1-0-0-0
Milton, Richard	0-1-2-0-0
Mimms, George	0-2-0-0-0
Mooney, Wm.	0-1-0-0-0
Moore, George	0-0-7-1-0
Moore, Maurice	6-4-33-34-5
Moore, Schenckg.	0-1-15-22-3
Mulford, Thomas	0-1-0-1-0
Murray, Jacob	0-1-0-0-0
Neale, Samuel	0-1-5-6-0
Neale, Thomas	0-1-7-7-0
Neale, Wm.	0-1-2-3-0
Nugent, Edmond	0-1-1-0-0
Ogdon, Wm.	0-1-0-0-0
Olive, John	0-1-0-0-0
Owram, Timothy	0-1-0-0-0
Parvesal (?), Isiah	0-1-0-0-0
Peabody, Joseph	0-1-0-0-0
Pennington, Wm.	0-1-0-0-0
Poller (Potter?), Robert	0-1-4-0-0
Pounds, John	0-1-0-0-0
Quince, Parker	0-1-19-11-1
Quince, Richard	-7-66-43-4
Ramsry (Ramsey?), James	0-1-0-0-0
Rieley, Richard	0-1-0-0-0
Robbins, Arthur	0-1-0-0-0
Robbins, Jethro	0-1-0-0-0
Robinson, John	0-1-0-0-0
Rogers, John	0-1-0-0-0
Roots, John	0-1-1-1-0

Rowan, John	0-1-19-11-1
Russ, John	0-1-0-0-0
Russ, Joseph	0-1-0-0-0
Russ, Thomas	0-1-0-1-0
Sampson, Jerema.	0-3-0-0-0
Sellers, Benjamin	0-1-0-0-0
Sellers, Elisha	0-1-0-0-0
Sellers, Jaconias	0-1-0-0-0
Sellers, James	0-1-0-0-0
Sellers, Joel	0-1-0-0-0
Sellers, Mathew	0-1-0-0-0
Sellers, Simon	0-1-0-0-0
Sessions, Thomas	0-1-0-0-0
Simmonds, Isaac	0-4-0-0-0
Simmonds, John	0-1-4-6-0
Simpson, Wm.	0-2-2-3-0
Smeeth, David	0-3-0-0-0
Smith, John	2-1-7-7-0
Snow, Robert	2-1-14-6-?
Soals, Gedion	0-1-0-0-0
Soals, Joseph	0-1-0-0-0
Soals, Silvanus	0-1-0-0-0
Stanaland, Garsham	0-1-0-0-0
Stanaland, John	0-1-1-1-0
Stanaland, Thomas	0-1-0-0-0
Stanbury, Wm.	0-1-0-0-0
Stevens, Charles	0-1-0-0-0
Stewart, Robert	0-1-0-1-0
Stone, Benjamin	0-1-3-2-0
Stone, Elias	0-2-0-0-0
Swaine, Arthur	0-1-1-0-0
Swaine, David	0-1-0-0-0
Swaine, Jonathan	0-2-3-4-0
Swaine, Judah	0-2-0-1-0
Teague, Wm.	0-1-0-0-0
Tharp, Samuel	0-3-0-0-0
Thomas, John	0-1-0-0-0
Tickle(?), Richard	0-1-0-0-0
Tiler, John	0-1-0-0-0
Tippins, Henry Thomas	0-1-0-0-0
Todd, Thomas	0-1-0-0-0
Todd, Wm.	0-1-0-0-0
Truett, John	0-1-0-0-0
Tryon, Governor	8-6-8-2-0
Turner, James	0-1-0-?-?

Vernons Estate	2-0-11-11-0
Waldron, Isaac	0-1-7-0-1
Walker, John	0-1-1-0-0
Walton (?), Christopher	0-4-3-3-0
Ward, Thomas	0-1-0-0-**0**
Watters (Walters?), Samuel	0-0-10-10-3
Wayman, Thomas	0-1-1-0-0
Weaver, Susannah	0-0-2-3-0
West, Arthur	0-1-0-0-0
West, James	0-1-0-0-0
West, Robert	0-1-0-0-0
Wilkinson, John	0-2-2-1-0
Willetts, JoBuck	0-1-0-1-0
Willetts, Samuel	0-1-0-0-0
Williams, Henry	0-1-0-0-0
Wilson, Richard	0-1-0-1-0
Wingate, Edward	0-2-3-4-0
Wingate, John	0-1-2-4-0

1772 Brunswick County, North Carolina Tax List
Saint Philips Parish

Adderson, Christopher	0-1-0-0-0
Allen, Elenor	0-1-1-0-0
Allston, Joseph	0-1-4-4-0
Ancrum, John	0-1-9-11-0
Anderson, John	0-1-0-0-0
Baccott, Samuel	0-1-0-0-0
Barrett, Wm.	0-1-0-0-0
Bassett, David	0-1-0-0-0
Bassford, James	0-1-2-0-0
Bearfield, Miles	0-1-1-0-0
Bell, James	0-2-0-2-0
Bell, James Junr.	0-2-1-1-0
Bell, John	0-2-0-0-0
Bellone, Michael	0-1-4-3-0
Benton, Job	0-1-0-0-0
Benton, Moses	0-2-0-0-0
Boone, Thomas	0-3-0-0-0
Cahoone, Macajiah	0-1-0-0-0
Cains, Christopher	0-1-1-3-0
Cains, John	0-1-0-1-0
Cains, Richard	0-1-0-0-0

Cains, Wm.	0-1-3-0-0
Caulkins, Elias	0-1-0-0-0
Caulkins, Wm.	0-1-0-0-0
Cheeseborough, John	0-1-0-1-0
Churs (Cheers?), John	0-1-0-0-0
Clifton, John	0-1-0-0-0
Conner, Morris	0-1-1-0-0
Corbett, James	0-1-1-1-0
Crandal, Elijah	0-1-0-0-0
Cumbo, David	0-1-0-0-0
Cumbo, Stephen	0-3-0-0-0
Daniell, Robert	0-1-2-11-0
Daniell, Sarah	0-0-2-5-0
Daniell, Stephen	0-1-4-4-0
Davis, Jane	0-0-0-3-0
Davis, Roger	2-1-15-17-1
Davis, Thomas	0-1-16-18-2
Davis, Wm.	0-2-10-6-1
Dement, Charles	
Dement, John	0-1-0-0-0
Drew, John	0-3-0-0-0
Dry, Wm.	2-2-40-40-6
Eagles, Richard. Estate	0-0-24-26-0
Eagleson, John	0-1-1-1-0
Eagon, Elizabeth	0-1-4-6-0
Earle, Joseph	0-2-0-0-0
Ellis, Robert	0-2-10-5-1
Etheridge, John	0-1-0-0-0
Etheridge, Samuel	0-2-0-1-0
Faulkner, Wm.	0-1-0-0-0
Fergus, John	2-1-1-2-0
Forristor, John	0-1-0-0-0
Fowler, Ann	0-0-0-2-0
Frankum, Joshua	0-1-0-0-0
Gallaway, John	0-1-0-2-0
Gallaway, Thomas	0-1-1-0-0
Gallaway, Wm.	0-1-0-2-0
Gause, Needham	0-2-3-2-0
Gause, Wm.	0-2-7-5-0
Generett, John	0-1-1-1-0
Gibson, Alexander	0-1-1-0-0
Godfrey, Wm.	0-1-1-1-0
Godwin, Ann	0-0-1-2-0
Gore, Wm.	0-1-0-0-0

Grange, John	2-1-20-34-6
Gressett, Wm.	0-3-3-4-0
Hall, Thomas	2-1-10-10-2
Hart, Abigal	0-0-0-1-0
Hasell, James	0-2-10-6-0
Hasell, Susanah	0-0-3-2-0
Hawkins, Wm.	0-1-0-0-0
Hewett, Ebenezer	0-1-0-0-0
Hewett, Elisha	0-1-0-0-0
Hewett, Hezekiah	0-1-0-0-0
Hewett, Jacob	0-1-0-0-0
Hewett, Joseph	0-2-2-0-0
Hewett, Philip	0-1-0-0-0
Hewett, Richard	0-1-0-0-0
Hickman, John	0-2-0-0-0
Hill, Wm.	2-1-1-4-1
Hilliard James	0-1-0-0-0
Hilliard, Jessey	0-1-0-0-0
Hines, Daniell	0-1-0-0-0
Hines, Jonas	0-1-0-0-0
Holden, Benjamin	0-2-0-0-0
Holmes, Edmond	0-1-1-1-0
Howard, Jetus	0-1-0-0-0
Howes, Robert	2-1-18-24-6
Jacobs, Zacheriah	0-1-0-0-0
Keeter, Charles	0-1-0-0-0
Lay, Enus	0-1-0-0-0
Lay, John	0-1-0-0-0
Lenoard, Samuel	0-1-0-0-0
Leonard, Henry	0-2-0-0-0
Leonard, Henry Junr.	0-1-0-0-0
Leonard, Samuel Junr.	0-1-0-0-0
Lewis, Jacob	0-1-0-0-0
Liles, Benjamin	0-1-0-0-0
Lockwood, Joseph	0-1-0-0-0
Lord, Wm.	2-1-12-8-0
Ludlam, Jeremiah	0-1-0-1-1
Ludlam, Joshua	0-1-0-0-0
Mackay, Arthur	0-1-0-0-0
Maclaine, Bryant	0-1-0-0-0
Marion, Isaac	0-1-5-6-0
Marlow, James	0-1-0-0-0
Marlow, John	0-0-0-1-0
McIlhenny, James	0-2-0-0-0
Mills, Wm.	0-3-0-0-0

104

Mimms, David	0-1-0-0-0
Mimms, George	0-3-0-0-0
Mooney, Wm.	0-1-0-0-0
Moore, George	0-0-7-1-0
Moore, Maurice retd. Since (?)	4-5-32-28-2
Munro, Hugh	0-1-0-3-1
Neal, Margaret	0-0-1-2-0
Neal, Thomas	0-2-6-10-0
Neale, Samuel	0-1-6-7-0
Nugent, Edmond	0-1-0-0-0
Ogden, Wm.	0-1-0-0-0
Pennington, Wm.	0-1-0-1-0
Phelps, Jacob	0-1-0-0-0
Potter, Miles	0-2-0-1-0
Potter, Robert	0-1-1-1-0
Pryor, Seth	0-1-1-0-0
Quince, Parker	0-1-2-9-2
Quince, Richard	2-5-99-51-5
Quince, Richard Junr.	2-1-23-23-0
Ris, John	0-1-0-0-0
Robbins, Arthur	0-1-0-0-0
Robbins, Jethro	0-1-0-0-0
Robeson, John	0-1-0-0-0
Rogers, John	0-1-1-0-0
Rogers, Richard	0-1-0-0-0
Roots, John	0-1-1-1-0
Rouse, Thomas	0-1-0-0-0
Rowan, John	6-5-20-18-3
Russ, Joseph	0-1-0-0-0
Savage, Frances	0-1-0-0-0
Sellers, Elisha	0-1-0-0-0
Sellers, James	0-1-0-0-0
Sellers, Joel	0-1-0-0-0
Sellers, Martha	0-1-0-0-0
Sellers, Simon	0-1-0-0-0
Sessions, Thomas	0-1-0-1-0
Simmonds, Isaac	0-5-1-0-0
Simmonds, John	0-1-8-6-0
Simpson, Willm, Jun.	0-1-1-0-0
Simpson, Willm, Senr.	0-3-4-4-0
Skipper, Clemonds	0-1-0-0-0
Skipper, Moses	0-1-0-0-0
Smith, Daniel	0-1-0-0-0
Smith, James	0-1-0-0-0
Smith, John	0-1-0-0-0

Smuth [sic], David	0-1-0-0-0
Snow, Robert	2-1-9-5-4
Souls, Gideon	0-1-0-0-0
Souls, Joseph	0-1-0-0-0
Souls, Silvenus	0-1-0-0-0
Stanaland, John	0-1-0-0-0
Stanaland, Samuel	0-1-0-0-0
Stanaland, Thomas	0-1-0-0-0
Stanton, John	0-1-0-1-1
Stevins, Alexander	0-2-0-0-0
Stone, John	0-1-0-0-0
Sturgis, Jonathan	0-1-1-0-0
Swain, David	0-1-0-0-0
Swaine, Arthur	0-1-0-0-0
Swaine, Jonathan	0-1-4-4-0
Swaine, Rebecca	0-1-1-2-0
Tharp, Samuel	0-3-0-0-0
Thomas, John	0-1-0-0-0
Todd, Thomas	0-1-1-0-0
Tyler, John	0-1-0-0-0
Vernon, Willm. Estate	0-2-9-13-1
Vines, John	0-1-0-0-0
Waldron, Isaac	0-1-8-8-1
Ward, John	0-1-0-0-0
Waters, Joseph Esta.	0-1-13-11-1
Waters, Samuel	0-1-17-18-1
Waters, Wm. Estate	0-0-5-3-0
Weaver, Susannah	0-0-2-3-0
Wells, Robert	0-1-1-1-0
West, Arthur	0-1-0-0-0
West, Merideth	0-1-0-0-0
West, Robert	0-1-0-0-0
White, James	0-2-3-1-0
Williams, Benedick	0-1-0-0-0
Williams, Henry	0-1-0-0-0
Willitts,	0-1-0-0-0
Willitts, JoBuck	0-1-1-0-0
Willitts, Mary	0-1-0-1-0
Wingate, Edward	0-2-4-5-0
Wingate, John	0-1-3-5-0
Woodside, Robert	0-1-0-0-0

Summary: Whites 238   Negro Men 526

Negro woman 515
Negro boys 46   In all 1325 taxables
Chair wheels 28 in all (i.e. carriages)

Among those residents was Major General Robert Howe (listed as Howes in the 1772 Saint Philips Tax List). He was an important southern leader, active in military matters of the time, circa 1776, advising national leaders such as George Washington.

The Revolutionary War Period - 1775

Shipwrecks

Since the days of ships entering waters, there have been shipwrecks. The remains of those ships and their treasurers continue to be located throughout the coastal waters of North Carolina, some documented, others not yet found.

In 1775, the ship, The *Elizabeth & Mary*, arriving from England, was lost while entering Cape Fear Inlet. There has been no salvage of this ship.

In 1784, a ship of unknown registry, the *Betsey*, sailing for Antigua, was totally lost near Cape Fear. The boat, *Impala*, sank in 1878 while sailing from Havana to New York with a large cache of diamonds and jewels. The gems were contained in a teakwood chest and worth $750,000. It was lost in a wreck a few hundred yards offshore from the Cape Fear River.

Brunswick County has recorded over 600 historical points of interest including seven Civil War ships resting in it's waters. Among those ruins are the remains seen at low tide off the east end of Holden Beach. Hidden beneath the waves are the historic ruins of one of those old ships including

107

the *USS Peterhoff.* Over 20 objects have been reclaimed from this wreck, dated about 1850-1874.

Many North Carolina, and Brunswick County residents participated fully in all aspects of the Revolutionary War. Many lost their lives, some on those ships and others on land. By 1776, North Carolina's Continental Congress representatives, Joseph Hewes, William Hooper, and John Penn, signed the Declaration of Independence.

Between 1776 and 1779, Gen. Robert Howe, a resident of Brunswick County, was transferred to the north and while there became commander of West Point, then involved in the defense of the Hudson River.

Notably, he was involved in the "affairs" of General Benedict Arnold. In 1779-80, Howe was president of the Arnold court-martial for his misconduct including the use of Army transportation equipment for personal service. Arnold was found guilty and sentenced to a reprimand. Howe died in 1786 after being elected to the North Carolina House of Commons, representing Brunswick County. A memorial remains in the Smithville Burying Ground, in Southport.

During the Revolutionary War, Brunswick Town was a major supply base. By the spring of 1776 several factors affected the decline of Brunswick Town, the hub of Brunswick County. Yet, Brunswick Town was named the county seat and remained so until 1779.

As the War years faded, by 1779, Lockwood Folly was named the county seat. Court was convened at the house of John Bell until a courthouse could be built in 1786. (Note: John Bell was listed as early as the 1769 Tax rosters.)

Colonial Plantations

Sixty-six prominent plantations on the Lower Cape Fear River are described in Colonel Alfred Moore Waddell's History of New Hanover County. These colonial plantations were a very refined and cultivated society. Classical learning, wit, and oratory, coupled with hospitality, entertainment, and festivity were an everyday part of their lives. However, the owners looked after their estates and kept well informed as to the political and social on-goings of the area, state and nation. Some even housed extensive libraries and valuable furnishings.

The family coach or gigs transported the residents to neighboring plantations or church. The gentlemen wore powdered wigs and knee-britches with buckled low-quartered shoes, and perhaps a gold or silver snuffbox.

Some of the more prominent plantation owners included:

Governor Burington of Governors Point, General Robert Howe of Howe's Point, Nathaniel Moore of York, Governor Arthur Dobbs of Russelboro, Roger Moore of Orton, James Smith of Kendal, Elaezar Allen of Lilliput, John Moore of Pleasant Oaks, Nathaniel Rice of Old Town Creek, John Baptista Ashe, of Spring Garden, later called Grovely, Chief Justice Hasell of Belgrange, Schencking Moore of Hullfields, John Davis of Davis Plantation, John Dalrymple of Dalrymple Place (who commanded Fort Johnston), John Anerum of Old Town, Marsden Campbell of Clarendon, Richard Eagles of

The Forks, Judge Alfred Moore of Buchoi, John Waddell of Belville, and Govenor Benjamin Smith of Belvedere. All of these plantations were below Wilmington, into the present Brunswick County.

Benjamin Smith
1756-1826
Governor of North Carolina from 1810-1811

The Quince's

Further north, on the northerly side of the Cape Fear, in the Wilmington area, was Rose Hill, the residence of the Quince family, and Rock Hill, the Davis family. These were two smaller and somewhat inferior rice plantations as compared to the large ones previously listed.

The Quinces were one of the first English settlers. Mr. Parker Quince was a merchant. Mr. William Soranzo Quince adopted the name of Hassell as his last name in an attempt to provide heirs for his mother, whose surname of Hassell would have died out with his generation. However, even with this

110

effort, he was not to have a son to keep his mother's progeny alive. His mother, Susanna Hassell, was the granddaughter of Chief Judge Hassell.

The Davis Rock Hill Plantation

The Davis Rock Hill Plantation belonged to Mr. Jehu Davis, and later his son, Thomas J. Davis. Both of these families left legacies of honesty and respectability.

Belville

The town of Bellville is located in Brunswick County's northeast corner along the Brunswick River and about five miles from the Cape Fear River. It lies at the intersection of highways 74-76 and North Carolina Highway 133/17. The town is located on portions of the former 280 Belville Plantation. Archibald McAlester owned the Belville Plantation in the late 1700's. Later it was the home of Governor Daniel L. Russell.

Governor Daniel L. Russell   1845-1908

Governor Russel died on this property in 1908. He was the Governor of North Carolina from 1897 – 1901.

A post office named Easy Hill was located in this vicinity in 1879 but was discontinued in 1889.

The Belville Plantation property was chartered in 1977 and later incorporated as the town of Belville in 1979. The town has a current population of 1440 residents.

The Brunswick Inn

The Brunswick Inn, of Southport (301 E Bay Street), was originally built as the summer residence of Benjamin Smith, founder of Smithville (Southport). (He was the 10th governor of North Carolina.) This mansion overlooks the mouth of the Cape Fear River. Tony, the whimsical resident ghost sometimes makes his presence known there. Tony was a harpist who played at the Inn and on local riverboats during the mid 1800's for formal balls. He drowned off Bald Head Island in 1882 in a boating accident. He has adopted the Inn as his home and roams the halls regularly.

Poverty in Brunswick County

Grand structure abounded throughout Brunswick County as the wealthy landowners built their plantation homes. Not always large, they still continued to exude the atmosphere of structure and grandeur. At the same time, there were those who lived in poverty within the grand plantations; some on the same lands and others nearby or removed and in remote areas like the Green Swamps. Many of these poor were content to live in poverty, although it seems the numbers choosing this lifestyle were small. Janet Schaw described some of them, as she saw it:

"Nature holds out to them everything that can contribute to conveniency, or tempt to luxury, yet the

112

inhabitants resist both, and if they can raise as much corn and pork, as to subsist them in the most slovenly manner, they ask no more; and as a very small proportion of their time service for that purpose, the rest is spent in sauntering thro' the woods with a gun or sitting under a rustick shade, drinking New England rum made into grog, the most shocking liquor you can imagine...These I speak of are only the peasantry of the country."

However, hand in hand, they worshipped together and built the county that now exists.

1790

By 1790 Brunswick County had grown, and many of the current surnames in the county are noticeable on the Census records. Several are included here to document the founding county residents.

1790 Brunswick County Census Records

Key:
1) Free White Male age 16 and up (including Head of Household)
2) Free White Males under age 16
3) Free White Females (including Head of Household)
4) All other free persons, except Indians, not taxed
5) Slaves
- -

		1	2	3	4	5	
22-1	Neal, Thomas	1	2	.	1	20	
22-2	Vernon, Eleanor	.	1	3	.	13	
22-3	Rundleson, Archibald	1	3	1	.	3	
22-4	Betts, William	2	3	2	.	5	
22-5	Richardson, Elizabeth	.	.	2	.	2	
22-6	Walters, Sarah ?	.	1	3	.	26	Watters
22-7	Vines, Samuel	1	2	4	.	.	

22-8	Turner, Amy	1	.	2	.	12
22-9	Graves, Benjamin	1	.	5	.	.
22-10	Holms, Moses	3	1	1	.	1
22-11	Hall, John Esq.	2	1	4	.	43
22-12	Grange, John	2	.	.	.	39
22-13	Taylor, Solomon,	1	3	3	.	.
22-14	Keater, Sarah	.	1	3	.	.
22-15	Boon, John	1	3	5	.	.
22-16	Fruman, James	2	.	7	.	1
22-17	Curray, Daniel	2	.	2	.	.
22-18	Allen, Cain Jr.	1	.	.	.	8
22-19	Root, John	1	2	6	.	16
22-20	Smith, James	1	1	4	.	.
22-21	Keater, Nehamiah	1	.	2	.	.
22-22	Keater, William	1	.	.	.	.
22-23	Norris, Thomas	1	.	2	.	.
22-24	Morris, Robert	1	.	1	.	.
22-25	Morris, Thomas	1	1	3	.	.
22-26	Jennots, Benjamin	1	.	1	.	.
22-27	Jennots, Winnie	.	.	2	.	.
22-28	Jennots, John	1	.	1	.	.
22-29	Pounds, John Sr.	1	.	.	.	.
22-30	Pounds, John Jr.	1	.	2	.	.
22-31	Pounds, Isaac	1	.	2	.	.
22-32	Skipper, John	1	.	3	.	.
22-33	Skipper, Moses	1	3	2	.	.
23-1	Skipper, Abraham	1	2	3	.	.
23-2	Flours, James	3	.	2	.	20
	Flowers ?					
23-3	Rowan, John	1	.	2	.	21
23-4	Allen, Drury	2	.	2	.	12
23-5	Newell, Thomas	2	.	4	.	.
23-6	Liles, Benjamin	1	2	5	.	.
23-7	Clark, Thomas	1	.	1	.	56
23-8	Mills, Jane	.	1	1	.	3
23-9	Skipper, James	1	.	2	.	.
23-10	Wheeler, William	1	.	2	.	.
23-11	Highsmith, John	3	.	3	.	.
23-12	Potter, James	1	3	3	.	.
23-13	Potter, Mills	3	1	.	2	
23-14	Leonard, Samuel	2	1	2	.	2
23-15	Carrol, John	1	1	3	.	.
23-16	Simpson, Elisha	1	3	4	.	.
23-17	Leonard, Henry	1	1	3	.	.
23-18	Sparksman, William	1	.	1	.	.

114

23-19 Williams, Margaret	2	.	2	.	.
23-20 Barrow, Huzzy,	1	.	3	.	.
23-21 Mills, Benjamin	1	1	3	.	9
23-22 Leonard, Eleanor	3	1	5	.	10
23-23 Gause, Benjamin	1	2	3	.	4
23-24 Aderson, John	3	.	7	.	2
23-25 Mills, William	1	2	1	.	.
23-26 Sullivan, Edward	1	3	2	.	4
23-27 Holms, John	1	.	.	.	.
23-28 Sellars, James	2	5	3	.	.
23-29 Potter, Miles	1	.	.	.	.
23-30 Harris, Richard	1	3	2	.	.
23-31 Sparksman, Levi	1	3	1	.	.
23-32 Sparksman, Richard	1	.	1	.	.
23-33 Johnson, John	1	2	1	.	.
23-34 Young, William	1	.	.	.	.
23-35 Holms, Joseph	1	.	.	.	.
23-36 Hays, John	1	3	4	.	.
24-1 Taylor, John William	1	.	.	.	.
24-2 Robbins, Benjamin	1	1	1	.	.
24-3 Robbins, Arthur	3	2	3	.	.
24-4 McMurray, William	1	1	2	.	.
24-5 Greer, John	1	2	3	.	.
24-6 Moore, Mary	.	3	3	.	5
24-7 Bell, James Sr.	1	.	2	.	9
24-8 Daniel, Stephen	2	3	3	.	8
24-9 Woodside, Robert	1	1	5	.	1
24-10 Gressel, Reuben	1	1	3	.	5
24-11 Gause, Charles	1	1	4	.	15
24-12 Swain, David	1	.	1	.	1
24-13 Bell, James Jr.	1	2	4	.	3
24-14 Folks, Shadrack	1	2	3	.	.
24-15 Wescut, John	1	1	1	.	.
24-16 Galloway, Nathaniel	1	1	1	.	3
24-17 Umphry, Joseph Humphrey ?	1	.	2	.	3
24-18 Galloway, Sarah	.	2	3	.	1
24-19 Long, Henry	1	2	3	.	1
24-20 Cain, John	1	1	5	.	9
24-21 Goodman, Henry	1	4	1	.	1
24-22 Sellars, Simon	1	1	2	.	1
24-23 How, Sarah ?	.	2	2	.	20 Howe
24-24 Goodman, William	2	1	3	.	3
24-25 Bell, Samuel	1	2	3	.	1

115

24-26 Gibberd, Retua ?	1	2	4	.	.		
24-27 Felps, Martha	.	1	1	.	.	Phelps ?	
24-28 Wescut, Jeremiah	2	1	1	.	.		
24-29 Price, Solomon	1	1	3	.	.		
24-30 Sellars, Mathew	2	1	5	.	2		
24-31 Hammer, Solomon	1	.	1	.	.		
24-32 Bell, Nathaniel	1	1	2	.	.		
24-33 Burley, Oxford ?	1	.	2	.	1	Beirley	
24-34 Morgan, William	1	2	2	.	.		
24-35 Alexander, James	1	2	3	.	.		
25-1 Sparksman, William	1	.	4	.	.		
25-2 Williams, Benjamin	1	2	3	.	.		
25-3 McDougal, Runnel	2	1	3	.	.		
25-4 Bennett, Daniel	1	1	3	.	.		
25-5 Swain, Joseph	2	.	3	.	2		
25-6 Dozier, Richard	1	3	3	.	2		
25-7 Boatright, William	1	.	1	.	.		
25-8 Gibbs, William	1	1	1	.	1		
25-9 Goodman, William	1	.	.	.	1		
25-10 Parker, William	1	2	3	.	11		
25-11 Clemmings, Timothy Clemmons ?	1	.	2	.	5		
25-12 Chain, James	1	1	2	.	3		
25-13 Rook, John	1	.	1	.	.		
25-14 Balloon, Daniel	1	1	4	.	16		
25-15 Bell, Robert	1	.	6	.	23		
25-16 Russ, Thomas	3	3	4	.	8		
25-17 Holden, Sarah	1	1	3	.	.		
25-18 Swain, Levi	1	2	2	.	.		
25-19 Swain, James	1	2	3	.	.		
25-20 Gause, Susanna	1	1	2	.	19		
25-21 Hewet, Philip	1	4	4	.	.	Huett ?	
25-22 Hewet, William	1	2	1	.	.	Huett ?	
25-23 Hewet, Ebenezer	1	2	2	.	.	Huett ?	
25-24 Clark, Jonah	1	3	2	.	5		
25-25 Clark, Henry	1	.	1	.	8		
25-26 Hewet, Joseph Sr.	2	1	.	.	1	Huett ?	
25-27 Hewet, Joseph Jr.	.	1	.	1	Huett ?		
25-28 Sharp, William	1	.	1	.	.		
25-29 Holden, Jobe,	1	2	3	.	.		
25-30 Holden, James	1	.	.	.	.		
25-31 Holden, Famus	.	.	1	.	.	??	
25-32 Hines, Betsey	.	.	4	.	.		
25-33 Singletary, Benjamin	2	.	1	.	.		

116

25-34	Willis, Henry	1	1	1	.	.	
25-35	Hewet, Ezekiel	3	.	2	.	.	Huett ?
25-36	Hewet, Robert	1	.	1	.	.	Huett ?
25-37	Hewet, Samuel	1	.	1	.	.	Huett ?
26-1	Gause, Bryant	1	.	3	.	18	
26-2	Stanley, Thomas	1	4	2	.	.	
26-3	Stanley, Samuel	1	2	3	.	1	
26-4	Tharp, Charles	1	.	5	.	.	
26-5	Hewet, Reuben	1	.	2	.	.	Huett ?
26-6	Robinson, John	1	3	3	.	.	
26-7	Hewet, David	1	3	3	.	.	Huett ?
26-8	Dudley, Jeremiah	1	1	1	.	3	
26-9	Ivey, Lewis	1	1	6	.	.	
26-10	Jones, William	1	.	1	.	.	
26-11	Holden, Benjamin	1	.	3	.	.	
26-12	Hankens, Dennis	1	2	3	.	46	
26-13	Daniel, Robert	1	2	3	.	14	
26-14	Tharp, Samuel	2	1	3	.	.	
26-15	Smith, Jeremiah	2	.	1	.	1	
26-16	Gause, John	1	1	1	.	7	
26-17	Foster, Electus Medus	1	3	1	.	15	
26-18	Sullivan,	1	3	3	.	.	
26-20	Craig, Lewis	1	2	3	.	.	
26-21	Jones, John	1	2	3	.	.	
26-22	McCree, Griffith McKinsey ?	1	1	3	.	30	
26-24	Clark, James	1	2	2	.	19	
26-25	Drier, John	1	2	1	.	.	Drew ?
26-26	Gause, Nedam	2	4	1	.	5	
26-27	Goodman, Henry	1	2	1	.	.	
26-28	Franks, Sarah	.	.	1	.	18	
26-29	Roberts, Patty	1	2	1	.	16	
26-30	Gause, William	2	3	3	.	37	
26-31	Clark, Henry	3	3	3	.	19	
26-32	Taylor, Mary	.	.	2	.	3	
26-33	Corners, John	1	.	4	.	.	
26-34	Wills, Henry	1	.	2	.	.	
26-35	Sellars, Mathew	1	2	2	.	.	
26-36	Sellars, Elisha	1	3	1	.	.	
27-1	Malsby, Samuel	1	3	2	.	.	
27-2	Quince, Richard	1	.	2	.	40	
27-3	Weathers, Thomas	1	.	3	.	23	
27-4	Lord, William	1	1	3	.	15	
27-5	Rulks, Samuel ?	3	1	3	.	6	Rooks

#	Name	C1	C2	C3	C4	C5	Note
27-6	McCallister, Archibald (McCalester)	1	.	.	.	70	
27-7	McCallister, James (McCalester)	1	.	.	.	13	
27-8	Wear, George	1	.	.	.	21	Ware ?
27-9	Davis, Thomas	3	1	3	.	35	
27-10	Supper, Isaac	1	2	.	.	.	
27-11	Supper, Clemmon	1	2	3	.	.	
27-12	Elkson, Samuel	2	.	2	.	.	
27-13	Elkson, Benjamin	2	.	6	.	.	
27-14	Supper, Jesse	1	1	1	.	.	
27-15	Butterland, Reddon	2	.	.	.	2	
27-16	McKethern, Gillard	1	1	2	.	.	
27-17	Howard, George	1	1	6	.	.	
27-18	Ward, John	3	2	4	.	.	
27-19	Hickman, Thomas	1	1	1	.	.	
27-20	Hickman, Samuel	1	.	2	.	.	
27-21	Runnles, William	1	2	3	.	3	
27-22	Soles, Silvenus	1	.	1	.	.	
27-23	Mandsfield, William (Mansfield ?)	2	2	3	.	.	
27-24	Sellars, James	1	.	1	.	.	
27-25	Little, Thomas	3	.	.	.	.	
27-26	Bennett, Joseph	1	1	2	.	.	
27-27	Boarman, Estherland	1	2	3	.	.	
27-28	Hill, Joel	1	2	3	.	.	
27-29	Hill, Ezekiel	1	3	4	.	.	
27-30	Colbert, James	1	.	2	.	2	
27-31	Connell, Redy	1	.	1	.	.	
27-32	Newell, Peter	1	1	4	.	.	
27-33	Aderson, James	1	1	4	.	2	
27-34	Taylor, Benjamin	2	2	7	.	.	
27-35	Gressel, William	1	3	5	.	12	
27-36	Taylor, Benjamin,	1	.	2	.	.	
27-37	Hargrove, Samuel	1	1	5	.	.	
28-1	Wingate, William	1	1	4	.	7	
28-2	Simmons, Benjamin	1	3	1	.	.	
28-3	Simmons, John	1	1	3	.	.	
28-4	Russ, John	2	3	1	.	1	
28-5	Floyd, Morris	1	2	4	.	.	
28-6	Sellars, William	1	3	4	.	.	
28-7	Sellars, Jordan	1	.	2	.	.	
28-8	Floyd, Bets	1	1	2	.	.	
28-9	Roach, James	1	.	4	.	.	
28-10	Ward, Milly	3	3	7	.	.	

28-11 Dugger, John	1	4	2	.	.
28-12 Edwards, Thomas	1	4	4	.	.
28-13 Stevens, Makijah	1	.	1	.	.
28-14 Soles, Timothy	1	.	2	.	.
28-15 Soles, Nathaniel	1	1	2	.	.
28-16 Goodman, Luke	1	1	2	.	.
28-17 Soles, Joseph	2	1	7	.	.
28-18 Jerret, Elias	1	1	4	.	.
28-19 Carter, William	1	.	.	.	.
28-20 Alford, Amy	1	2	3	.	.
28-21 Mooney, William	1	.	8	.	7
28-22 Bick, John	1	2	4	.	.
28-23 Reeves, Solomon	1	5	3	.	.
28-24 Hickman, Samuel	1	1	3	.	.
28-25 Sugs, ? Ezekiel	2	2	3	.	.
28-26 Gooden, Jonas	3	.	2	.	.
28-27 Arnold, Eleanor	.	1	3	.	.
28-28 Simmons, Ann	2	2	2	.	.
28-29 Simmons, John	1	.	2	.	.
28-30 Norris, Frederick	1	.	2	.	.
28-31 Norris, William	1	.	2	.	.
28-32 Norris, Jerulia	.	.	2	.	.
28-33 Benson, Nathan	1	1	2	.	.
28-34 Marlow, Nathan	1	1	5	.	.
28-35 Simmons, Thomas	3	1	2	.	.
28-36 Simms, William	1	3	3	.	.
28-37 Duncan, Elias	1	3	3	.	.
28-38 Mooney, John	2	3	2	.	.
29-1 Stevens, Alexander	1	1	6	.	3
29-2 Counsel, Hardy	1	1	3	.	.
29-3 Simmons, John	1	.	.	.	.
29-4 Smith, Simon	1	2	2	.	.
29-5 Clark, Benjamin Jr.	1	3	1	.	.
29-6 Hardy, Andrew	1	1	2	.	.
29-7 Soles, Markinne	1	3	1	.	.
29-8 Powell, Abraham	1	3	2	.	.
29-9 Powell, Jacob	1	1	2	.	.
29-10 Cox, John	1	2	3	.	2
29-11 Connell, Edward	2	1	3	.	4
29-12 Williams, Benjamin	1	1	2	.	.
29-13 Soles, Benjamin	1	.	1	.	.
29-14 Williams, Moses	1	1	2	.	.
29-15 Mills, John	1	2	3	.	.
29-16 Gressel, George	1	2	2	.	17
29-17 Simmons, Moses	1	2	4	.	1

29-18 Russ, Francis	1	2	2	.	.	
29-19 Simmons, Isaac	1	2	1	.	5	
29-20 Stevens, Joshua	1	2	2	.	.	
29-21 Abbott, William	2	.	1	.	.	
29-22 Canniday, John	1	.	7	.	.	
29-23 Gore, Jonathan	1	3	5	.	.	
29-24 Wingate, Sarah	1	.	1	.	7	
29-25 Stevens, Mathew	2	2	4	.	.	
29-26 Rhoads, John ?	1	.	3	.	.	Rhodes
29-27 Reeves, Mark	1	2	1	.	.	
29-28 Rhoads, Mary ?	1	.	1	.	.	Rhodes
29-29 Rogers, John	1	1	7	.	.	
29-30 Smith, James	1	1	3	.	2	
29-31 Thomas, John	3	1	2	.	.	
29-32 Lay, John	2	3	2	.	.	
29-33 Gore, James	1	1	2	.	.	
29-34 Ellis, Mary	.	1	2	.	.	
29-35 Smith, John	1	.	3	.	.	
29-36 Cox, Elijah	3	2	5	.	.	
29-37 McKeather, Alexander	1	.	1	.	.	
29-38 Cone, Elisha	2	1	2	.	.	Gore ?
30-1 Norris, Thomas	1	.	2	.	.	
30-2 Smithars, John	1	3	3	.	.	
30-3 Jordan, Thomas	1	.	2	.	.	
30-4 Smith, John	3	3	3	.	2	
30-5 Simmons, Benjamin	1	3	1	.	.	
30-6 Simmons, John	1	1	3	.	.	
30-7 Sellars, Mathew	1	.	1	.	.	
30-8 Clew, ? George	1	1	3	.	.	
30-9 Outlaw, Palatrah ?	1	1	2	.	.	
30-10 Benton, Hardy	1	2	4	.	.	
30-11 Benton, Joab	1	3	2	.	.	
30-12 Lay, Joseph	1	.	1	.	.	
30-13 Stanley, Hugh	1	2	3	.	.	
30-14 Mooney, Thomas	1	2	1	.	.	
30-15 Stanley, Nedam	1	1	1	.	.	
30-16 Benson, Abraham	1	2	3	.	4	
30-17 Stanley, Margaret	.	.	2	.	2	
30-18 Mink, Lucretia	.	5	2	.	.	
30-19 Murrrel, William	1	1	3	.	.	
30-20 Gore, William Esq.	1	3	2	.	2	
30-21 Dupree, Lewis Esq.	1	2	2	.	34	
30-22 Alston, Francis	2	2	2	.	60	

30-23 Howell, James	1	.	.	.	.
30-24 Egle, Joseph	1	3	1	.	29
30-25 Moore, Alfred	.	.	.	.	48
30-26 Flanican, William Flannigan	1	.	5	.	.
30-27 Dry, William	1	.	.	.	2
30-28 Ward, Frederick	2	.	.	.	6
30-29 Smith, Benjamin Esq.	2	2	14	2	221
30-30 Richards, Nicholas	1	3	1		

In 1804, circuit rider Reverend Francis Asbury, described Brunswick as "an old town; demolished houses, and the noble walls of a brick church; there remain but four houses entire". British redcoats had burned the town. By 1816 most that was destroyed by the British was never rebuilt and only two or three wooden homes were all that remained.

George Washington Visits the Gause Manor-1791

A letter dated 25 April 1791, and written by Mrs. Jane Anna Simpson to her sister, on the day of a reception in Wilmington, for General George Washington, describes his visit. "This day he dines with the gentlemen of the town; in the evening a grand ball and illumination; tomorrow takes his leave. I believe the light horse are to escort him on a day's journey on his way Chas'ton." Mrs. Simpson continues to say that Mrs. Quince has given up her house to the Generals and she stays with our uncles."

Upon Gen. Washington's visit across the river to General Smith, at his plantation Belvedere, he was met by a group of thirteen young ladies, representing the thirteen colonies, all dressed in white, leading him to the large brick plantation home, strewing flowers along his route. "Wilmington," wrote General Washington, "has some good houses, pretty compactly built." He continues to say that Monday, the 25th, he attended the ball in Wilmington with sixty-two ladies, illumination and bonfires." It is after this Wilmington visit that he continued into Brunswick County.

In 1791, George Washington, then President, was said

to have ridden a stagecoach or horse and carriage, down the Waterway Road to visit the William Gause Manor. The two were said to have had breakfast and at some point, President Washington hung his "underwear" on the oak tree near the manor. Could Mr. President have taken a "dip" in the ocean, or was this a "handkerchief" as remembered by Mrs. Mary Piggot, 80 years of age in 2007, as she relayed stories of her childhood and an earlier era. President Washington did not spend the night, but continued his travel to the Little River and further into South Carolina. Regardless, the Washington visit is well documented and the over 200-year old oak remains as a testament to the history of the area.

Gause's tomb (the owner of the famous plantation) is visible on old Blueberry Farm Road, about a mile from the location of the Washington Oak Tree.

George Washington Tree

Old Stage Coach Road

During this era (late 1800's), stagecoaches remained the primary method of travel for families and especially the ladies. Highway 179, leading from Shallotte through the Ocean Isle, Sunset Beach and Calabash area, is the same path that many took and was known as the Old Stage Coach trail. This was the main path that post-Revolutionary stagecoaches took when visiting the southeastern coast of Brunswick County. Just off of the Stage Road, near Ocean Isle, is the infamous Waterway Road with its picturesque oak trees, dripping in moss, forming a canopy to welcome visitors.

Southport

Southport was originally incorporated in 1792 as Smithville, named for Governor Benjamin Smith who was also an officer for the Revolution. In 1877 town leaders changed the name to Southport in order to make the small port seem more like THE port of the South. Their plan failed. Southport kept its new name, and remained a small town, barely affected by the heavy shipping traffic to Wilmington.

Dr. W. G. Curtis wrote about Southport in 1905. (Curtis was the quarantine surgeon for the Port of Wilmington for thirty years.)
"Smithville was reached from Wilmington by the line of ocean steamers which were a continuation of the great line to the south. These were four steamers named "The Gladiator," the "C Vanderbilt, the "Governor Dudley" the "North Carolina," the last of which was a spare ship to be used in case of accident to any of the others. They were commanded respectively by Captain Isaac B. Smith, Captain Sterrit, and Capt. Bates, and were very popular, making their trips for many years to Charleston, South Carolina without accident. They started daily from Wilmington on the arrival of the northern train. Breakfast, and dinner were served on board

between Wilmington, and Smithville, and they were fine repasts as they had the markets of Charleston, and Wilmington to rely upon, with all the luxuries they afforded. These steamships took passengers, and freight for Smithville, and made their landing at a wharf near where the steamer *Wilmington* now has her landing. Returning from Charleston they stopped at the same wharf and breakfast served between Smithville, and Wilmington. I will here mention the name of a woman quite celebrated in the annals of Smithville; her name was Mrs. Mary Duffy, who kept an eating-house on the waters edge, which was long patronized by the citizens of Smithville, especially by the pilots. For over twenty-five years Mrs. Duffy arose about three o'clock in the morning, and prepared breakfast for all passengers intending to go up in the steamer. A cup of coffee, or anything else wanted by the pilots, who wanted a morning meal before going to sea in search of vessels. There were several fine deck boats which were very fast, and able to go to sea in all weather; each of these pilot boats corried as many pilots as were necessary, and sometimes did not come into port again until they had put all their pilots aboard incoming vessels. The bar at that time had about 12 feet of water upon it, consequently vessels coming into this port must be of that draft, and built to carry from 1000 to 2000 barrels of naval stores; they also brought from the northern markets what ever freight was offered, and this was nearly all the northern freight because the railroad was very uncertain. Mrs. Duffy was remarkable in her powers of seeing and hearing, and her business was, in addition to supplying meals to wake up passengers who wished to take the steamer to Wilmington as these steamers entered port before light in the morning. It was necessary that Mrs. Duffy go by the sense of hearing, and she could always hear these boats which were side wheelers, far enough out to sea to enable the passengers she had collected to get up and dress, and go down to her establishment for a cup of coffee before going on the steamship wharf; as may be well imagined Mrs. Duffy was a very important character in the life of Smithville, and she was duly appreciated by all the citizens of Smithville as a good, and faithful woman; she lived to a great age and all through the war she continued the same occupation so far as the war would permit but her house was finally burned and her business was destroyed, and she retired to live with her daughter in the house which is now the rectory of St. Philips Episcopal Church, and ended there her long and useful life regretted by all but by none more than the children of Smithville to whom she supplied cakes which were so celebrated as to acquire the name of "Duffy Cakes." This steamship line was discontinued on the completion of the railroad, called The Wilmington & Manchester, which carried all through passengers for southern ports or cities. As may be well imagined, this left Smithville aground upon the shoals, and what to do was a matter for serious consideration. How to get any where from Smithville was a difficulty not easily solved; there were few horses or vehicles of any kind in Smithville, but the river was there at any rate, and if you did not wish to go by land, and ride in a cart you could take a boat, of which there were plenty, and plenty of skillful boatmen to manage them; but neither of these modes of travel suited the public. Mr. Elijah Owen who kept an old fashioned house of entertainment in Smithville had two horses but no buggy; besides one of these horses was an ancient quadruped whose business it was to attend to the transportation of all persons who died to their last resting place, and his services might be required at any moment, and in consideration of these services, he was granted the freedom of the town, and was pastured in the streets of Smithville, from which place he did not wish to go. The other horse was, during the intervals between courts, mostly engaged in transporting people in the country, and ploughing fields belonging to "Uncle Elijah." So the people sat down, and waited, and waited for the arrival of the Rev. Mr. Pickett, and his wife who travelled the circuit in a "one horse shay," and being a man of varied resources of entertaining the people they were always glad to see him approach. The Rev. Mr. Pickett was a man who preached the gospel strictly on Sundays and during the rest of the days of the week, he sat and smoked his pipe in peace, and left his parishoners to enjoy life in their own way. At this time the people of the churches, and their preachers had'nt gone into politics, or any of the side issues which at the present day perplex the minds of the people, and draw their attention away from sacred things; so when the time came, when this reverend gentleman was expected, the citizens who had been sitting on logs or in boats gazing out upon the broad Atlantic for ships to heave in sight turned their backs upon the river, and the ocean, and gazed out in the direction of the country anxiously awaiting his approach that they might grasp his friendly hand in their own, and bid him welcome. It may be well here to remark, that though they were mostly engaged in maritime pursuits they did not forget that there was a better country ahead of them to which sooner or later they must all travel, and they wanted to have the way pointed out to them so they would not be likely to get ashore or lost in any fog which might arise."

In the absence of steam communication it was found necessary to utilize the river as the best way for getting to Wilmington, so one or two enterprising men provided sailing packets on which they embarked and if the wind was fair they made good time to the city. If the wind was ahead however or a dead calm and they had to anchor it has come down to us by common report that they had a pretty good time on board; plenty to eat, and something also to drink which seemed to keep up their spirits while they waited for some body on board, to stick jack knives in the main mast, and whistle for the wind. These adventurous people always arrived in Wilmington Some-Time, which was sufficient. Capt. Samuel Potter, and Capt. Samuel Price were captains in whom they could put implicit trust, and as they were not in a hurry they did not complain. But the necessity of a better mode of travel between Wilmington, and Smithville, soon led to the establishment of a steamboat passenger line by Mr. A. H. Van Boklen the largest distiller of turpentine in the city of Wilmington.

He put on the line the steamer "*Spray*" greatly to the satisfaction of Wilmington, and Smithville, but her schedule

126

was only for summer trade, and at the close of the summer season she was laid up, and soon afterward she was burned. This steamer was under the command of Capt. John B. Price, a Cape Fear pilot of marked ability, and well fitted for the business. She brought down all the summer residents, of whom there were now a great many, and her decks were crowded with passengers, and excursionists. It was about this time that the first tugboats ever on the Cape Fear River were put into service. One of these was the "*Mariner*" under command of Capt. John Davis; the other was the "*Equator*" under command of Jacob A. T. Price. These tug boats however, did not wish to carry passengers and only did so as a favor; so that the means provided for travellers was very unsatisfactory. They assisted greatly in towing of vessels which was all (that) was wanted by the merchants of Wilmington. The time of their service on the Cape Fear River was very short as the war which shortly afterwards begun captured nearly every thing which floated upon the sea. The summer residents of Smithville did not however depend upon these tugboats as they came to Smithville for fun and enjoyment and did not care much whether they went to Wilmington or not until the season was over. They were planters along the Cape Fear River, and retired merchants of Wilmington, and they formed the most delightful society in Smithville for they believed in Smithville as a most delightful place of residence, and were interested in everything that was done and participated in all the amusements of the place. But we are now getting close upon a time when every amusement and every interest commercial or other wise was to feel the dreadful shock of impending war, and go out of existence, leaving Smithville as lonesome and bereft of all pleasure as its worst enemies could desire. In the next chapter of these reminiscences I will go back, and give some account of what happened in more peaceful times."

"..there were many others who ought to be mentioned and whose names ought not to be forgotten. Mr. Thos. Mellhenny, Frederick J. Lord, Philip Prioleau, Dr. John H. Hill. Owen D. Holmes, Dr. Fred Hill, Thos. Cowan, and

Henry N. Howard, were all rice planters from the Cape Fear River, men of education and refinement who spent their summers in Smithville, and were friends of that town to the very last. Mr. Robt. W. Brown also had a fine residence in Smithville, and after a long life as a commission merchant in Wilmington, he loved to spend his summers in ease and tranquility. These gentlemen have all passed over the river, and are forever at rest from their labors, and they leave behind them a record of being Southern gentlemen than which there can be no higher reputation to be desired. There were many others scattered through the county who never lived in Smithville, but they were well known to all its inhabitants as good citizens, and men of the highest worth; many of them sat in the county Board of Magistrates, making the county court of Brunswick the equal of any in the state of North Carolina."

".....Mr. Owen D. Holmes, and family and Dr. John H. Hill were on their plantations of Kendal and Lilliput trying rather vainly to keep up their spirits as there were newspaper reports that Fort Fisher would shortly be attacked by a great force of the enemy. The writer well remembers (and at this period of time it seems like a huge joke) that Doctor Hill insisted that if the Yankees came about his plantation that he would have one shot at them at any rate; but he thought better of this the next day when he gathered together his negroes and started to the interior of the country. Mr. Owen Holmes did the same thing and escaping as they thought into Sampson County where they thought no enemy would ever discover them. But sad and bitter was their experience for they got right in the tract of Sherman and his bummers and all the negroes who had been so carefully taken to this place of safety went over to the enemy and assisted them in their work of destruction and depredation." (Walter G. Curtis)

"In reviewing the period which elapsed from the close of the war up to the election of Governor Vance it will be seen that wise and patriotic men whose names should be known and inscribed upon the pages of history were laboring continually to restore peace and prosperity and in doing this they had to act with great judgement and discretion. It is impossible to name all these men........ While the Democrats of Brunswick county, and I think of the whole state, acted on the principle of restoring peace and making a genuine, happy and reunited country in whose breast patriotism was the moving principle. Col. John D. Taylor, William Watters, Owen D. Holmes, D. S. Cowan, Saml. R. Chinnis, D. C. Allen, John M. Bennett, John Mercer, Wilson McKethan, Saml. And Jabez Frink, John H. Mintz, D. L. Butler, Jesse Lancaster, Peter Rourk, Rufus Galloway, David Gilbert, S. J. Standland, Thomas G. Drew, Francis Moore, W. G. Curtis, and a host of others equally as good, whose names there is not sufficient space to record, were the men who worked in season and out of season to bring back peace to Brunswick county and to the state. These men were assisted as opportunity offered, by nearly every member of the legal profession who practiced at the Brunswick bar, and they were always ready to come over from New Hanover and other counties to help us. " So says Walter Gilman Curtis. His detailed accounts of Southport from 1848 through 1900 are a "must read" for all local genealogists and others interested in a more detailed description of its history.

Brunswick County Jail

The old Brunswick County Jail was built in 1904 for a cost of $6,738. The jail was built to replace the old city jail that was destroyed by fire. The jail was used until 1971 when a new jail was built to the rear. The Southport Historical Society has maintained the old jail since 1984.

The jail is a two-story brick building. It includes two cells, constructed of flat iron bars wrapped together. Each of the two jail cells includes four bunks. There is another jail section on the second floor. The Old Brunswick County Jail is located at the corner of Rhett and Nash Streets in Southport.

Brunswick County Jail

Last Buffalo Hunt in NC

To close out the century, the last recorded buffalo hunt was conducted in North Carolina. In 1799, Joseph Rice kills the last bison, or buffalo, seen in the Asheville area. The way of the Indians is almost gone. No mention of buffaloes can be located for the southeastern North Carolina area at that time, but reason dictates that if not buffalo, other forms of sustenance would soon be harder to locate and the infringement of the white men into the Indian territories would drive them further inland. The area would be forever changed as colonial settlers claimed their land.

Chapter 5

Colonial Life

Life in the 1700's

Life in the early to late 1700's varied greatly sometimes dependent upon the financial status of the individual. The plantation owners lived a very different existence than their loyal slaves. On the other hand it could be extremely challenging to all as they faced the Native Americans, nature, and the new lands. They were presented with a myriad of challenges each and every day. The passages contained herein are but a taste of typical events in their lives..

Clothing

The colonists first wore gray clothing. Later, the women started to wear yellow and orange colored clothes. Young girls wore shifts (white shirts) over their long dresses or skirts. Bonnets were a necessity for the girls.

Men wore trouser (short pants), long socks and black shoes. Young men wore shifts and trousers just like the men. The boys wore vests over their shifts even in the summer. The soldiers wore hats with curled ends so that when it rained they would not get wet, at least not their faces.

Colonial Williamsburg: 18th Century Clothing http://www.history.org/history/clothing/index.cfm gives us an excellent description of the clothing in the 1700's. "Their working clothes were practical, simple, and were different when they worked for something different. It was easy to guess a man's job from the clothes he wore. For example, it was common for a doctor to wear a neat black suit and for a farmer to wear a worn out hat, a long, loose linen shirt, woolen breeches, and simple leather shoes. Men had a lot of shoes and some of their shoes looked like a modern woman's shoes. They usually had buckles. Wealthy men wore fragile pumps on formal occasions." "Men had tall boots to protect their knees when going through thorns in a hurry."

"In the eighteenth century, middle-and-lower class woman wore simple cotton and linen dresses, but wealthy woman wore beautiful gowns made from expensive materials. There were two main types of gowns: the open robe and the closed robe. Before donning the gown, the lady had to put on her undergarments."

The shift was one of the most important garments for a woman. They were made of linen usually with drawstrings at the neck and the sleeves. Sometimes it was finished with lace.

"The corset (or in other words stays) have narrow strips of whale bone, metal, or wood to mold the shape of a woman by putting it around their waists, and having a maid put their foot on the woman's back. The maid would then pull with all of her might at the tightening strings. Corsets gave proper shape and beauty to the woman's body. The hoops gave width to the hip of the woman, and served as pockets beneath the gown. The stockings were constructed of knitted wool, linen, cotton, or silk (and)…were held up by ribbon like underwear tied up above the knee. Ladies fashionable shoes were made of variety of silks and leathers. After all of these undergarments, the lady then put on the actual gown!! The bodice was on the upper part of the gown with the skirt permanently on the waistline."

"The stomacher was a separate decorative triangular-shaped part of the dress, either stitched, hooked, or straight pinned to the bodice of the gown, or the corset beneath. The under part of the gown was the petticoat, a skirt worn beneath the gown.

A gown was the main part of a woman's dress. There were two main types of gowns: the robe anglaise and the robe francais (sack). The sleeve had ruffles attached (to) the gown or to the shift (an undergarment).

"The cap completed the appearance of the woman in the gown, and prevented the need to fix the hair. The cap kept the hair away from the dust and dirt. Usually made of cotton or linen, the cap had many shapes, size, and design." So went the description of ladies wear. (A complete description of men's clothing is located at the colonial web address previously mentioned.)

Candle Making & Basket Making

The colonists used lanterns and candles for light. They made the candle from beeswax and bayberries and braided cotton string for the wick. They melted the beeswax and dipped the string into it over and over until they had a candle.

The settlers (or their slaves) made their own baskets by weaving together thin strips of wood, mostly oak. They dipped the strips in water so it would be easier to handle and shape. It took several days to complete a basket which might be was used to carry, store and gather items and food. Examples of early basket making techniques are still evident today, especially on Highway 17 as you approach Charleston, South Carolina and see the many women selling their wares along the roadside.

Food

The settlers had to provide their own food. They grew corn and scraped it off the cob. Then it was sometimes mashed. They churned their own butter, dried apples and peaches, and preserved any food sources available. Winters were long and summer was the time to prepare for the non-growing seasons. Depending upon the current regulations, they drank coffee, wine apple cider, water, milk or beer.

They cooked over a fire and had pans that had legs so that when you put the pan over the fire it wouldn't burn. Their main staples were grown in the summertime and "shot " in the winter when the men hunted wild game. The coastal residents added fish, clams, oysters and other seafood to their diet, offering a ready supply of rations. Their ingenuity at growing, trapping, hunting, and catching food was only matched by their determination to survive in this new world.

Punishment

In Old Brunswick Town, they were two types of punishment. One was the stocks and the other the pillory. The pillories were used to hold the hands and heads. The stocks held the feet. Punishable offenses in the stocks or pillory included gambling on Sunday, playing on Sunday, or gossiping any day.

The jails, unlike today, were not used as places of punishment. They were used to hold the accused until the time of trial. They were used to hold prisoners who could not afford to pay fines levied upon them by the courts. Punishments, other than fines, were often swift and public...the stocks or the pillory. The pillory was considered a worse punishment than the stocks and it was common for onlookers to throw fruit or rotten vegetables at the criminal. Also used for punishment were the whipping posts and the ducking stool that was dipped into water for short periods of time.

Stocks

The Ducking Stool

Children were even sometimes "bound out". The court contracted with someone for the child to serve as his or her apprentice for a number of years. Sometimes the punishment for a crime was for people to "work it off" by being sold to someone as a servant for a period of years. Even lack of attendance at church was sometimes punishable by a fine. Colonial punishment was sometimes harsh.

Although it is unknown exactly which of these punishments was common or used in Brunswick County, one can assume that common Virginia punishments such as these were also used by the residents of southeastern North Carolina.

Toys and Games

Long ago kids didn't have much time to play. If they did, they played with dominos made from bone or cards. However, the cards were unlike modern cards and did not have numbers on them. They had dots and the kids had to count the dots. Sometimes they might have homemade toy soldiers. The only toy allowed on Sunday was Jacob's Ladder, a testament to the influence of the spiritual on everyday life. Other examples of colonial toys included the Yo-Yo, puzzles, hoops, kites, jump ropes, spinning tops, hopscotch, leap frog, bow & arrows, see saws, bubble blowing, marbles, rocking horses, swinging, and jack straws (or pick up sticks), many of which are played by the local children of today.

A **Jacob's ladder** is a colonial toy consisting of blocks of wood held together by strings or ribbons. When the ladder is held at one end, blocks appear to cascade down the strings. However, this effect is a visual illusion which is the result of one block after another flipping over. (Shown is Master Jacob A. Fisher.)

The toy is called Jacob's Ladder because its seemingly endless tumbling of blocks is said to resemble a dream of angels continuously ascending and descending a ladder to heaven, as dreamed by the biblical patriarch Jacob (Genesis 28:12). Because of the Biblical connection, and because it was a "nice quiet toy", Puritan children were allowed to play with it on Sundays.

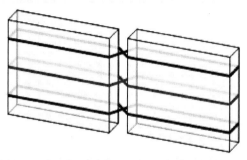

A Jacob's ladder is usually constructed of six wood blocks. The toy depends on a counterintuitive arrangement of interlaced ribbons which allow each block to act as if hinged to the next one at either of its two ends. The same mechanism is used in the 1980s toy Rubik's Magic but with plastic strings run diagonally across squares, with the result that the squares can hinge along either of two *adjacent* sides.

The Personalities of the Cape Fear

In an old volume published in Dublin, Ireland, in 1737, Doctor John Brickell, a traveler to the Cape Fear region of North Carolina described them as:

"The planters by the richness of the soil, live after the most easier and pleasant manner of any people I have ever met with, for you shall seldom hear them repine at any misfortunes in life, except the loss of friends, there being plenty of all necessaries convenient for life; poverty being an entire stranger here, and the planters the most hospitable people that are to be met with not only to strangers but likewise to those who by any misfortune have lost the use of their limbs or are incapable to work and have no visible way to support themselves; to such objects as these, the country allows fifty pounds per annum for their support. So there are no beggars or vagabonds to be met with strowling from place to place as is common amongst us. The country in general is adorned with large and beautiful rivers and creeks, and the woods with lofty timber, which afford most delightful and pleasant seats to the planters, and the lands very convenient and easy to be fenced in, to secure their stocks of cattle to more strict boundaries whereby with small trouble with fencing, almost every man enjoy to himself an entire plantation. These with many other advantages, such as cheapness and fertility of the lands, plenty of fish, wild fowl, and venison and other necessaries that this country naturally produces had induced a great many families to leave the more northerly plantation, and come and settle in one of the mildest governments in the world, in a country that with moderate industry may be acquired all necessaries convenient for life, so that yearly we have abundance of strangers that come among us from Europe, New England, Pennsylvania, Maryland, and from many of the islands, such as Antigua, Barbadoes, and many others, to settle here; many of whom with small beginnings are become very rich in a few years. The Europeans or Christians of North Carolina are a straight, tall, well-limbed active people, their children being seldom or never troubled with rickets, and many other distempers that the Europeans are afflicted with, and you shall seldom see any of them deformed in body. The men who frequent the woods and labouor out of doors, or use the waters, the vicinity of the sun makes impressions on them; but as for the women who do no expose themselves to weather, they are often very fair, and well featured as you will meet with anywhere and have very brisk and charming eyes; and as well and finely shaped as any women in the world. The girls are most commonly handsome and well featured, but have pale or swarthy complexions, and are generally more forward than the boys, notwithstanding the women are very shy in their discourses, till they are

138

acquainted. The girls are not only bred to the needle and spinning, but to the dairy and domestic affairs, which many of them manage with a great deal of prudence and conduct, though they are very young. Both sexes are very dexterous in paddling and managing their canoes, both men and women, boys and girls, being bred to it from their infancy. The women are the most industrious in these parts, and many of them by their good housewifery make a good deal of cloath of their own cotton, wool and flax, and some of them weave their own cloath with which they decently apparel their whole family through large. Others are so ingenious that they make all the wearing apparel for husband, sons, and daughters, down at disappointments and losses, and seldom immoderately grieving of any misfortunes in life, excepting the loss of their nearest relations."

What a legacy to leave...these early colonists with the graces of peace and selflessness.

Social Gatherings During Colonial Times

Social gatherings in the 1700's were frequent and unsparing in their preparations. The often occurred at the plantations at Brunswick, Orton, Kendal and Lilliput where large parties went for weeks and together traveled from house to house for boundless hospitality. Those known for their social gatherings were:

"We might tell of Colonel Maurice Moore, "King" Roger Moore, McLean, McGuire, General Robert Howe, General James Moore, Judge Alfred Moore, Governor Benjamin Smith, Colonel William Dry, Samuel and John Swann, Edward Mosely, Alexander Lillington, John Baptista Ashe, the elder Cornelius Harnett, William Hill, William Hooper, General Thomas Clark, Chief Justice Allen, Archibald MacLaine, the Eagles', the Quince's, James Hasell, Robert Halton, Armand DeRosset, William Lord, Benjamin Heron,

Rev. Richard Marsden, Captain Edward Hyrne, Col. James Innes, Col. Thomas Merrick, the Claytons, the Rutherfords, the Rices, the Rowans, the Watters', the Strudwicks, and their associates of New Hanover County, of which the Brunswick and Wilmington settlements were a part, whose character and fame, as scholars and soldiers and statesmen, were not equalled by the citizens of any other settlement in the country at that period. And we might recall, how, in the memorable days of excitement caused by the attempted enforcement of the odious stamp act, a sturdy band of patriots with Ashe and Waddell at their head, marched up the avenue of stately trees to Tryon's palace, over yonder, and in clear and emphatic terms, with arms in their hands, resisted for the first time on this continent, the established authority of their Sovereign Lord, the King."

James Sprunt went on to describe the society debs of the time:

"There are society women upon whom the mantle of the old-time lady has fallen, through nature or heritage, whose social gifts are the sum of many gifts, the crown of many womanly virtues. One finds them everywhere; women who cherish the fine amenities, who are gracious, intelligent, tactful, kind and active in all good works; who understand the art of elegant living as well as the intrinsic value of things, and hospitable homes for the pleasure of their friends. It is such as they who represent the finest flower of our womanhood, and help to preserve the traditions of gentle manners which are in the way of being trampled out in the mad march of something we call progress. It is for these to ostracise vulgarity, to put up the delicate barriers which have been permitted to be let down between the pleasant comradeship of men and women, and the loud note of familiarity, to temper the sordid spirit of commercialism with the refinements of that higher class of intellect which sees things not only as they are, but as they ought to be."

140

"You should impress upon the minds of those for whose moral and intellectual training you are responsible, the importance and usefulness of knowledge, and be prepared to make some sacrifice for its acquisition, or this great object may not be obtained. It is more to be desired than riches. Daniel Webster told the students of Amherst that the great business of life was education. He also said: "If we work on marble, it will perish; if we work upon brass, time will efface it; if we rear temples they will crumble into dust; if we work on immortal minds, and imbue them with good principles, with the fear of God and love of their fellowmen, we engrave on these tables something that will brighten for all eternity." I think it was Lord Brougham who said that ignorance is the mother of vice and it was the great philosopher, Edmund Burke who remarked, "Education is the cheap defense of nations." "And what, says Taylor, is our defense? Not standing armies, not the daily sight of military tramping the earth with saber and bayonet, but the children of the people, going from their homes to their schools, and from their schools to their homes, carrying in their hands the testament, and the spelling book. This is our strength, and in this we have put our trust." Mr. James Sprunt, c. 1900."

July 4th Toasts in 1805

For over 200 years the city of Southport has celebrated our nations' independence during the July 4th celebration in a big way with recent accounts of over 50,000 visitors during that time. Victorian homes line the city, a testament to its heritage.

Despite the changing times, one source of entertainment remained among the early settlers, the scattered drinking houses. Although habitual drunkenness was frowned upon, there were no restrictions upon moderate drinking. Still celebrated today, the 4th of July celebration was one of those "moderation times" and an occasion for merriment and patriotism. The highlight of the day was a big feast with a series of toasts. Those offered on July 4, 1805 were:

1. July 4th
2. The President of the United States
3. The Governor of North Carolina
4. The North Carolina Legislature
5. George Washington
6. The Flag of the United States
7. The United States Army and Navy
8. That the expedition of the United States against the Tripolitans may succeed
9. The pine trees, the staple commodity of North Carolina
10. Joshua Potts, the founder and promoter of Smithville
11. The recovery of General Smith and the population of Smithville
12. May the wounds received in virtuous causes be speedily healed
13. The Land we live in
14. May political divisions cease
15. The memory of the brave patriots who fell in the cause of liberty
16. The Fair Sex

This tolerance of drinking was to wane somewhat by 1833, especially in the Lockwood Folly area with the foundation of a "temperance society". Hence the county was soon to usher in the Civil War era, and in many areas, building and politics continued.

Plantation Memories

In 1944 Fanny C. Watters wrote her <u>Plantation Memories</u>, accounts from the plantation days of North Carolina. Like those related, they surely must have been representative of life on the plantations of southeastern North Carolina. Several samples are quoted to provide a flavor of plantation life.

The Carpenter:

HE was in the loft of the barn doing some work with two other Negroes helping him, when he lost his balance and fell through the floor. When his helpers reached him, they said, "Unker Abrum, is yu hurted? He ain say nuthin. We took im up, an drug im doun de fo stept tu de canal. He haid nock all de stept gwine doun, but e ent cum tu. E stil look lack e ded.

"We dip im in de water an dat brot im tu. E open e eye, an sot up, an look roun, an e say, 'Way my hammer?' "

Coots:

COOTS would appear just before frost. We would get them when we returned to Clarendon, from Summerville. They were water birds and webfooted. The negroes would pole bateaux through low water and find them perched in bushes and weeds above the water and thrash them off with sea myrtle bushes and put them in bags. Sometimes they would get a bushel of them. It is a delicious bird, better than partridge, in fact, the most delicious I have ever eaten.

Black Walnuts:

TWO big trees were in the yard. As the walnuts ripened and fell, they would be picked up and spread where the sun would shine and left until thoroughly dry. Then they would be hulled. Father had the carpenter make such a nice thing for hulling them: a board a yard and a half long and twelve inches wide; from the middle of the board an auger hole was bored on each side, four inches from center, just large enough for the nut to fall through. A negro man sat at each end of the board, placed a nut over the hole and knocked it through with a wooden mallet, leaving the hull above the board.

Black Walnut Bread

CREAM together half cup of sugar and one egg until light. Sift two cups of flour, three level teaspoons of baking powder and half teaspoon of salt together; then add one cup of milk, more or less, making a stiff batter. Add one cup of walnuts chopped, not fine. Let rise twenty minutes; bake as light bread.

Feeding the Hounds:

Each day a large pone of corn bread was baked for the hounds. Father would feed them after our breakfast. They would gather and loll around until they saw him come out on the porch. Then they would form a circle in front, each in his own place, sitting straight up.

When things were quiet, "Toby," a big Muscovy drake would waddle up and take *his* place between *any* two of the dogs and watch *his* chance. Father would call "Dash" and toss a piece of bread to him, "Clay" and toss his piece, "Toby" and toss his piece. They were all on the lookout and seldom missed catching, even "Toby." When the pone was consumed, they were satisfied and went their different ways.

Myrtle Wax:

Negroes would be sent to the woods to gather myrtle berries. They were tiny, grey-green, waxy and very fragrant. Mother made wax from them to polish the mahogany tables. The tables would be waxed, rubbed with a cork, then with a flannel cloth. Then they would shine like glass.

Nannie:

ONE of the Negro men, coming from his work late one afternoon, brought Mother a tiny fawn he found in the woods. Mother raised it on the bottle, from a tiny spotted fawn to a grown deer. It was as gentle as one of the dogs. A big wooden
144

bowl would be put in the yard with corn bread, "pot licker," potatoes, dumplings, all cut up together. I have seen Nannie, one of the hounds, Toby, chickens and the cat, all eating together. Every now and then Nannie would butt them from the bowl. Then one morning Nannie was missing. We heard the hounds in full cry (one who had eaten out of the bowl with her). In a few minutes we saw her bounding home with the hounds close behind. She cleared the fence, dashed in the house, into my room and jumped on my bed, muddy feet and all! 'Twas a frolic for her and the dogs, but if they had caught her in the woods so far from home I am sure they would have killed her.

The Plantations:

"ON THE east side of the Cape Fear River is Wilmington, North Carolina. On the west, bordering on the river, are the plantations. The fields are flooded from the river by canals, with floodgates, near the mouth of the river (which is thirty miles from Wilmington). The water is brackish and cannot be used for flooding the fields, so the planters use fresh water ponds."

"They could not live in summer near tidewater, so built summer homes sixteen miles from the river, in the pinewoods, and called the village Summerville. They returned to their winter homes after frost."

(The original Fanny Watters Plantation Memories book is located in the New Hanover Public Library.)

1800

In 1808 the county seat of Brunswick County was moved to Smithville, later named Southport, a very historical town full of antique shops and movie sets. Its picturesque location allows one to view two lighthouses at one time and contemplate the blockade-runners during the civil war battles, only to imagine the loss of life during that era.

Southport contains beautiful and spacious colonial homes that remain today. Many of them are recognized for their exquisite architecture and design.

Health Issues

Health was a primary concern in the early colonies. There was a lack of medical knowledge and standards of sanitation were low. Brunswick County was subject to "plagues, pleurisies, smallpox, malignant distemper (sic) and bilious complaints." To combat these germs and diseases, any incoming ship, which had a disease aboard, required that the holds of all vessels be washed with vinegar and smoked with brimstone. These precautions, however, did not alleviate all the contagious diseases or prevent occasional epidemics. The results of those maladies are seen in the graveyards throughout the county with mother and children alike buried side by side. In those unfortunate days, smallpox played no favorites, sometimes killing entire families, sometimes leaving only one or two spared from deadly diseases.

Notably in 1819, yellow fever swept through neighboring New Hanover County and into Brunswick County. As in 1862, many families fled Wilmington in 1819 during this disease ravage. Just as the summer disease had almost ended its destruction, a great fire hit Wilmington, beginning on Dock Street and engulfing over three hundred houses of all descriptions, business and residence alike.

Ships

The ships during colonial times had a cabin for the captain only. Other crewmembers slept on hammocks or on the deck. They used sand timers to tell time. They rang bells to signal different work schedules. The crew had precisely seven minutes to store their hammocks and get ready before they had to be at their stations. Obviously time was of the essence.

146

There were rocks in the bottom of the ships to keep the boat even and to slow the boat down. The bathrooms were called the head. The front of the ship is called the prow and the back was called the stern. These beautiful ships majestically sailed the coastal shores of North Carolina.

Chapter 6

Cemeteries Tell the Story

Meet the Settlers

Throughout Brunswick County, colonial cemeteries abound in the midst of current residential and rural communities alike. They tell the story of the early colonists, their lives and deaths. Some of these historic locations are included in recent photographs, showing the burial practices of the time as communities and towns began to develop in southeastern North Carolina.

Frink-Long Cemetery - 1700 – 1800's

The Frink-Long Cemetery attests to some of the residents from the 1700- early 1800's in the southern portion of Brunswick County. The Reverend Reuban Joseph Long, his wife M. Jennett, and Samuel Frink appeared to be the oldest gravesites in the Frink-Long Cemetery, located inconspicuously off the Old Georgetown Highway, near Capeside Wynn Road, just down from the Pearl Golf Course. Several grave markers appear to have been vandalized and others deteriorating. The Rev. Reuban Long, born 1822, and Samuel Frink, born 1824, may well have entered into battle together during the Civil War as most men joined the forces of gray. The Reverends wife, M. Jennett Long, had inscribed on her gravestone, "Her end was Peace," a most calming conclusion to what must have been a life of penance as a preacher's wife in the mid 1800's. She died in December of 1896. The photo of Samuel Frinks' headstone shows wooden

149

stakes in the background, which mark long forgotten gravesites, soon to blend into the environment.

Last Will and Testament of Samuel Frink – 1790

In the name of God, Amen! I, Samuel Frink, of the county of Brunswick and State of North Carolina, being in a low state of health, but thanks to God of sound mind and memory, do make and ordain this my Last Will and testament in manner and form following:

First, I bequeath my soul to Almighty God, and my body to the Earth, to be buried in a decent Christian manner on the Plantation whereon I now live under a Cedar Tree at the discretion of my executors. And as touching (?) and concerning the worldly estate God hath been pleased to bless me with I leave in manner and form following:

First, I desire all my just debts to be paid by the sale of any of my property either real or personal as my Executors shall think proper, or, if they find it convenient, by XXXX XXXX, I give and bequeath to my beloved wife, Sarah, five negroes named Hagar, Caesar, Cuff, Joe and Hannah, one third part of all my horses, cattle, hogs and sheep, one feather Bed and furniture to her and her heirs forever. I also xxx unto my beloved wife, Sarah, during her widowhood all the rest and residue of my estate, real and personal. XXX, I give and bequeath to my nephew, Samuel Frink, two Negro boys, named Jack and Bob to him and his heirs. XXX, all the rest and residue of my Estate real and personal I give and bequeath to all the children of my brother, Dewies Hankins, except his daughter, Elizabeth Gause, and all the children of my brother,Thomas Frink, to be equally divided amongst them. And lastly, I do xxxx, constitute and appoint my trusty friends Masters Hankins, Alexicus Madorr Forster, and John Frink, when he comes to the age of twenty-one years, Executors to this my last Will and Testament, and I do hereby revoke all former Wills by me heretofore made, certifying and confirming this as my Will. In witness whereof I have bexxxxxx, set my hand and seal this fifth day of May, Axxx Domini One thousand, seven hundred and ninety.

Samuel Frink

Executors: Dewis Hankins
              Elizabeth Gause

Filed in the Clerks office the 20th day of July A. D. 1795.

___

(Note: XXX indicates illegible letters or words).

Interesting note: A Samuel Fletcher Frink committed suicide on the banks of the Calabash River after coming back from fighting in the Civil War. His descendents say that "somehow" the gun he shot himself with was thrown into the Calabash River. It is said that his father, Samuel Frink, left the area after this incident and perhaps headed to the Atlanta, Georgia area.

Another interesting legend about the Frink family involves the slaves. In the 1700's and early 1800's, it was a common practice for families to "loan" each other their slaves, especially when a large work project might be involved such as building a new barn, or major plantings. It is said that when area slaves were "loaned" to the Frink plantation owners, the slaves would plead with the Frink family to "buy" them as they were treated most kindly by the Frink family. It is said that descendents of those slaves today, still greet the Frink elders with respect and gratitude for their kind care.

*Rev. Reuben Long Headstone
Located in same Frink Cemetery.*

Live Oak Road Cemetery - 1700 – 1800's

A burial ground rests just off Seaside Road, Live Oak Road Cemetery where bricks are stacked and crypts are evident. They mirror the burial practice of several cemeteries in the Holden Beach and Seaside areas with crypts built of homemade brick, encasing the final resting place. The crypts of the Live Oak Cemetery appear to be the same relative age as the Holden Cemetery, and if so, date back into the 1700's to early 1800's. No gravestones identify the bodies laid to rest there. The brick was once thought to be the same type as the ballast used on ships, which came into the area.

The cemetery location is about ¼ mile down a road that leads to the "Brooks property" and the waterfront where sailing vessels used to dock. It sits amidst the vacation homes and trailers in the area.

Old time residents remember dogwood trees grown at the base of each grave. Six of them marked specific burial spots. Remnants of depressions and brick crypts show evidence of at least eight burials in this approximately 50-foot by 25-foot cemetery. A colonial home would have been nearby as cemeteries were often placed so that "momma" could see the spot from the kitchen window. In addition, many were placed with the bodies lying east-west.

Kind souls have protected this site with a split-rail fence and placed prayer benches for visitors to think and reflect upon times long ago. It is said that a hermit lived nearby for many years and only moved when Sea Trail was purchased from the International Paper Company.

Note: In the Ocean Isle waters, schooners were caught, full of liquor, during the prohibition period. To avoid prosecution, many bottles were broke and left scattered in the nearby woods. Some say the remnants of those bottles remain the woods surrounding and near the Live Oak Cemetery.

Job Holden Cemetery – 1700 – 1800's

St. Philip's Parish Head of Household listing in 1763 lists one Benjamin Holden. Benjamin Holden is one of the very first families settling in the Holden Beach area after which Holden Beach was named. His plantation was located in the present Sea Aire Estates development. Benjamin Holden and his family arrived to this area in 1756. This was one of the earliest settlements for Holden Beach. The Holden home place was passed down through several Holden family members until it eventually was sold to Wallace Styron; the Holden family reserved the one-half acre family cemetery. The cemetery was neglected for many years and eventually bulldozers destroyed all but two grave markers. It is located in Sea Aire Estates III, Block E, Lot #16.

After passing through multiple land transactions, in March 1995, the cemetery was deeded back to "Job Holden Cemetery" and titled to preserve its historic significance and the early resting place of Benjamin A. Holden and his family members. One tombstone marker remained, as well as, one vault. The present cemetery is located at the north end of Carstens Street in the Sea Aire Estates III and was just recently (in the 1990's) discovered and preserved by present day descendents and brothers, Lynn and Alan Holden.

Tombstone of Elizabeth A. Holden, wife of W. M. Holden, who died February 20, 1852.

Among the ruins of this cemetery is a brick foundation, which is likely a crypt. It is shown above.

Orton Plantation Cemetery – 1800's

The Orton Plantation Cemetery contains the remains of the following:

1. Mary Ivie , wife of Warren Winslow of Fayetteville & daughter of John D Toomer ; Born May 12, 1811; Died May 22, 1845

2. Louisa Catharine, Eldest daughter of JG & MA Burr; Born Feb. 1, 1843; Died Sept 6, 1852; Aged 9 Yrs 7 Months & 6 Days

3. "King" Roger Moore.
   Granted 8000 Acres by the Lords Proprietors in 1720. He built older part of Orton mansion in 1725 (below):

3. John Hill MD; Died May 9, 1847; Aged 51 Yrs

4. James A Berry who died 22 November 1832; Aged 32 Years ; Brave Generous and Kind, Honourable and Devout, a Gentleman and Christian

5. Catharine Ann Berry; Relict of James A Berry; Born 3rd October 1803; Died 20th August 1844.

Sea Trail Frink Cemetery – 1800's

Inside the well-known golf course Sea Trail, off highway 179, near the River Creek Condominiums, is a small cemetery with well-known residents. William Frink and his wife, Annie, are buried among a mother with her five children, apparent victims of a plague or disease, which devastated that family. Stories say that those children died of typhoid as it raged through southeastern North Carolina area. Mr. and Mrs. William Frink, both born in the late 1700's and buried in the Sea Trail Cemetery, must have been infants or nearly newborns when President Washington made his breakfast visit to the Gause Manor. The famous S. Bunn Frink, political statesman is buried in this same graveyard. Small original ground markers are no longer present but have been replaced by more modern markers by "caretakers" of this small resting place.

Two Last Wills and Testaments can be found at the Brunswick County Courthouse describing the descendents of Samuel Frink and Martha Frink. Samuel lists his wife, Sarah and leaves her five negroes named Hagar, Caesar, Cuff, Joe and Hannah, along with one third part of all of his horses, cattle, hogs and sheep, one feather bed and furniture as well as land and other personal property. He also mentions his nephew, Samuel Frink. He mentions the children of his brother Davies Hankins (note different last name?), Hawkins daughter Elizabeth Gause, and also lists a brother Thomas Frink. He lists his trusty friends: Masters Hawkins, Alexius Madora Forster and John Frink. 5th day of May in 1790.

In Martha Frinks Last Will and Testament, dated the 20th of August 1790, she references her son, Davies Hankins, and her son, Samuel Frink's Will. This would make Martha the mother of Samuel Frink. She lists Elizabeth Gause, wife of Needham Gause and leaves her a slave. Her grandson, masters Hawkins and Samuel Frink are also referenced. She also lists another grandson, John Frink, then under age 21. With Wills such as these, one begins to grasp a notion of the life of the early residents and how they were related. Many legal documents exist which document the early years of southeastern North Carolina. They are located at the Government Complex in the Register of Deeds office and the Clerk of Courts office. Many local residents have taken advantage of this wealth of information to put together extensive family genealogies. In addition, a few individuals such as John Holden have written of local history.

Gause's Tomb

William Gause, plantation owner, and host to George Washington, is buried in this tomb, located in the Ocean Isle Beach area. Slowly disintegrating, it lies as a testament to his wealth and status.

Last Will and Testament of William Gause

In the name of God, Amen! I, William Gause of the State of North Carolina and County of Brunswick, being in perfect mind and memory, thanks be to God, calling to mind the mortality of the flesh, and knowing that it is appointed unto all men once to die, do make and ordain this my last will and testament in form and manner following: that is to say, first I recommend my soul into the hands of Almighty God from whom it received its birth, trusting in the merits of our blessed Savior Jesus Christ for a glorious resurrection, and my body to it's original dust to be buried in a decent Christian like manner at the discretion of my Executors which are here after named. And as touching (?) such worldly goods which are here after named. And as touching (?) such worldly goods whence with it has pleased God to bless me with, I give, devise and bequeath in manner and for following.

I give, devise and bequeath unto my son Samuel Gause, all the negroes ever in his possession also his proportionable part of the debts due me, or money in hand, if any.
I dispense unto my daughter, Elizabeth Gause, all the negroes delivered her on her marriage, also little Gilbert and Mariah with two cows and calves, one steer and two yearlings, also her proportionable part of the debts due me or money in hand, if any. To her and the lawful issue of her body.

I devise unto my son William one half of my plantation whereon I now live, beginning at the mouth of the Indigo branch running xxx the same to the first westernmost head thereof, from thence a direct course to the head of the Negroe Branch, there with xx branch to the Swamps, thence a parallel line to the back line of all the surveys including and joining the said Plantation whereon I now live, containing all (close ?) lands on the westernmost side of the aforesaid line, including Killvurts and Morgans, ecept one half of Tubbs Beach and the marsh adjoining it, also one hundred acres on Shallotte
162

Swamp joining his (cowxxx place?). Also all the negroes and stock that I have given xxx since marriage with Lancaster and his proportionable part of the debts due me, and money in hand, if any to xxx and his heirs forever.

I dispose unto my daughter Martha the Negroes and stock delivered her since her marriage with a proportionable part of the debts due me and money in hand if any to her and the issues lawful of our body.

I devise unto my son Peter one half of my Plantation on Settle went whereon I now live (except fifty-acres adjoining and including the dwelling house to his mother during her life) being the easternmost half beginning at the mouth of the Old Indigo branch, encurring xxx   xxx   xxx to the first westernmost xxxx xxxx to xxx being the division line already mentioned to my son William with one half of Tubbs Beach and XXX marsh adjoining thereto.

Also all the land which I purchased last – from my son Samuel Gause, where he lived, and all the land I purchased from John Gause, joining the land I purchased from Samuel Gause with a late survey of fifty-acres giving the aforesaid lands on and in Little River Savannah. Also, one hundred acres on the head of Shallotte. XXX by the name of the cowpren Place with the following Negroes, viz. Ned, Bellah, George, York, Billy, Quanriah (?), Bella's child Ned, Bellahs child Harry, Caesar, Cuffy, Zuanriahs, and Patty and the future issue and increase of such as are females, also Tom at the death of my wife E. Gause, and one half of all my stock of all kinds to be proportioned off to him immediately after my decease, with xxx proportionable part of the debts due me, and money in hand, if any to him and his heirs forever. But in case he should die before he arrives to the age of twenty one years, or marries, then all the negroes with their increase and all other property to be equally divided among my surviving children, and should any of them die then their children to receive the distributive share of such child increased.

I dispose unto my loving wife, Elizabeth Gause fifty acres of land including my dwelling house during her natural life and after her demise, with Tom, to descend to my son Peter which I have allowed unto her as a full portion of her xower, with the following negroes: Beaclsford, Charles, Jenny, Tom, Peter, Dinah, Zuash, Flora, Aaron, Hagar, Jack, York, and Sopilia with her proportionable part of the debts due me, and money in hand, if any. Also one half of my stock of all kinds, during her natural life, and after her decease the negroes with their increase, with all other property to be equally divided among my children now living. I also give unto her the use of my household and kitchen furniture during her natural life, and after her decease for the beds and furniture with the remaining part of the household and kitchen furniture to be delivered to my son Peter, with all the plantation told, But in case my son Peter should marry before the death of my wife, E. Gause, my will is that one half the household and kitchen furniture be delivered to him on his marriage.

XXX, I devise unto my grandsons, Benjamin William Gause and William Wilson, all my lands on the west side of Lockwoods Folly River to be equally divided between them by my executors according to its value. Lastly, I do xxxx and aprprocite (?) my beloved sons Samuel Gause, William Gause and Peter Gause when he arrives to the age of twenty one years and my son in law, John Gause, Junior, Executors to this my last will and testament and do hereby revoke all wills by me made heretofore and declare and pronounce this to be my last Will and testament. In witness whereof I have hereunto set my hand and seal this xxx day of May in the year of our Lord one thousand eight hundred and one.

N. B. My xxxx and xxx is, in the division of the Plantation where I live, between my sons William and Peter, that the division line already mentioned shall be the boundary between xxx whither there should be an equal number of acres or not. This added before signed.

Signed, sealed and declared to be the last Will and Testament of the testator in the presence of all of us.

Wm Gause

Elisha Sellars
Mary Sellars
Thomas Sellars
J. Gause, Jun.

This was (to) certify that I was present at the signing and sealing of this my husband's last will and testament and am fully satisfied with the contents thereof. Witness my hand this ninth day of May, 1801. Elizabeth Gause

(Note: XXX or xxx indicates illegible letters or questionable spellings ?).

    The current Smithville Burying Ground, a local cemetery in Southport, pays tribute to many of the early settlers with graves dating back into the 1700's. Located on East Moore and South Rhett Streets, this graveyard was

established about 1804 for the burial of lost river pilots, monuments to entire crews and families who lived and died by the sea. Stoic elegies memorialize Southport's past residents as no other site can. Many of the names immortalized on these stones live on among descendents still living in the area today.

Andrew Jackson – Potter Cemetery, 1825

Located off Rock Creek Road between Town Creek and Greenhill road, the historical Andrew Jackson-Potter Cemetery graces the woods. The residents were born in the early 1800's. This is one of the oldest cemeteries in the county. While some tombstones stand tall, others have begun to disappear from the environment. Note a Last Will and Testament exists for Miles Potter, dated October 1798 that lists his four sons, Miles, James, John and Robert. Ages suggest that perhaps the following may be his grandsons.

1840

The residents below, are buried somewhere in the county…or most of them are presumed to be. We can only use the Census Records to document their existence. By 1840 Brunswick County had documented the ages of its residents through more detailed census records, which also listed Freed persons of color as well.

1840 Brunswick County Census Records

Peter L Sellars
1 male 20-30, 1 male 30-40
1 female 15-20, 1 female 20-30, 1 female 30-40, 1 female 60-70
1 slave female 10-24

Samuel Potter
1 male 5-10, 1 male 40-50

Daniel Leonard
1 male 10-15, 3 males 15-20, 1 male 20-30, 5 males 40-50
1 female 10-15, 1 female 50-60
1 slave female under 10, 1 slave female 10-24, 1 slave female 36-55

Moses McKethan
1 male under 5, 2 males 5-10, 1 male 10-15, 1 male 60-70
1 female under 5, 2 females 5-10, 1 female 20-30, 1 female 40-50

Daniel Harrell 1 male 20-30, 1 male 50-60

Ivey Jones 1 male 20-30, 1 female under 5, 1 female 15-20

Ezekial Smith
2 males 5-10, 1 male 50-60
1 female under 5, 1 female 5-10, 1 female 20-30

G.W. Carrol 1 male 15-20, 3 males 20-30

W.P. Hall
1 male under 5, 1 male 5-10, 1 male 30-40, 1 female under 5, 1 female 5-10, 1 female 20-30 , 1 male FCP 10-24

James Ellis 1 male 20-30, 1 male 50-60, 1 female 20-30, 1 female 30-40, 2 females 60-70 , 1 slave male 10-24

Alexander Campbell 1 male 30-40, 1 male 70-80, 2 females 20-30, 1 female 30-40, 1 female 60-70 , 2 slave males 10-24, 4 slave males 24-36, 2 slave females under 10, 2 slave females 10-24

Moses King 1 male 60-70, 1 female 60-70, 1 slave male under 10, 2 slave females under 10

James Bird 1 male under 5, 1 male 10-15, 1 male 30-40, 2 females 5-10, 1 female 10-15, 1 female 20-30 , 4 slave males under 10, 3 slave males 10-24, 2 slave males 24-36, 2 slave males 36-55, 1 slave male 55-100, 7 slave females under 10, 2 slave females 10-24, 6 slave females 24-36, 3 slave females 36-55, 1 slave female 55-100

Eldred Freeman 1 male 5-10, 1 male 40-50, 1 female under 5, 1 female 5-10, 1 female 15-20, 1 female 40-50 , James L Warren, 3 males under 5, 1 male 30-40, 1 female 30-40 , 2 slave males under, 10, 1 slave male 10-24, 2 slave females under 10, 1 slave female 24-36

Stephen Hall 1 male 20-30

Samuel Sellars 1 male under 5, 1 male 30-40, 1 female 30-40

Michael Chinners 1 male under 5, 1 male 10-15, 1 male 40-50, 1 female 5-10, 1 female 20-30

Nehemiah Peavy 2 males FCP under 10, 4 males FCP 10-24, 1 male FCP 36-55, 1 female FCP under 10, 1 female FCP 36-55

Nathan Peavy 2 males FCP under 10, 1 male FCP 24-36, 1 female FCP 10-24 , 2 slave males under 10, 3 slave males 10-24, 1 slave male 24-36, 1 slave male 36-55, 2 slave females under 10, 3 slave females 10-24, 2 slave females 36-55

Asa Jacobs 1 male FCP under 10, 2 males FCP 10-24, 1 male FCP 36-55, 3 females FCP under 10, 1 female FCP 10-24, 1 female FCP 24-36

David D Allen 1 male under 5, 1 male 5-10, 1 male 15-20, 1 male 30-40, 1 female 10-15, 1 female 30-40

James H Allen 1 male under 5, 1 male 20-30, 3 females 5-10, 1 female 30-40

Amos Braddy 2 males 20-30, 2 females 15-20, 1 female 50-60
1 slave male under 10, 2 slave males 10-24, 1 slave female under 10, 1 slave female 10-24

John Browning 1 male under 5, 1 male 40-50, 3 females 5-10, 1 female 30-40 , 5 slave males under 10, 3 slave males 10-24, 4 slave males 24-36, 2 slave males 36-55, 4 slave males 55-100, 6 slave females under 10, 5 slave females 10-24, 6 slave females 24-36, 2 slave females 36-55

Hosea McKethan 1 male 20-30, 1 female under 5, 1 female 20-30

Caleb Little 1 male under 5, 1 male 15-20, 1 male 30-40, 1 female 5-10, 1 female 15-20

Elias Pottervine 1 male under 5, 1 male 5-10, 1 male 30-40, 1 female under 5, 1 female 10-15, 1 female 15-20, 1 female 20-30

John Evans 1 male 5-10, 1 male 10-15, 1 male 20-30
1 female 10-15, 1 female 15-20

Caleb Rennulls 1 male 40-50, 1 female 50-60

Felix King 2 males under 5, 1 male 20-30, 1 female 20-30

Stephen King 1 male 30-40, 3 females under 5, 1 female 20-30
2 slave males under 10, 2 slave males 10-24, 2 slave males 55-100
2 slave females under 10, 3 slave females 10-24, 2 slave females 24-36

William Thornton 2 males 5-10, 1 male 40-50, 1 female 5-10, 2 females 10-15, 1 female 15-20, 1 female 30-40

Samuel Jordan 1 male 10-15, 1 male 30-40, 1 female 15-20, 1 female 50-60 , 1 slave female 10-24

John Vines 1 male under 5, 1 male 15-20, 1 male 30-40, 1 male 60-70, 1 female 15-20, 1 female 50-60 , 1 slave male 10-24

Daniel Webb 4 males FCP 10-24, 1 male FCP 55-100
1 female FCP under 10, 4 females FCP 10-24, 1 female FCP 55-100 , 3 slave males under 10, 5 slave males 10-24
3 slave females under 10, 1 slave female 10-24, 1 slave female 36-55
James Abram 1 male FCP 10-24, 1 female FCP under 10, 1 female FCP 10-24

Mary Freeman 4 males FCP 10-24, 3 females FCP 10-24

Daniel Patrick 1 male FCP 10-24, 1 male FCP 36-55, 4 females FCP under 10, 1 female FCP 24-36

Henry H Williams 1 male 5-10, 1 male 20-30, 1 female under 5, 1 female 5-10, 1 female 15-20 , 2 slave males under 10, 4 slave males 10-24, 1 slave male 24-36, 2 slave females under 10, 2 slave females 10-24, 2 slave females 24-36

James W McCoy 1 male 20-30, 1 female 10-15

Mary L Bryant 1 female 10-15, 1 female 40-50, 1 female FCP 10-24

Samuel R Lock 3 males 5-10, 2 males 10-15, 1 male 30-40, 1 female 5-10, 1 female 10-15, 1 female 60-70 , 1 male FCP 24-36

Martha Jordan 2 males under 5, 1 male 30-40, 2 females under 5, 2 females 5-20, 1 female 30-40 , 1 slave male under 10, 1 slave female 10-24, 1 slave female 55-100

Simpson Register 1 male under 5, 1 male 10-15, 1 male 40-50 4 slave males under 10, 3 slave males 24-36, 1 slave male 36-55, 1 slave male 55-100 , 5 slave females under 10, 1 slave female 10-24, 3 slave females 24-36, 1 slave female 36-55

William Baldwin 1 male 30-40, 2 males FCP under 10, 1 male FCP 10-24

John Skipper 2 males 15-20, 1 male 50-60, 1 female 10-15, 2 females 15-20, 1 female 50-60 , 2 slave males under 10, 1 slave males 10-24, 1 slave male 24-36, 1 slave male 36-55, 2 slave females under 10, 1 slave female 10-24, 1 slave female 24-36

Jere Smith 2 males 5-10, 1 male 40-50 2 females under 5, 2 females 5-10, 1 female 15-20, 1 female 50-60, 1 female 60-70 , 1 slave male under 10
John Browning 1 male 15-20, 1 male 50-60, 1 female 10-15, 1 female 20-30, 1 female 40-50 , 1 slave male 55-100, 1 slave female 10-24, 1 slave female 36-55

John G Hall 1 male 30-40, 1 slave male 36-55

Joshua Newell 1 male under 5, 1 male 30-40, 1 female under 5, 1 female 5-10, 1 female 30-40, 1 female 50-60 , 3 slave males under 10, 1 slave male 10-24, 3 slave males 36-55, 1 slave female under 10, 3 slave females 36-55

William Smith 1 male 5-10, 1 male 10-15, 1 male 15-20, 1 male 40-50, 1 female under 5, 1 female 5-10, 1 female 15-20, 1 female 40-50 , 2 slave males under 10, 2 slave males 10-24, 1 slave female under 10, 1 slave female 10-24

Charles W Taylor 2 males under 5, 2 males 5-10, 1 male 30-40 1 female under 5, 1 female 20-30 , 2 slave males under 10, 2 slave males 10-24, 2 slave males 36-55, 2 slave females under 10, 2 slave females 10-24, 1 slave female 24-36, 1 slave female 36-55, 1 slave female 55-100

George W Lennon 1 male under 5, 1 male 5-10, 1 male 10-15, 1 male 30-40, 1 female under 5, 1 female 20-30 , 1 slave male 10-24

George W Hall 1 male 20-30

Benjamin Ivey 1 male 50-60, 1 female 15-20, 1 female 50-60

Samuel Stanley 1 male 5-10, 1 male 10-15, 1 male 15-20, 1 male 20-30, 1 male 40-50, 1 female under 5, 1 female 15-20, 1 female 40-50

Uriah Hewett 2 males under 5, 1 male 5-10, 1 male 10-15, 1 male 30-40, 1 female under 5, 1 female 5-10, 1 female 30-40 3 slave males under 10, 1 slave male 24-36

Lewis Hewett 2 males 5-10, 1 male 30-40, 1 female under 5, 1 female 5-10, 1 female 20-30 , 1 slave male under 10, 3 slave males 10-24, 2 slave males 24-36, 1 slave male 36-55, 2 slave males 55-100, 4 slave females under 10, 1 slave female 10-24, 2 slave females 24-36, 1 slave female 36-55

Edward Clemmons 1 male 5-10, 1 male 15-20, 1 male 40-50 1 female under 5, 1 female 5-10, 1 female 10-15, 1 female 30-40 1 slave male 24-36, 1 slave female under 10

Hezekiah Robeson 1 male 20-30, 1 female 10-15, 1 female 15-20 1 slave male under 10, 2 slave males 36-55, 2 slave females 36-55

Timothy Clemmons 1 male 70-80, 2 females 15-20, 1 female 40-50

J Simmons 1 male under 5, 1 male 5-10, 1 male 15-20, 1 male 30-40, 1 female 5-10, 1 female 30-40

John Morgan 1 male 5-10, 2 males 10-15, 1 male 40-50, 1 female 10-15, 3 females 15-20, 1 female 20-30

172

Elisha Sellars
1 male under 5, 1 male 5-10, 1 male 10-15, 1 male 40-50
1 female 10-15, 3 females 15-20, 1 female 20-30, 1 female 40-50
3 slave males under 10

John Holden 3 males under 5, 1 male 5-10, 1 male 50-60, 1 female under 5, 1 female 30-40

John L Hewett 1 male 40-50

James W Phelps 2 males 20-30, 1 female 10-15, 1 female 15-20, 1 female 20-30, 1 female 50-60

Wm Holden 2 males under 10, 1 male 5-10, 1 male 30-40
1 female 30-40 , 3 slave males under 10, 1 slave female 24-36

Nathaniel Galloway 1 male 10-15, 1 male 40-50, 1 female 15-20, 1 female 40-50 , 1 slave male under 10, 3 slave females under 10, 1 slave female 10-24, 1 slave female 24-36

Joel Cason 1 male 15-20, 1 male 40-50, 1 female under 5, 1 female 5-10, 1 female 10-15

W.C. Mooney 1 male 30-40, 1 female under 5, 1 female 20-30

Moses Hewett 1 male 10-15, 1 male 15-20, 1 male 40-50, 1 female under 5, 2 females 5-10, 1 female 20-30, 1 female 30-40

James Bell 1 male 10-15, 1 male 20-30, 1 male 50-60
1 female 40-50 , 1 slave male under 10, 1 slave male 10-24, 2 slave males 24-36, 1 slave male 55-100, 2 slave females under 10, 1 slave female 10-24

Alfred Galloway 1 male 5-10, 2 males 10-15, 2 males 15-20, 1 male 40-50, 1 female 30-40

Mathias Hewett 1 male under 5, 1 male 5-10, 1 male 30-40, 1 female under 5, 1 female 20-30

John Rutland 1 male 20-30, 1 male 70-80, 1 female 15-20

Edward Hewett 1 male under 5, 1 male 30-40, 2 females under 5, 1 female 5-10, 1 female 10-15, 1 female 20-30 , 1 slave male 10-24
1 slave female under 10, 2 slave females 10-24

N.W. Rulk 1 male 5-10, 1 male 30-40, 1 female under 5, 1 female 20-30 , 1 slave male under 10, 1 slave male 24-36

Timothy C Clemmons 2 males under 5, 2 males 5-10, 1 male 40-50, 1 female under 5, 1 female 5-10, 2 females 10-15, 1 female 15-20, 1 female 40-50

Joel Reaves 1 male 10-15, 1 male 50-60, 1 female under 5, 1 female 20-30, 1 female 40-50 , 2 slave males 36-55, 1 slave female 24-36

Samuel Hewett 1 male 70-80

John Robeson 1 male 70-80, 5 slave males under 10, 6 slave males 10-24, 2 slave males 24-36 , 8 slave females under 10, 3 slave males 10-24, 3 slave males 24-36, 3 slave females 36-55, 1 slave female 55-100

John Robeson Jr 2 males under 5, 1 male 30-40, 2 females under 5, 1 female 20-30 , 2 slave males 10-24, 2 slave males 24-36, 2 slave males 36-55, 1 slave male 55-100; 4 slave females under 10, 2 slave females 10-24, 1 slave females 24-36, 1 slave female 36-55, 1 slave female 55-100

George Kirby 1 male under 5, 1 male 5-10, 1 male 40-50, 1 female 10-15, 1 female 20-30, 1 female 40-50
Francis Price
1 male 60-70
1 female 5-10, 1 female 10-15, 1 female 15-20, 1 female 60-70

Benjamin Gause
2 males 10-15, 1 male 40-50
1 female 5-10, 1 female 50-60
3 slave males under 10, 1 slave male 55-100
1 slave female 36-55, 1 slave female 55-100

Job Holden
1 male 80-90, 1 female 70-80
11 slave males under 10, 7 slave males 10-24, 2 slave males 24-36, 3 slave males 36-55, 2 slave males 55-100
9 slave females under 10, 2 slave females 10-24, 2 slave females 24-36, 6 slave females 36-55, 4 slave females 55-100

Mary Hemmway
1 female 15-20, 1 female 30-40, 1 female 70-80
10 slave males under 10, 10 slave males 10-24, 9 slave males 24-36, 6 slave males 36-55, 4 slave males 55-100

11 slave females under 10, 7 slave females 10-24, 6 slave females 24-36, 7 slave females 36-55, 1 slave female 55-100

Edward Clemmons
1 male under 5, 1 male 70-80
1 female 15-20, 1 female 30-40
9 slave males under 10, 5 slave males 10-24, 3 slave males 24-36, 3 slave males 36-55, 1 slave male 55-100
7 slave females under 10, 5 slave females 10-24, 6 slave females 24-36, 4 slave females 36-55

Neal Galloway 2 males 15-20, 1 male 60-70, 1 female 20-30, 1 female 50-60 , 1 slave male under 10, 4 slave males 10-24, 1 slave male 24-36, 2 slave males 55-100, 4 slave females under 10, 2 slave females 24-35

Nathan Arnold 1 male 20-30, 1 female under 5, 1 female 15-20

Abigil Holden 1 male 5-10, 2 males 10-15, 1 male 15-20, 1 female 5-10, 2 females 10-15, 1 female 30-40, 1 female 70-80

James Holden 1 male 70-80, 1 female 70-80
James Hilburn 1 male 10-15, 1 male 15-20, 1 male 50-60, 1 female under 5, 2 females 5-10, 1 female 10-15, 1 female 15-20, 1 female 40-50

Luke Hilburn 1 male 10-15, 1 male 20-30, 1 male 50-60, 1 female 10-15, 1 female 40-50

John Liles 1 male 15-20, 1 male 40-50, 1 female 50-60

Hugh Mathews 1 male 60-70, 2 females 50-60, 1 FCP male 10-24

Vaun Bird

Saml Stanley 1 female 15-19

Abram Otway 1 female 10-19, 1 fe 40-49, 1 slave female under 10, 1 slave female 24-35

NN Nickson

DB Evans   1 female 5-9, 2 female 15-19, 1 fe 40-49

Isaac Hewett 1 female under 5, 1 fe 5-9, 1 fe 10-14, 1 fe 30-39; 2 FCP females under 10, 1 FCP female 24-35
Jacob Combo

John Sellars 1 female under 5, 1 female 10-14, 1 female 15-19, 1 female 30-39

Alfred Hewett 1 female under 5, 1 female 20-29

Sterling Arnold 1 female 20-29, 1 female 50-59

Joseph Hewett 1 female under 5, 2 females 5-9, 1 female 15-19, 1 female 40-49

Mary Hewett 1 female 40-49

Randall Hewett 1 female 40-49

Uriah Hewett 3 females 5-9, 1 female 15-19, 1 female 20-29

John Hewett 1 female 50-59

Wm L Litchfield 1 female 5-9, 1 female 10-14, 1 female 30-39
Wm Holden 1 female 30-39

Elijah Hewett 2 females 5-9, 2 females 10-14,1 female 30-39

Saml Robeson 2 females 10-14,1 female 15-19

Redman Mercer 1 female 10-14,1 female 40-49,19 slave females under 10,9 slave females 10-23,6 slave females 24-35,5 slave females 36-54,2 slave females 55-100

John J Drew 1 female under 5,1 female 5-9,1 female 20-29,3 slave females under 10,1 slave female 10-23,3 slave females 24-35

Wm H Drew 1 female under 5, 1 female 15-19

William Willitts 1 female under 5, 1 female 5-9, 1 female 20-29, 1 slave female under 10

Gilbert Cox 1 female 30-39

Wm Coleman 1 female 20-29

John Coleman

John A Potter 1 female 40-49, 1 slave female under 10

Unknown female 5-9, 1 female 10-14, 1 female 15-19, 1 female 20-29, 1 female 40-49

Unknown 1 female under 5, 1 female 20-29

Unknown 2 females under 5, 1 female 20-29

Unknown 1 female 20-29

Unknown 1 female 20-29

Uriah Sullivan 1 female 15-19, 1 female 20-29, 1 female 60-69

James Montgomery 1 female 20-29

Lewis Westcoat 1 male under 5,1 male 5-9,2 males 10-14,1 male 30-39,7 slave males under 10,3 slave males 10-23,2 slave males 36-54,2 slave males 55-100,1 female 30-39
1 female 40-49, 9 slave females under 10, 2 slave females 10-23, 3 slave females 24-35, 3 slave females 36-54, 2 slave females 55-100
Susan Bennett 1 male under 5, 1 female 20-29

Saml Hewett 3 males 5-9, 1 male 30-39, 1 female 10-14, 1 female 30-39

Saml A Laspier 1 male 5-9, 1 male 40-49, 2 slave males 10-23
1 slave male 24-35, 1 female under 5, 1 female 30-39, 1 slave female 10-23

Elijah Owen 1 male 5-9, 1 male 20-29, 1 male 30-39, 1 female 40-49

Sarah Faulk 1 male 5-9, 1 female 20-29, 1 female 50-59

Henry Stanley 1 male under 5, 1 male 5-9, 1 male 40-49, 1 slave male 24-35, 1 female 10-14, 1 female 15-19, 1 female 40-49

Luke P Swain 1 male under 5, 1 male 30-39, 2 females 5-9, 1 female 10-14, 1 female 30-39

John Adkins 1 male 20-29, 1 male 30-39, 1 female 40-49

John Dozier 1 male under 5, 2 males 20-29, 1 female 20-29

John Spencer 2 males 10-14, 1 male 15-19, 1 male 30-39, 1 female 10-14, 1 female 15-19, 1 female 70-79

Danl Smith 2 males 10-14, 1 male 15-19, 1 female 5-9, 1 female 10-14, 2 females 15-19, 1 female 20-29, 1 female 50-59

Willis Sellers 1 male 20-29, 1 male 60-69, 1 female 20-29

Robt Sellars 1 male 15-19, 1 male 20-29, 1 female 15-19

Arthur Pinner 1 male under 5, 1 male 20-29, 1 female 20-29

James G McKithen 1 male under 5, 1 male 5-9, 1 male 10-14, 1 male 40-49, 3 slave males under 10, 1 slave male 24-35, 1 female under 5, 2 females 5-9, 1 female 10-14, 1 female 15-19, 1 female 40-49, 2 slave females under 10

James Howard 2 males under 5, 1 male 30-39, 1 female under 5, 1 female 5-9, 1 female 10-14, 1 female 30-39

Robt Woodsides 2 males under 5, 1 male 30-39, 1 male 50-59, 1 female 50-59

Ann Bell 1 female 15-19, 1 female 50-59

James Biggs 1 male under 5, 2 males 10-14, 1 male 20-29
1 male 40-49, 1 slave male 10-23, 1 slave male 24-35, 1 female under 5, 2 females 5-9, 1 female 40-49, 1 slave female 10-23

James O Hale 1 male 30-39, 1 female 30-39

John Marlow 1 male 5-9, 3 females 5-9, 1 male 20-29, 1 female 20-29

William Pearse 1 male 20-29, 1 male 60-69, 1 female 20-29, 1 female 60-69

John Parker 1 male 20-29, 1 male 50-59, 1 female 10-14, 1 female 50-59, 1 female 80-89

John Beck 3 males 10-14, 1 male 40-49, 2 females 10-14, 1 female 40-49

Malliki Hughes 1 male 10-14, 1 male 15-19, 1 male 20-29, 1 male 50-59, 1 slave male 10-23, 1 female 5-9, 1 female 10-14, 1 female 15-19, 1 female 50-59

Mary Pinner 2 males under 5, 1 male 5-9, 1 female 10-14, 1 female 30-39

Gabl Long 1 male under 5, 1 male 5-9, 1 male 30-39, 1 female under 5

Zackariah Russ 2 males under 5, 1 male 20-29, 1 female under 5, 1 female 15-19, 1 slave female 55-100

Danl McKithen 1 male 20-29, 1 female under 5, 1 female 15-19

William Gause 1 male under 5, 3 males 10-14, 1 male 60-69, 1 female 30-39

William Gore 1 male under 5, 1 male 5-9, 1 male 10-14, 1 male 30-39, 2 females 10-14, 2 females 15-19, 1 female 30-39

Benjamin Hickman 1 male 5-9, 1 male 30-39, 5 slave males under 10, 3 slave males 10-23, 6 slave males 24-35, 4 slave males 36-54 1 slave male 55-100, 1 female under 5, 1 female 5-9, 2 females 10-14, 2 females 15-19, 1 female 30-39, 2 slave females under 10, 6 slave females 10-23, 5 slave females 24-35, 3 slave females 36-54 3 slave females 55-100

Saml Standley 1 male 30-39

Ann Long 2 males 15-19, 1 female 5-9, 2 females 10-14, 1 female 15-19

Josiah Bingham 1 male 10-14, 1 male 15-19, 1 male 40-49, 1 female 5-9, 1 female 30-39

Saml F Standley 1 male 30-39, 1 female under 5, 1 female 30-39

Gabl Long 1 male 20-29, 4 slave males under 10, 2 slave males 10-23, 3 slave males 24-35, 2 slave males 36-54, 1 female 20-29, 2 females under 5, 6 females 5-9, 5 females 10-14, 3 females 15-19, 3 females 20-29

Esam Lay 1 male 20-29, 1 female under 5, 1 female 20-29

Ann Suggs 1 male under 5, 1 female under 5

Wm H Patterson 1 male under 5, 1 male 10-14, 1 male 30-39, 1, female under 5, 1 female 20-29

Arthur Benton 3 males under 5, 2 males 5-9, 1 male 30-39, 2, females 10-14, 1 female 15-19, 1 female 30-39

David Gilbert 1 male 20-29, 1 female under 5, 1 female 15-19

Allen R Benton 1 male 15-19, 1 male 20-29, 4 slave males 24-35, 1 female under 5, 1 female 20-29, 4 slave females under 10
3 slave females 24-35

Joseph Lay 1 male 60-69, 1 slave male 55-100, 1 female under 5
1 female 20-29

Willis T Sellars 3 males 5-9, 1 male 30-39, 2 females 5-9, 1 female 20-29

Job Raburn 2 males 5-9, 3 males 15-19, 1 male 30-39, 2 females 5-9, 2 females 15-19, 1 female 30-39

Mary Faulk 2 females 30-39

Isam Cumbo 1 FCP male under 10, 1 FCP male 10-23, 1 FCP male 36-54, 1 FCP female 24-35

Joseph Scull 1 male 5-9, 1 male 10-14, 1 male 40-49, 1 female under 5, 1 female 5-9, 1 female 15-19, 1 female 30-39

Thos Watson 2 males under 5, 2 males 5-9, 1 male 10-14, 1 male 30-39, 1 female 15-19, 1 female 30-39

Alfred Boon 1 male under 5, 1 male 30-39, 2 females under 5, 1 female 20-29, 1 female 60-69

Zadock Williams 3 males under 5, 2 males 5-9, 1 male 15-19, 1 male 40-49, 1 female 5-9, 1 female 10-14, 1 female 40-49

James Williams 1 male under 5, 1 male 20-29, 1 female 20-29

Wm H Williams 1 male 15-19, 1 male 20-29, 1 male 40-49, 1 female 10-14, 1 female 40-49

Wm Watson 1 male 20-29, 1 male 30-39, 1 male 60-69, 1 female 10-14, 2 females 15-19, 1 female 60-69

Thos Graves 1 male 30-39, 2 slave males under 10, 1 slave male 24-35, 1 slave male 36-54, 1 female 15-19, 1 female 40-49, 2 slave females under 10, 1 slave female 24-35

Wm Liles 1 male 30-39, 2 slave males under 10, 2 slave males 10-23, 1 female under 5, 1 female 20-29, 2 slave females under 10, 2 slave females 10-23, 1 slave female 24-35

Benj Liles 1 male 20-29

Benj Watson 1 male 40-49, 2 females under 5, 1 female 30-39

Stephen Mints 2 males under 5, 1 male 20-29, 6 slave males under 10, 5 slave males 10-23, 1 slave male 24-35, 1 slave male 36-54, 1 female 20-29, 1 slave female under 10, 7 slave females 10-23
7 slave females 24-35

Wm Roberts 1 male 5-9, 1 male 10-14, 1 male 50-59, 1 slave male under 10, 2 slave males 10-23, 1 slave male 24-35, 2 females 15-19, 1 female 40-49, 2 slave females under 10, 1 slave female 10-23, 1 slave female 36-54

A.D. Moore 1 male under 5, 1 male 5-9, 2 males 10-14, 1 male 40-49, 2 females under 5, 1 female 5-9, 2 females 15-19, 1 female 30-39

Watty Register 1 male 30-39, 1 female 15-19

Judy Register 1 male 30-39, 1 female 60-69

Isaiah Mitchell 2 FCP males under 10, 2 FCP males 10-23, 1 FCP male 36-54, 4 FCP females under 10, 2 FCP females 10-23
1 FCP female 36-54

John Hooper 1 FCP male under 10, 1 FCP male 24-35, 1 FCP female 24-35

Danl A Flemming 1 male 40-49, 2 females 15-19, 1 female 30-39

James Parker 1 male under 5, 1 male 30-39, 1 female under 5
1 female 20-29

Stephen Williams 1 male 30-39, 1 male 70-79, 4 slave males 36-54, , 1
female 20-29, 1 female 40-49

Benj Roberts Jr 1 male under 5, 1 male 20-29, 1 female 20-29

Wm A Robins 1 male under 5, 1 male 5-9, 1 male 10-14
1 male 30-39, 2 females 5-9, 2 females 10-14

Randall Hall 1 FCP male 10-23, 1 FCP male 55-100, 1 FCP female 36-
54, 1 FCP female 55-100

Henry Mears 1 male 20-29

Nathan Williams 1 male 5-9, 1 male 15-19, 1 male 40-49, 1 female 5-9,
2 females 15-19, 1 female 40-49

Benj Roberts 2 males 20-29, 1 male 50-59, 2 females 15-19, 1 female 30-
39

John Jordan 1 male 5-9, 1 male 60-69, 1 female 15-19, 1 female 60-69

Ann Swain 1 male 15-19, 1 female 40-49

John Phillips 2 FCP males 10-23, 1 FCP male 36-54, 1 FCP female under
10, 1 FCP female 24-35

Wm Baldwin 1 FCP male 24-35, 1 FCP female under 10, 1 FCP female
10-23

Heron Allen 1 FCP male 24-35, 2 FCP females under 10, 1 FCP female
10-23

James Potter 1 FCP male under 10, 1 FCP male 55-100, 3 FCP females
under 10, 1 FCP female 10-23, 1 FCP female 36-54

Effy Freeman, 1 FCP male under 10, 3 FCP males 10-23, 2 FCP females
10-23, 1 FCP female 36-54

William Hewett 1 male under 5, 1 male 30-39, 2 females under 5
1 female 10-14, 1 female 30-39

182

Nehemiah Keeter 1 male under 5, 1 male 20-29, 2 females under 5, 1 female 20-29

Winny Adams 1 female 5-9, 1 female 30-39

George Smith 1 male 30-39, 1 female under 5, 1 female 20-29**Richd Sullivan** 1 male 20-29, 1 female 50-59

Wm Pickett 1 male 20-29, 2 males 30-39, 1 female 30-39

Alexr Lewis 2 males under 5, 1 male 5-9, 1 male 30-39, 1 female under 5, 1 female 15-19, 1 female 30-39

David Godwin 2 males under 5, 1 male 5-9, 2 males 10-14, 1 male 30-39, 1 female 15-19, 1 female 30-39

Nathl Potter 1 male 5-9, 1 male 50-59, 2 females 10-14, 1 female 15-19, 1 female 20-29

John Jacobs 1 FCP male 10-23, 1 FCP male 36-54, 8 slave males under 10, 10 slave males 10-23, 10 slave males 24-35, 6 slave males, 36-54, 5 slave males 55-100, 2 FCP females under 10, 1 FCP female 36-54, 7 slave females under 10, 9 slave females 10-23, 10 slave females 24-35, 7 slave females 36-54, 4 slave females 55-100

James Jacobs 1 FCP male 36-54, 3 slave males under 10, 2 slave males 10-23, 1 slave male 24-35, 1 slave male 36-54, 5 FCP females under 10, 1 FCP female 10-23, 1 FCP female 36-54, 3 slave females under 10, 5 slave females 10-23, 5 slave females 24-35, 2 slave females 36-54, 1 slave female 55-100

Charles Skipper 2 FCP males under 10, 1 FCP male 10-23, 1 FCP male 36-54, 2 FCP females under 10, 1 FCP female 36-54

John Freeman 1 male under 5, 1 male 5-9, 1 male 10-14, 1 male 30-39, 1 female 40-49, 2 females 50-59

Franklin Carrol 2 males 5-9, 1 male 20-29, 1 female 20-29

John Peavy, 1 FCP male 10-23, 1 FCP male 36-54, 2 FCP females 10-23, 1 FCP female 36-54

Charles Skipper 1 FCP male under 10, 1 FCP male 10-23, 1 FCP male 24-35, 2 FCP females under 10, 1 FCP female 24-35

David Daniel 1 male 20-29, 1 female 20-29

Jessee Freeman 3 FCP males 10-23, 1 FCP male 36-54, 1 slave male 24-35, 4 FCP females under 10, 1 FCP female 24-35, 1 FCP female 36-54

Elizabeth Freeman 1 FCP male under 10, 1 FCP male 10-23, 10 slave males under 10, 4 slave males 10-23, 10 slave males 24-35, 2 slave males 36-54, 4 FCP females under 10, 1 FCP female 24-35, 2 slave females under 10, 5 slave females 10-23, 4 slave females 24-35, 3 slave females 36-54, 1 slave female 55-100

Wm Patrick 1 FCP male 24-35, 5 slave males under 10, 5 slave males 10-23, 6 slave males 24-35, 1 slave male 36-54, 1 slave male 55-100, 3 FCP females under 10, 1 FCP female 10-23, 1 FCP female 36-54, 7 slave females under 10, 10 slave females 10-23, 3 slave females 24-35, 2 slave females 36-54, 1 slave female 55-100

John Jacobs Jr 2 FCP males under 10, 1 FCP male 24-35, 10 slave males under 10, 11 slave males 10-23, 9 slave males 24-35, 3 slave males 36-54, 3 slave males 55-100, 1 FCP female under 10, 1 FCP female 24-35, 10 slave females under 10, 12 slave females 10-23, 8 slave females 24-35, 4 slave females 36-54, 4 slave females 55-100

Saml Jacobs 1 FCP male 55-100, 5 slave males under 10, 9 slave males 10-23, 3 slave males 24-35, 2 slave males 36-54, 3 slave males 55-100, 2 FCP females 10-23, 1 FCP female 55-100, 3 slave females under 10, 6 slave females 10-23, 3 slave females 24-35

John Edey 1 FCP male under 10, 1 FCP male 10-23, 1 FCP male 36-54, 1 slave male under 10, 2 slave males 10-23, 1 slave male 24-35, 1 slave male 36-54, 1 slave male 55-100, 2 FCP females under 10, 3 FCP females 10-23, 1 FCP female 36-54, 1 slave female under 10, 1 slave female 10-23, 1 slave female 55-100

Jeremiah Edey 1 FCP male 10-23, 1 FCP male 55-100, 1 FCP female 10-23, 1 FCP female 55-100

Jeremiah Edey Jr 1 FCP male 24-35, 1 FCP female 24-35

Henry Jacobs 1 FCP male under 10, 1 FCP male 36-54, 3 slave males under 10, 2 slave males 10-23, 4 slave males 24-35, 1 slave male 36-54, 3 FCP females under 10, 1 FCP female 24-35, 1 slave female under 10, 5 slave females 10-23, 2 slave females 24-35, 1 slave female 36-54, 1 slave female 55-100

Alfred Jacobs, 1 FCP male under 10, 1 FCP male 36-54, 8 slave males under 10, 12 slave males 10-23, 3 slave males 24-35, 5 slave males 36-54, 2 slave males 55-100, 2 FCP females under 10, 1 FCP female 24-35, 5 slave females under 10, 13 slave females 10-23, 10 slave females 24-35, 1 slave female 36-54, 1 slave female 55-100

John Freeman 1 FCP male under 10, 1 FCP male 10-23, 1 FCP male 24-35, 1 FCP female 24-35

James Smith 1 FCP male under 10, 1 FCP male 24-35, 1 FCP female under 10, 1 FCP female 24-35

Neal Davis 3 FCP males under 10, 1 FCP male 24-35, 3 FCP females under 10, 1 FCP female 24-35

Archy Freeman 2 FCP males under 10, 1 FCP male 24-35, 1 FCP female under 10, 1 FCP female 24-35

William Smith, 2 FCP males under 10, 1 FCP male 24-35 , 3 FCP females under 10, 1 FCP female 24-35

Ezekial Jones 1 FCP male under 10, 1 FCP male 24-35, 3 FCP females under 10, 1 FCP female 36-54

Allen Jones, 1 FCP male under 10, 1 FCP male 24-35, 1 FCP female under 10

Shadrick Bird 6 males under 5, 1 male 30-39, 1 male 90-99, 2 females under 5, 1 female 15-19

Meady Asby 1 male 5-9, 1 male 50-59, 1 female 15-19, 2 slave females under 10, 1 slave female 10-23, 1 slave female 24-35, 1 slave female 36-54

James Potter 2 FCP males under 10, 2 FCP males 10-23, 1 FCP male 24-35, 1 FCP male 36-54, 22 slave males 10-23, 7 slave males 24-35, 3 slave males 36-54, 1 FCP female under 10, 1 FCP female 24-35, 18 slave females under 10, 10 slave females 10-23, 9 slave females 24-35, 4 slave females 36-54

185

Elias Freeman 1 FCP male under 10, 1 FCP male 10-23, 1 FCP male 36-54, 2 FCP females under 10, 4 FCP females 10-23, 1 FCP female 24-35, 1 FCP female 36-54

John Brown 1 FCP male under 10, 1 FCP male 24-35, 2 FCP females 10-23

Frederick J Hill 1 male 10-14, 1 male 40-49, 2 females 15-19
1 female 40-49

John H Hill 2 males 5-9, 1 male 30-39

George Bennett 1 male under 5, 1 male 5-9, 1 male 20-29, 1 female 10-14, 1 female 15-19

William Taylor 1 male under 5, 1 male 10-14, 1 male 30-39, 1 female 5-9, 1 female 20-29

Brown Robbins 1 male under 5, 1 male 20-29, 1 female under 5 , 1 female 20-29

Richd Harris 1 male under 5, 1 male 10-14, 1 male 30-39, 1 female under 5, 1 female 5-9, 1 female 30-39

Henry Taylor 1 male 20-29, 1 female 15-19

William Hankins 2 males under 5, 1 male 30-39, 1 female 15-19

Enock Robbins 1 male 20-29, 1 female under 5, 2 females 5-9, 1 female 10-14, 1 female 20-29

Gabl Holmes
(blank)
(blank)

Thos F Davis
(blank)

(blank)

Edwd B Dudley

186

(blank)
(blank)

A J DeRossett
(blank)
(blank)
Wm B Robeson Jr 1 male under 5, 1 male 5-9, 1 male 20-29, 1 female 5-9, 1 female 10-14, 1 female 30-39

Benj Chinnis 1 male 30-39, 2 females under 5, 1 female 20-29

Joel Robbins Jr 1 male under 5, 1 male 30-39, 1 female under 5, 1 female 30-39

James Moore
(blank)
(blank)

John Swann
(blank)
(blank)

Bryant Ganey 3 males 5-9, 1 male 20-29, 3 females under 5, 1 female 20-29

Alexr Webb 2 FCP males under 10, 1 FCP male 36-54, 1 FCP female under 10, 1 FCP female 24-35

John Ward, 1 male under 5, 1 male 20-29, 1 female 20-29

Mary Sikes 1 female 70-79

Ebenezer Hewett 1 male 80-89
note: Ebenezer Hewett, age 95, is listed as a Pensioner for Revolutionary or Military Services in this census

Elizabeth Rogers 1 female 30-39

Saml Millender 1 male 5-9, 1 male 40-49, 2 females 10-14, 1 female 40-49

Hartford Jones 1 male 30-39

David Taylor 1 male 40-49, 1 female under 5, 3 females 10-14, 1 female 15-19, 1 female 20-29

William B Mears 1 male 20-29, 3 females 5-9, 1 female 20-29

Note: There is a **John Cason**, age 100, listed as Pensioner for Revolutionary or Military Services in this census. The only person A person matching that description was a male, aged 90-99, living in the **Shadrick Byrd** household.

FCP = free colored person

A Free Colored Person was a category on the 1790-1840 Census (listed as other in 1790). The census taker used his own discretion to determine who fit into this category so total accuracy is unlikely. A free colored person could be a black person who was not a slave or a person with mixed black/white heritage or another origin who had dark skin or in some fashion did not fit the census takers idea of what "white" entailed. No Indians were listed as a racial category, nor were Hispanics or Asians identified. Some of these persons may well have been laid to rest in the Winnabow or Holden Beach Slave Cemeteries.

Winnabow Slave Cemetery

Rumor has it that an old Slave Cemetery is located behind the Winnabow Fire Department in the northern part of the county. The cemetery is no rumor. Neither is the Slave denotation. This is the final resting place of many former slaves from the northern part of Brunswick County, many who were members of St. Mary's Zion Church, once located in this area; now relocated, not far away.

Most of the residents are unknown. Pictured are three of the remaining, standing, headstones that date in the early 1920's. Additional graves are very evident in the adjacent area with depressions in the ground still visible in July of 2007, the possible final resting place of former slaves. A small cast iron angel remains at the site of one long forgotten, possibly a portion of a cast iron fence that may have surrounded a prized garden or entryway. Is the angel reminiscent of an hourglass with wings denoting the wings of time? Or is this symbol a representation of a deeper spiritual belief? Although the answer will never be known, the sentiment is obvious. The cemetery was appears to have been formerly decorated and tended. Today it is beginning to meld into the woodland. Several headstones, no longer legible, rest in their fallen places, cracked and worn but still a remembrance placed by a loved one long ago. Many depressions in the ground lay testament to others buried in this location. May God bless those departed souls.

190

Winnabow Slave Cemetery

All that remains of St. Mary's Zion Church, near the Winnabow Slave Cemetery that formerly was located on the original thoroughfare from Shallotte to Wilmington, and lies abandoned in the woods, a stairway to heaven.

The Stairway to Heaven

Hewett Cemeteries

A cemetery just off of the Holden Beach causeway holds testament to the burial of Mary Hemingway. Two headstones and a partial brick fence are all that remain of a once manicured resting place. A doublewide trailer reportedly sits on top of at least two additional gravesites and possibly as many as nine more. As of August 2007, portions of this historical brick wall line the flower gardens of the current owners lot. Married to Joseph Hewett (deceased by 1842), Mary is presumed to be one of the individuals buried in this cemetery. Her headstone testifies to that. She was the sister of Job Holden, daughter of Benjamin Holden, Senior and Abigail Leonard. Benjamin and Abigail came down from Cape May with the Hewett clan and others. Abigail and Hannah, the wife of Joseph Hewett, Sr. were sisters and the daughters of Henry Leonard and his wife, Hannah.

Mary left her legacy with a detailed will giving very specific instructions for her burial. She requested that her final resting place be covered in brick, in "like manner as was his (her husband) and both to be enclosed in a brick wall, the expense thereof to be paid out of the legacy hereinafter bequeathed to my nephew, John Holden." The remainder of her will contains a listing of much of her property including hundreds of acres, cattle, hogs, sheep, slaves, horse & gig, household items, ox cart, cash, and "my plantation, known as the Taylor Plantation." Land holdings describing acreage adjoining Job Holden and "my seashore plantation".

Mary is documented to be the sister of Job, daughter of Benjamin A. Holden, Sr. and Abigail Leonard. Joseph Hewett, in his Will of 1812, identifies his wife, Mary, and marks his property lines at Standberry Creek, Oxpen Creek, Mulberry Mill and Plantation. Local roadways in 2007 document these names at Stanbury Road, Oxpen Road, and Mulberry Street.

Joseph Hewett also left a Last Will and Testament, dated 6 May 1812, where he bequeaths to his wife, Mary, "all my Negros, stock of horses, cattle, sheep and hogs, with all my money, with all my notes and what other debts due by account with my bank stock, household furniture and plantation tools, to be at her own disposal to do with as she shall think fit." Included in that will was the mention of land lying on Bacon Sound and including Beach Marsh and upland adjoining and out to Stanberry Creek and Oxpen Creek and Mulberry Mill. This will was signed in the presence of a shaky – handed Benjamin Holden, Joseph Robert _____, Thomas Hewett, James Chaison, son-Phillip Hewett, Robert Hewett, James Chaison (?). (Is this a derision of the "Caison" surname, found currently in the same portions of the Holden Beach area?)

The Hewett and other historic cemeteries dot the landscape throughout Brunswick County leaving a legacy of the early colonists.

Mrs. Ouida Hewett, Mr. Grover Holden, and other descendents of the aforementioned colonists, continue to work for the preservation of neglected burial grounds and other little known historical locations. One such cemetery is severely neglected and located on Kinston Street, directly between two mobile homes.

Grover Holden and Ouida Hewett

The Kinston Street Cemetery is the final resting place of Mrs. Mary Holden Hemingway, buried sometime after her Last Will and Testament, which was dated 13 October 1842. She and her deceased husband, Joseph Hewett, are partially surrounded by a crumbling brick wall, slowly disintegrating into the environment. According to Mrs. Ouida Hewett, when Joseph Hewett came to the area, he brought two Indians with him. One headstone can be seen in the photo, leaning at this time (August 2007). Another is shown downed, whether by age or vandals, in the next photo.

This massive headstone once held the epitaph of the person buried there. They are partially shielded by the partial enclosure sitting among a residential neighborhood, beside the massive oak, which shades the area. Ms. Ouida Hewett and Mr. Grover Holden are not the only residents who recall a minimum of six to seven additional headstones formerly known to be at this location. They are working to restore this historic cemetery and protect it from further deterioration. Currently a mobile home and small storage shed sits atop additional gravesites. Sitting just off of the Holden Beach Causeway, its historic importance to longtime residents is evident. Just ask the descendents. Mary Hemingway gave a special glimpse into life in the mid 1800's through her Last Will and Testament and relatives want to protect this historic site.

Mary Hemingway Last Will and Testament

North Carolina State Archives: Records of Wills 1764-1954, pages 179-181, File Number 122, Last Will and Testament of Mary Hemingway, 12 October 1842.

IN THE NAME OF GOD, AMEN!

Know, all men, by these presents, that I, Mary Hemingway, of the county of Brunswick in the state of North Carolina, calling to Mind the Mortality of the flesh & that it is appointed unto all to die, do declare and constitute THIS, my Last Will & Testament in manner & form following, to wit:

1st, I commend my soul to Almighty God, who gave it, and my body to the earth to be decently buried by the side of the grave of my former husband Joseph Hewett & my grave to be covered with brick in like manner as his was and both to be enclosed in a brick wall, the expense thereof to be paid out of the legacy hereinafter bequeathed to my Nephew John Holden.

Secondly, my will & desire is that my negro Man Slurry and his wife Nancy for their long & faithful service to me, be placed in the possession & under the care of my nephew John Wescoat freed or exempted from the duties of a slave or servant during their natural lives. I also place in his possession My negro Man Friday, and two cows & calves for their support, after their death the said negro Friday to be the property of John Wescoat. My will is that John Wescoat come and take the two cows & calves before my stock is divided.

Third, I give & bequeath to U. W. Rourk one yoke of oxen before my stock is divided his choice.

Fourth, My will is that my stock of cattle hogs & sheep be equally divided half and half out of the one half I give John Holden, Junr. His choice of one yoke of oxen and two cows & calves & the remainder of that half to be equally divided among the surviving children & wife of William Holden, decd – John Holden, Jr. excluded.

5th. The remaining half of my stock of cattle, hogs & sheep I leave to the use of Sarah Gause during her natural life – I also leave her one half of my household & kitchen furniture at her death the remaining property to be equally divided among her daughters.

6th, I give to my grand Nephew John Holden, Jr. my plantation, known by the name of the Taylor Plantation. If the said John Holden should die leaving no lawful issue the said land to belong to John Holden, Senr.

7th, I give to my two grand Nephews, Saml. Stanaland & Peter Thomas Stanaland 250 acres of land lying between Job Holden and my seashore plantation well known by the name of the Simpkins land – should Peter Thomas die leaving no lawful issue Saml. Stanaland to inherit the whole reserving also to Sarah Gause their Mother a farming privilege during her natural life.

8th, I give & bequeath to my sister (?) Holden my horse & gig – should she not be living at my death I give it to Sarah Gause.

9th, I give to my niece Mary Taylor five hundred dollars in a note I hold against Dr. S. B. Everett – I give to my niece Mary Taylor, one silver ladle, six silver table spoons, six silver tea spoons all marked J H M, one scissors, silver chain.

10th – I give to my Nephew William Wescoat three hundred dollars in a note I hold against U. W. Rourk.

11th-I give to my niece Elizabeth Robinson one half of my household and kitchen furniture – also my Negro woman Elcy & her boys Cuff & Henry & her future increase if not disposed of otherwise.

12th – I give to my Nephew Thomas Holden my boy Slurry.

13th – I give to my grand niece Lydia Mince my boy Robert.

14th – I give my boy English to U. W. Rourk & John Wescoat share and share equal.

15th – I give to my grand niece Molly Holland Robinson a negro girl Mary Ann, Elcy's daughter.

16th – I give to my grand niece Amelia Stephens a Negro girl named Rose, Charity's daughter. I also give her two hundred & sixty dollars in a note I hold against U. W. Rourk – Should she die without issue Ephraim D. Gause to inherit the whole – should they both die without lawful issue Lydia Mince to inherit the same.

17th – I give to U. W. Rourk my ox cart and my negro man named Rentz – I also give to Sophia Ruouk my side saddle and bridle.

18th – I give to Thomas H. Rourk my Negro boy named Whitfield.

19th – I give to my nephew John Wescoat a negro woman named Charity & her son Fuller with all her future increase if not disposed of otherwise.

20th – I give to my Nephew Lewis Wescoat my negro girl named Beck with all her increase if not disposed of otherwise.

21st – I give to my niece Elizabeth Stanaland my Negro girl named Sarah, Elcy's daughter.

22nd – I give to my niece Sarah Cha???oy my Negro girl named Flora Jane.

23rd – I give to my Nephew John Holden, Senr. 100 acres of Salt Marsh including the ford at Cedar landing j- also one note I hold against himself for one hundred and fifty dollars & the interest.

24th – I leave all the remainder of my property not otherwise disposed of Real & Personal, with U. W. Rourk and John Wescoat for the special purpose of paying all expense and

198

charges of my burial and enclosing the graves as is directed in the first item, and defending my will. If any difficulty should occur and after all necessary expenses are settled, the residue thereof, if any remains I give to John Holden, Senr.

25th - & lastly I do hereby constitute & appoint my two trusty friends U. W. Rourk & John Wescoat Executors of this my last will & testament & moreover I do hereby revoke and make void all other wills or parts of wills heretofore by me made & declare this only to be my last will & testament – In witness whereof I the said Mary Hemingway have hereunto set my hand and seal this 13th day of October in the year of our Lord, 1842.

Mary Hemingway

Signed, sealed & declared by the Testator to be her last will & testament in presence of us who at her request & in the presence of each other have hereunto subscribed our names –
James Bell   Robt. Woodside   Anthony Clemmons
This is to certify that I annex this to my Will as a Codicil in the manner & form following –

In the 8th Item of my will where I have given my horse & gig & harness to Sister Sarah Holden, she being in a low state of health, I revoke that part of said will, and I now give to my Nephew John Wescoat's wife Mary Wescoat the said horse & gig & harness. I also give to Sarah Gause fifty dollars in cash or notes that may be on hand at my death. In the 16th item of my will where I have given a negro girl and two hundred & sixty dollars in notes to Amelia Stephens & Ephraim D. Gause, I now revoke that part where E. E. Gause is concerned & give the said girl and two hundred & sixty dollars to Amelia Stephens above.

In witness whereof I have hereunto set my hand & seal this 24 July 1843.

Joseph Hewett, former husband of Mary Hemingway, is also buried at this location. Mary references his gravesite in her will. In Joseph Hewett's land deeds, one finds a transaction where he sold land to Hope Ridgway from South Carolina in 1764 for Twenty Pounds. The size of the parcel was 120 acres. Reubin Hewett originally owned this land, received it in a land grant and had sold it (or perhaps given it in a Will) to Joseph Hewett. In this contract, Mr. Ridgeway agreed to pay the back rent on this property from the date of the first patent...held by Reubin Hewett. The contract was signed by Joseph Hewett and Hannah Hewett. Hannah must have been a co-property owner. Perhaps his first wife? Samuel Willets and Joseph Newton witnessed this deed.

This is but one example of the grand scale of land sales of the era. Ultimately he and the very wealthy future wife of his, Mary Hemingway, ended their time on this land at the cemetery shown in the picture above, amidst a summer vacation trailer lot, beside a dog pen and next to a metal storage building. Perhaps other relatives are even buried underneath the storage building and trailer located in the

Holden Beach area. Advocates continue to attempt to restore the dignity to this cemetery that it deserves.

Stone Chimney Slave Cemetery

Mary Hemingway's Last Will & Testament, listing many slaves, brings up the question of the location of other county slave cemeteries. Little is known or has been written of the burial grounds of slaves in Brunswick County. Their final resting places seem to have disappeared into the landscape. While one is suspected in Winnabow, another is known to be located in the Holden Beach area, on Stone Chimney Road.

Headstones and markers were very expensive and burial customs of the slaves did not usually include permanent markers for each site. The slave cemeteries were rarely laid out in a nice neat row, arranged by families, or otherwise planned to present a beautiful "garden-like" display. Instead, they were often placed in distant parts of the slave owner's property, sometimes designating one particular piece of land as the slave burial grounds for the entire community. Such is the case of the cemetery hidden among the woods just off of Stone Chimney Road, near Stanbury Road close to Holden Beach.

On August 14th, 2007, the author and Ms. Bertha Bryant, with her Uncles Eugene Hewett and Emmitt Grissett, attempted to determine the exact location of the large cemetery which was almost forgotten. Earlier descendents had spoken of the "Slave Cemetery" located at this location but no one seemed to know the exact location, nor was it documented or identified in any manner. Mr. Hewett, Mr. Grissett, Ms. Bell, and the author entered the "approximate location" where the elderly Hewett and Grissett were "told" the cemetery was located. Another uncle, Mr. Jesse Bryant (80+ years old), was "sure" it was "there somewhere". These three distinguished gentlemen prayed for the cemetery to be located and gravesites identified in order to protect and preserve this historic location for future generations.

Amid the mosquitoes, the redbugs, and briars, the "one" remaining and remembered headstone was located. A small two-foot by one-foot simple monument lay among the other sunken graves of previous slaves and their descendents. A pink flag was affixed to the nearest tree to expedite finding the same location in a few weeks when specially trained Human Remains Detection canines would re-visit this site to pinpoint as many gravesites as possible. Most importantly, the location had now been established. Three elderly men, probably the last remaining descendents recalling this cemetery, walked with their niece, Ms. Bertha Bell, at the historic site. They were already making preservation plans, a deed born in the heart.

Shown below is Mr. Eugene Hewett (left), Ms. Bertha Bell (center), and Mr. Emmitt Grissett (right), descendents of the slaves buried in the cemetery directly behind them, just inside the woods line on that day of discovery (August 14, 2007).

The one remaining tombstone, that of Willie Fullwood, testifies to his birth as 8 February 1888 and his death on the 17th of March 1897 at nine years old. Additional words on the tombstone were not legible and the supposition of his demise from typhoid or smallpox could only be suspected. Was he related to the Benjamin Fullwood, a black man who once owned most of Long Beach? A son? A brother? Another descendent?

Very near Willie Fullwood's gravestone are two wooden stakes, made from lighter wood, and speared into the ground; obvious gravesites among other ground depressions. Each was dutifully flagged for further investigation and reports. Tears welled as the extent of this "find" began to sink in and the history of black ancestors was once again found, recorded, and preserved. A sense of family enveloped the three as they looked upon this site for the first time, realizing the impact of their actions. A piece of local history would be preserved. Their heritage was not forgotten. Emmitt Grissett and Eugene Hewett had located the one remaining headstone in the Stone Chimney Slave Cemetery.

This cemetery served the entire black community from the coastline to the north end of the present Highway 17, including the Royal Oak and Supply areas.

It was not restricted to certain families and open to all, following no particular burial plan or design as is evidenced by the located grave sites.

Some people did not have a desire or need to mark graves. They felt the body was destined to return to the earth and earthly monuments were not necessary. Other people "were very superstitious and thought if they had a tombstone that the devil would find them." So relates Jeff Phillips, a Brunswick County resident.

Wooden "lighter" stakes, barely visible, mark a grave of a former slave.

Four generations had passed this way as Ms. Bertha Mae Bryant Bell remembered her family history. Her great-grandparents, Mr. John Jack Bryant (1811 – 1 Nov 1887) and Mrs. Holland Lancaster (1826-1 July 1889) were slaves brought to Brunswick County by Mr. Jesse Lancaster, believed to be from Pitt or Craven County, North Carolina. Their son, James (Jim) Bryant married Louvenia Hemingway (perhaps a servant (or relative) of Mary Hemingway?). Their son Harry Bryant married Annie Bryant Bryant and begat Ms. Bertha Mae Bryant (Bell). One can only speculate that some of them are buried in this very Slave Cemetery, exact location unknown, but approximate locations now marked.

Mr. Jesse Lancaster, slave owner, deeded a portion of his land to his faithful servant, Mr. John Jack Bryant. Descendents later purchased this same land and remain there today. A daughter of Mr. Lancaster is buried near one of the descendents home, the burial place of that child once covered in seashells and last seen about fifty years ago, reportedly placed just "before a run"...a former drainage ditch which often marked land borders. Plans are also being made to locate this gravesite in order to protect it. It most likely dates to the early part of the 1800's and most certainly prior to the sale of the land to Mr. Bryant.

Ms. Bertha Bell, retired school counselor, and preservation coordinator for the Stone Chimney Slave Cemetery.

Riley Hewett Cemetery

Many members of the Cedar Grove Church are buried in the Riley Hewett Cemetery, located off Turkey Trap Road, near the church. Riley Hewett deeded the first acre of land for use as a community cemetery about the 1930's. This would have been about the time of the last burial in the slave cemetery off Stone Chimney Road that had served as a community cemetery until that time. Many "lighter" sticks or stakes are evident as the only markers of those buried at the Riley location. These graves are presumed to be some of the oldest at the Riley Cemetery and sometimes marked with household items such as a "pitcher", "vase", or other household item. Among those presently in the cemetery is the beautiful purple Depression glass vase, broken in two pieces, marking the grave of Rebecca Gore Bryant, who died circa 1912. Family members plan a more permanent marker soon.

Sometimes the exact locations of the graves have been lost as well-intentioned cemetery tenders "picked up" items left as markers. Not unlike some other cemeteries in the area, a few graves are covered in seashells or other identifying emblems.

Slaves could not afford the elaborate headstones and did what they could for those gone before them. These graves are dated from about the 1930's to about 1950's with birth dates ranging back to the mid 1800's. More recent burials include crypts encompassing the vaults of the deceased, some more elaborate than others, but all providing a testament to those loved family members buried there. May God rest their souls.

Chapter 7

The Civil War Era

By 1845 the state of North Carolina held the title to Brunswick Town. The Orton Plantation, and the remains of Brunswick Town eventually became museums welcoming visitors to archaeological remains.

In 1848, the Prices Creek Lighthouse was constructed.

Prices Creek Lighthouse Photograph by John Muuss

It stood only 20 feet tall. Made of red brick, it is one of eight lighthouses along the Cape Fear River, which were built to illuminate a 25-mile stretch between the Cape Fear

River and Oak Island. (Long Beach merged with the town of Yaupon Beach in 1999 to form the town of Oak Island). Two others were built on Oak Island, two at the Upper Jettee and the remaining two at Orton's Point and Campbell's Island. During the Civil War, Prices Creek served as a Confederate signal station, helping the blockade-runners to navigate the river. The Confederates destroyed all of the stations as they lost control of the region. By the late 1880's all of these lighthouses had been replaced by unattended beacons. The Prices Creek Lighthouse is still visible (about 200 yards away) from the ferry as it takes it trip between Fort Fisher and Southport.

Oak Island Lighthouse

Completed in 1958, the Oak Island lighthouse rose 169 feet above the water. It was completed at a cost of $110,000. A misconception is that the lighthouse itself is 169 feet tall. The actual structure is 148 feet tall, but it stands on a slight rise. Therefore, the height of the light above the water is 169 feet, and it is so reported on nautical charts. It does not contain the typical lighthouse spiral staircase but a series of ladders with 131 steps to the 11-foot tall lantern gallery.

The Oak Island Lighthouse Friends describe this historical location with the following: "In 1761, a hurricane carved out an inlet near the mouth of the Cape Fear River, which soon became the most popular route to Wilmington, North Carolina's largest port. Because of the increased traffic in this aptly named 'New Inlet', two range lights were built on Oak Island, located on the west side of the river mouth. First lit on September 7, 1849, these lights were often referred to as the 'Caswell Lights' because of their proximity to Fort Caswell.

The Oak Island light is located on property that has been in use as a US Coast Guard station since the 1930s, and prior to that it was a US Lifesaving Station. The current Coast Guard station was recently reconstructed after a fire completely destroyed the ten-year-old building in 2002. The new station house is built over the footprint of the lost station, and closely resembles the older station.

"unlike the other Cape Fear River range lights, the Caswell Lights were free-standing brick towers, with a separate 1.5 story cottage for the keeper. The original brick beacons were in use only a few years before the Civil War extinguished all the lights on the Carolina coast. Both range lights were destroyed by retreating Confederate troops, who preferred to blow up the structures rather than see them fall into Union hands. Of course interested parties had no intention of allowing New Inlet to remain dark for long, and in 1865, plans (were made) for new standing twenty-seven feet above sea level, and a rear beacon, a sophisticated four-level structure with living quarters. Unfortunately, like their predecessors, these range lights survived less than 20 years. Another hurricane in 1893 damaged the front beacon and keeper's house beyond repair. But this time, because changes in shipping routes had decreased,(along with) the number of vessels along that part of the Cape Fear River, the damaged range lights were decommissioned with no plans to repair them." (Lighthouse Friends).

1850 - Mt. Misery Road Haunting

Mt. Misery Road runs along the Cape Fear River, and about 1850, when people owned slaves, the road ran all the way to Fayetteville. Slave ships would dock at the Cape Fear River and march the slaves along this road, all the way to Fayetteville. This was a 90-mile hike and many slaves died of heat exhaustion. Some of these slaves still haunt Mt. Misery Road, near Leland, in the northern portion of Brunswick County. Multiple folks have reported that late at night moaning and chains can still be heard.

Many slaves succumbed during their 90-mile march to Fayetteville, North Carolina during the Civil War. A "feeling of dread is said to still overcome motorists" while driving on Mt. Misery Road today. The name says it all. More than one miserable event has occurred at this location. The death of slaves is but one.

1860 - Statistics

By 1860, Brunswick County was reported to have 258 slave owners, each owning anywhere from 1 to 4 slaves; 61 had from 5 to 9; 4 owned from 10 to 19; 27 owned from 20 to 49; 12 owned from 50 to 99; and 4 owned from 100 to 199. Only one owned as many as 200 slaves. There were 15 grist (flour) plants, 5 sawmills, 10 rice threshing plants, 41 turpentine operations (crude plants), and 13 turpentine distilleries, which employed 335 people. Rice was the great money crop in the county. Cattle and hogs ran wild in the woods. Some of these wild hogs remain today. There was no commercial salt water fishing business at that time (prior to the Civil War). After the war, many things changed.

Note that a Grist Mill Road remains off highway 130 between Shallotte and Holden Beach, former home of one of the Grist Mills that once served the community.

The Maco Light

Not far from Mt. Misery Road, in northern Brunswick County, N.C., are the ghost train lights near Maco, formerly called Farmer's Turnout. The Maco Light is located about 15 miles outside of Wilmington into Brunswick County. On a fateful night in 1867, a slow freight train was puffing down the track. In the caboose was Joe Baldwin, the flagman. As the caboose slackened speed, Joe looked up and saw the beaming light of a fast passenger train bearing down upon him. The caboose was struck by the oncoming train and in the process Joe's head was severed and thrown to one side of the track. His lantern was tossed to the opposite side of the track. Rescue efforts could not locate his head and his body was buried without it. (Note: Farmer's Turnout is near the Hood Creek area.)

"Thereafter on misty nights, Joe's headless ghost appeared at Maco, a lantern in its hand. If one stands on the trestle, an indistinct flicker is seen on the tracks moving up and down, back and forth. The beam will swiftly move forward, grow brighter, then move back and disappear.

Throughout the years, many have come from miles around to catch a glimpse of the Maco Lights. College students from across the state have taken road trips to Maco to document the ghostly apparition. Many have tried to attribute them to swamp gasses or vehicle lights from nearby roads.

It is said that during one investigation, all traffic was routed away from Maco and no cars were allowed to approach the area.... and yet the unearthly light still appeared. On one occasion, a machine gun attachment from Fort Bragg encamped at Maco to solve the mystery, or at least shoot it down, but they did neither. Joe Baldwin, or whatever is the ghostly source for the Maco light, continues. No studies have yet dismissed Joe Baldwin and his search for his head.

Some say the Maco lights are the spirit of Baldwin, swinging a lantern as he searches for his severed head. Others maintain it is the ghost of an Indian warrior killed in battle, while another old legend said it was the phantom of a black ``witch-woman.''. Ghostly lights are nothing new to the folklore of the Deep South. Since Indian times, stories about mysterious flashing lights and wispy halos of color floating in the night have entertained and terrified generations.

It is said that the light often appears to be very small and then grows to the size of the lantern that Joe Baldwin must have been carrying. It has been reported here since 1873 and has been seen by literally thousands of people since that date. In 1886, an earthquake stopped the light for a short time but when it came back there were 2 lights for a short time. In 1889, the light was even seen by then president, Grover Cleveland.

In 1977, the railroad tracks were removed and the swamp has reclaimed the haunting grounds. Since that time, fewer sightings of Joe Baldwin have been reported. Perhaps he is now at rest or perhaps just fewer seek him out.

USS Peterhoff - 1863

The *USS Peterhoff* contributed its civil war era 30-pound parrot rifle to the University of North Carolina at Wilmington where it rests on a grassy lawn. This rifle was a part of the armament of the blockade-runner assigned to the North Atlantic Squadron. The ship was a British iron-hulled steamer that left England in January of 1863 for Mexico. On the 6th of March 1864, the *USS Monticello* was steaming close to shore and was blundering into the line of blockade-runners watching the Cape Fear at New Inlet. The Captain, acting

Ensign Joseph Hadfield, thought he was approaching a blockade-runner, but instead was on a collision course with the *Peterhoff*. The *Monticello* plowed into the *Peterhoff*, which promptly sank in five fathoms of water within half an hour. The crew was rescued although they lost all of their possessions.

In order to keep the confederates from salvaging anything from the *Peterhoff*, other blockaders (the *Mount Vernon* and *Niphon*) were sent to destroy as much as possible. The Yankees cut the mast and chopped up the rigging. The guns that were reachable, such as a 30-poiund Parrot rifle, were dumped overboard. This rifle was recovered in 1974 by a group effort of the North Carolina Division of Archives and History, and UNC-Wilmington.

Additional guns from the *Peterhoff* are on display at Fort Fisher and the Carteret County Museum of History in Morehead City.

Blockade Runners

The Underwater Archaeological Reconnaissance and Historical Investigation of Shipwreck Sites in the Lockwood Folly Inlet (Brunswick County) reported in 1986 that surveys produced data to support identification of two sites identifying the wrecks as the blockade- runners *Elizabeth* and the gunboat *USS Iron Age*. In addition, the *Bendigo* was investigated, confirming the identity. Recommendations were made to document these threatened vessels, their structure, and possibly salvage the associated cultural material.

(Visitors to any of these sites need to be aware of the enveloping waters as the tide comes in. Don't get caught on the sand bar during in-coming tides or you may be in danger. Safety is paramount.)

Museums up and down the coast of North Carolina proudly protect and display the many artifacts recovered from the North Carolina shipwrecks. The artifacts uncovered by underwater explorations date from prehistoric (Native American), Civil War and present day tragedies.

The North Carolina Underwater Archaeologists describe the Atlantic Graveyard as a definite link to the past. "Throughout the centuries the people of North Carolina have lived in close contact with the waters of the state. Before the arrival of Europeans the Indian inhabitants relied upon the rivers and sounds as a source of food, and a means of transportation and trade. The Indians built wooden dugout canoes and developed a variety of ways to catch fish. During the winter many tribes would camp along the coastal sounds living off the readily available supply of oysters and other shellfish." Some of their canoes remain today, a testament to their residency.

"Early European settlers used these same avenues of water as a means to explore and settle the interior of the state. Gradually settlements grew to port towns such as Edenton, Bath, New Bern, Beaufort, Brunswick, and Wilmington. In addition, smaller communities and plantations had their own landings along the waterways. Down these rivers traveled the products of the new land: lumber, naval stores, tobacco and cotton. In exchange, ships from the other colonies, the West Indies and Europe brought to the major ports manufactured goods and other materials needed by the colonists." Brunswick County participated in these activities providing valuable ports and products.

"During the nineteenth century paddlewheel steamboats came into use on the rivers of the state. Carrying passengers and cargo, often with a barge in tow, the steamers made their way well into the interior of the state on major rivers and their tributaries such as the Cape Fear, the Neuse, the Tar, the Roanoke and the Chowan. With the coming of the twentieth century, railroads and highways gradually replaced the rivers and sounds as a means of transporting goods. Today Wilmington and Morehead City serve as the state's major overseas shipping ports."

"Naval warfare in the waters of the state has also left a legacy of shipwrecks and other underwater archaeological
214

sites. This is particularly true of the Civil War. Along the southeastern coast of North Carolina underwater archaeologists have investigated the remains of 29 Civil War period shipwrecks. Most of these wrecks were blockade-runners attempting to evade the Union ships and enter the Cape Fear River. Wilmington, situated 20 miles up the river, served as the last major Confederate port open to blockade runners and the valuable cargoes they brought to the south. In addition to the blockade runners, divers have located the remains of four Union warships and two Confederate gunboats."

"In the central and northern coastal areas other reminders of the Civil War have been found. In 1977 a survey and recovery project was conducted in Roanoke River adjacent to Fort Branch, a Confederate earthwork fortification near Hamilton, North Carolina. The project resulted in the recovery from the river of four cannon and hundreds of smaller Civil War period artifacts. This material has been preserved and is on display at the Fort Branch Museum in Hamilton."

"The North Carolina Underwater Archaeology Branch (UAB) was created by the General Assembly in 1967. The UAB is charged with "conducting and/or supervising the surveillance, protection, preservation, survey and systematic underwater archaeological recovery of shipwrecks and other underwater archaeological sites throughout the state. By working with individuals, dive clubs, educational institutions and others the Underwater Archaeology Unit is compiling and inventory of underwater archaeological sites throughout the state."

North Carolina Archaeology, Underwater Branch.
http://www.arch.dcr.state.nc.us/ncarch/underwater/underwater.htm

Blockade Runner *Annie*

In 1864, the Confederate blockade-runner *Annie*, carrying $50,000 in gold coins contained in a keg and stowed in the captain's quarters sank off the northern end of Smith's Island opposite Southport. It was trying to pass through Union batteries. This ship has never been salvaged. It's treasure remains. In the 1930's, a boy found a small cache of gold coins at the mouth of the Cape Fear River while digging for fishing worms. Are there more treasures?

Fort Anderson

The 19th century confederate fortification - Fort Anderson is well preserved. During the Civil War, Fort Anderson was build atop the old village. Large gun platforms remain, evidence of the Revolutionary port, razed by British troops.

Col. William Lamb and Maj. John Hedrick constructed Fort Anderson about 1861-62 as a confederate stronghold. It protected Wilmington, a major blockade-running port. Slaves and Indians moved dirt and sand one shovel at a time during its construction. It eventually held nine seacoast cannons, movable field artillery, and large underground chambers, which sheltered the garrison and volatile black powder supply during bombardments. Lamb later commanded Fort Fisher, located just downstream.

By February 1865, after the fall of Fort Fisher, Union forces attacked Fort Anderson. The Fort Fisher commanders retreated to Fort Anderson in January-February 1865 when federals finally captured Fort Fisher and Wilmington. After three days of fighting, the Confederates evacuated the Fort. There was another one-day fight north of the site at Town Creek before the Federals occupied Wilmington on February 22, 1865. Much blood was shed. Many lives were lost.

In 1900, at the invitation of the North Carolina Society of the Colonial Dames of America, Captain E. S. Martin described Fort Anderson and its involvement in the Civil War:

"Our pilgrimage of patriotism is accomplished, and we stand on hallowed ground. Hallowed by the many memories that cluster around this historic spot. By the memory of those men of might-those grand in soul, the founders of this town, once the capital of the colony, who controlled its destinies; of those who reared that sacred edifice and after life's fitful fever, sleep their last sleep in yonder churchyard; of those who, with lofty patriotism and fierce courage were ever ready to defend their rights, their homes and altars and were the very first to defy the power of imperial England and to lead in the grand drama of the Revolutionary War. Truly a glorious story but one I shall not enter upon today. …Of those around that old church to do battle with hands and hearts like their fathers before, in the Lost Cause, the gallant dead of the Confederate Army. Of those brave men and the storm of war that raged around this old town I am here to speak today."

"Sunday, January 15th, 1865, was a day of storm in this section. The forces of the United States had gathered by land and sea around Fort Fisher on the opposite side of the river, and, after the most terrific bombardment in all history had silenced every gun on the land face of the fort. Attack after attack by the fleet had been made upon the fort and on that Sunday afternoon the grand assault was made by the army, which, after gallant resistance on our side was repulsed. But later in the evening of that day the attack was renewed with greater success, our men reduced in numbers being driven from travers to travers, from gun chamber to gun chamber, parapet to parapet, desperately fighting against overwhelming odds. Those of us at Fort Caswell could see by the flash of the guns the lines of enemy gradually advancing and our men retiring, their firing growing less and less. Between nine and ten o'clock that night there was for a time, silence and darkness. Then from the midst of the darkness a single rocket shot high into the heavens and bursting fell in myriads of stars. We knew then that Fort Fisher had fallen. Not surrendered. Instantly on the sea, as far as the eye could reach, there burst forth from the fleet the most superb display of fireworks it has ever been my fortune to see. Battle lanterns, calcium lights, magnificent rockets, blue lights and every description of fireworks flashed forth in one grand and imposing picture that meant, to us a tale of sorrow, but to them one of rejoicing. Fort Fisher had fallen!"

"On Monday following Fort Holmes, erected on Smith's Island, commanded by Col. John J. Hedrick and garrisoned by the Fortieth N. C. Regiment was evacuated, the works destroyed, and these troops carried by steamers to Smithville. The defenses of Oak Island composed of Fort Caswell under the immediate command of Major Alexander MacRae, Fort Campbell, commanded by Lt. Col. John D. Taylor, Thirty-six N. C. Regiment, and other inner works all under the command of Col. Charles H. Simonton, were evacuated. Fort Pender, at Smithville was also evacuated and the troops from all of these forts were gathered here at Fort Anderson where they were allowed to remain unmolested from the 19th of January to the 17th of February of the same year. In the mean time the Federal fleet had entered the river in force, and lay at anchor below the fort. On the 16th of February Schofield's corps arrived at Fort Fisher, was transported by steamer to Smithville that night and marched from there on the 17th to attack this fort. Our lines were here and constituted a part of the exterior lines of the defenses of the city of Wilmington."

"The fort proper was commanded by Col. Hedrick with the Fortieth N. C. Regiment; on his right was Moseley's Battery of Whitworth guns, then came the light artillery around this church, then Maj. MacRae's command and on our extreme right Colonel Simonton's Regiment and other South Carolina troops, the whole under the command of General Johnson Hagood, afterwards Governor of South Carolina. His head quarters were on the road towards Orton."

"On the morning of February 17th, 1865, the monitors and gunboats of the Federals moved up near the fort and opened fire while the army under Gen. Schofield advanced upon our lines. Shells from the monitors and gunboats were bursting incessantly over this place some of which destroyed many of the tombs around the church. Standing upon that parapet I saw an eleven-inch Dahlgren shell strike that church and glance, then burst, a large piece passing between Colonel Hedrick and myself cutting his sword from his side. All day Friday and Saturday the bombardment continued and Saturday night some time after midnight, the evacuation of the fort took place. I being (Chief of Artillery and Ordinance) on the Staff of the Commanding General at that time, was sent down into the fort late at night to execute certain orders after the troops had departed, and thus was the last man to leave the fort. Some of the dead were still in the gun chambers and along the lines while some had been carried into that sacred edifice and lay there with their pale faces turned towards the silent stars above them. While here I heard the enemy mustering their forces for storming the works on Sunday morning. By putting your ear to the ground, as we all know, you are enabled to detect the movement of masses of men. After the execution of my orders I hastened on and soon joined our troops. On Sunday the battle of Town Creek took place, and a portion of our command under Colonel Simonton was there captured. It is well that you have this commemorative service. It is well to recall the character of our forefathers, to brush from their tombs the dust that has gathered upon them in the years that are gone. It is honorable, that those who bear the names keep the graves and boast the blood of these patriotic men should tenderly revere their memories and dwell with pride upon their exalted virtues. Thus gazing long and intently upon them we

219

may pass into the likeness of the departed, may emulate their virtues and partake of their immortality."

By Captain E. S. Martin

Remaining today are earthen walls with green emplacements reminiscent of the stronghold of yesterday.

Fort Caswell

The batteries at Fort Caswell were named in honor of Richard Caswell, member of the Continental Congress, Revolutionary War soldier, and first governor of North Carolina. The armament once contained an area of over 2, 300 acres and was the headquarters of the coastal defenses of the Cape Fear region. Col. Charles A. Bennett commanded the post. It consisted of mortars; direct and rapid fire guns, and a mine defense.

Fort Caswell bunkers remain a testament to the embankment during the Civil War battles. Photography by John Muuss.

Fort Fisher

Fort Fisher was built of mostly earth and sand, ideal for absorbing the shock of heavy explosives. It was equipped with 22 guns and bordered by 12-foot high walls, 45 and 60-foot high.   Ft. Fisher was sometimes referred to as the Gibraltar of the Sea.   It was a mammoth, L-shaped fortification of sand and sod.

By 1865, the supply line through Wilmington was the last remaining supplies route open to Robert E. Lee's Army of Northern Virginia.

Fort Fisher fell after a massive attack from January 12 to the 15th, 1865 where a 32-pound seacoast gun remains as a testament to Shepherd's Battery. On January 15th, more than 3,300 Union infantry, including the 27th U. S. Colored Troops assaulted the land face. After several hours of hand-to-hand combat, Fort Fisher fell.

Fort Fisher is reportedly haunted by both Union and Confederate Soldiers. Individuals visiting the Fort Fisher site have reported several mysterious events. Union soldiers and General Whiting have been seen up on the mounds crying out "organize the counter attack." This sometimes occurs during major storms or weather events.

Inside the park visitor's center, pamphlets have been noted to fly off the shelves. Unexplained lights have been seen from the bridge area where a sentry was killed during the war. Occasionally a man in uniform is spotted in the vicinity, both inside the building and out, walking the grounds. Although unidentified, he certainly must represent the brave soldiers who so courageously defended this location.

The alert visitor to Fort Fisher may catch a glimpse of the Confederate General William Whiting who was imprisoned by the Union following his unsuccessful defense of the fort. Many of the men who died at this historic Civil War Battle, linger on these bloody grounds. Union and Confederate soldiers join together to walk these bunkers.

Winnabow and the Town Creek Skirmishes

Major battles occurred on the bluffs of Town Creek during the Civil War which resulted in much death and suffering. This skirmish line extends throughout the length of Town Creek and is well documented. Much blood was shed along the creek banks.

Just off of highway 133 heading from Town Creek/Winnabow area toward Southport, lay a huge mound...described as a hill. As Brunswick County locals know, there are few "hills" in Brunswick County. However, in this one location, reportedly behind a store off of highway 133, the area is known to have been the location of a mighty battle during the Civil War. Few accounts are known of this battle, or the details of its importance to the development of events to come. It is known that there was a heavy casualty count for both the northern and the southern armies at this location. That almost forgotten hill is soaked with the blood of brothers, family, friends and foe alike. The spirits of those brave soldiers continue to walk that hill in remembrance of that deadly day.

Elmira, the Death Camp of the North

While many died during the battles in southeastern North Carolina, many more were captured and taken into custody, often sent to the northern prisons like Elmira. Elmira became final resting place for many Brunswick County and countless North Carolina soldiers.

Elmira opened on the 6th of July 1864 and closed on the 11th of July 1865 with over 12,000 prisoners passing through its doors during that one-year period. Over 3,000 of them died there leaving their Carolina legacies in the north. Many of the North Carolina prisoners, and particularly the Brunswick County prisoners, hailed from the Fort Fisher battles. The greatest numbers came from the January 1865 battles where death and capture tolls were the greatest at the Ft. Fisher engagements. The very first prisoners were described in great detail in the following passage from Elmira, Death Camp of the North by Michael Horigan: "The rebs, who arrived yesterday, wore all sorts of nondescript uniforms; besides the regular dark, dirty grey. Some had nothing on but drawers and shirts. They were a fine looking body of men physically, taller than average, for the most part, made up of two classes, the old and the young, the middle age having a small representation. They did not exhibit a high degree of intelligence but looked to be men that would go where they are told, let what might happen: although lean and lank, yet evidently possessing the vigor and litheness to go through thick and thin. Of course they laughed and joked among themselves. They marched off lively toward Barracks No. 3 from the depot, seemingly gratified by their recent change of base." A member of the 30th North Carolina ranks, A. J. Madra of Tarboro, would be the first man to enter the gates of Elmira.

Sadly, enroute to Elmira and loaded with prisoners, two trains at King and Fuller's Cut, collided in the mountains and only a few survived this accident. In the confusion of the accident, five Confederates managed to scramble to safety and escape into the rugged Pocono Mountains. They were never heard from again. The prisoners, which did not survive, were buried along the railroad tracks in a trench 76 feet long, 8 feet wide and 6 feet deep. This mass grave with pine coffins was filled in and marked.

As many other places in this nation of ours, great bloodshed has preserved our freedom and rights. Along with these great battles, families suffered, loved ones died, and both children and parents alike mourned their losses. Some of the brave people who fought so courageously have not yet gone to their hereafter. Their spirits still walk those familiar battlefields. Be respectful and solemn as you visit these locations.

Chapter 8

Post Civil War Era

1870 - The Committee Tree

The Committee Tree of Stone Chimney Road

Deep into the Lancaster/Bryant parcel is an oak tree, a rather large and historic one. Under this tree, a committee regularly met and established the Cedar Grove Missionary Baptist Church. Mrs. Annie R. Bryant scripts the story in her own words. "In the year of our Lord 1872, just after the Civil War ending the dark days of slavery, a group of Negro Brothers and Sisters who were worshipping at the mount

Pisgah Baptist Church (a predominantly white church) of Supply, North Carolina, decided that they would rather have a church, pastor and officers of their own. They did not feel that they had the freedom that rightfully belonged to them in Mount Pisgah Church. They were restricted to a special area, which had been fenced off in the church for them to worship. Realizing that this was against Bible teachings, they started getting together to make plans to establish a church of their own. They continued to worship at Mount Pisgah while making plans for their own church. They held meetings under a large oak tree, which they called the Committee Tree. It was under the shade of this tree, with faith in God and under the leadership of the late Rev. Moses Louder, the church was organized."

Mrs. Bryant continued with her description of the first Church established by this group of parishioners: "The first Church was a log structure which was erected between the Stone Chimney Road and a place called Sandhill. The Church was built under a large cedar tree with other cedars growing nearby. From these cedar trees, the church obtained its name, Cedar Grove Missionary Baptist Church. Through the years, the spot on which the first church was built has remained clear and it is referred to as a sacred spot because no trees have grown on it. In the year of our Lord 1958, the cedar stump under which the first church stood was taken up for preservation. It had decayed but there was enough to preserve. The stump was cleaned, varnished and put in a small building on the church grounds to serve as a memorial to the founders of the first church."

Interestingly, the treasurers of Cedar Grove Church have kept a family tradition of service by following each other in their duties as church treasurer; one son after another. The first treasurer was James Bryant (1872-1924); then his son, Harry Bryant (1925-1969) and now Harry's son, James H. Bryant, who has served since 1966.

228

Among those thought to be buried in the nearby Slave Cemetery is Wade Bryant (named after John Jack Bryant's brother), born 3 Jan 1843 and died 20 June 1920. He married Rachel Brown. Also, perhaps buried there is Andrew Bryant who died on 12 October 1912 and married Valley Hankins. Known to be positively buried there and reportedly the last person buried in this cemetery is Mr. Pompey Marshall Bryant, who married Pherby Hewett and died on the 29th of November 1929. Dates and information have been recorded by their descendent, Ms. Bell, from family Bibles.

Brick / window casing protecting the original Cedar Stump which was the namesake of Cedar Grove Baptist Church.

Navassa

Navassa is located in the northern section of Brunswick County with the natural boundaries of the Cape Fear River on the north, the Brunswick River to the east, and Sturgeon Creek to the south. In the early years Navassa served as an industrial and transportation center. The railroad bridge was the primary means of freight transportation. Additionally, ferries provided easy access to neighboring areas.

Because of the "high bluffs" that came right to the edge of Cape Fear River from the west, and a land mass between Navassa and Wilmington that would allow the construction of Railroad tracks across Eagle's Island, the

Railroad Company decided to build a bridge across the Cape Fear at Navassa two years after the Civil War ended in 1867. Because of the war, the south's economy was struggling and land costs were pretty cheap. Building this bridge allowed two Railroad Companies (Atlantic Coast Line and The Seaboard Airline) to connect Wilmington with Charlotte and the interior counties of South Carolina. This laid the groundwork for early industry to develop.

Some prudent businessmen led by Donald McRae realized the distinct advantages of locating a fertilizer factory at this location. For years the turpentine industry had been shipping their products to the West Indies without having a product to bring home upon their return. In 1856 large Guano deposits were discovered on Navassa Island, a small barren Island about 15 miles off the coast of Jamaica. McRae and his business partners made arrangements to have the returning ships loaded with the Guano rock and consequently built a factory and named it after the island. They were able to use the Railroad to ship their finished product to the interior of the state for sale. They built the Navassa Guano Factory in 1869.

The Guano mined for processing in Navassa was from Navassa Island, located between Jamaica and Haiti. It brought limestone and calcium phosphate produced from the tectonic uplifting of the coral reefs. Peruvian guano was in essence bird-droppings. Although processing discontinued in 1898, the name guano became synonymous with fertilizers. This industry later became important in neighboring Wilmington.

Meares Bluff became the first post office in 1875 but ceased operations in 1886. In 1903 Mr. Simeon D. Chinnis resumed the mail service. At that time the name Navassa was established although the town was not officially incorporated until 1977. The population of the Town now numbers about 1600 citizens. That number includes the two newly annexed communities of Phoenix and Old Mill.

1880

President Cleveland's
Visit to Northwest

Of interest is one particular political event that occurred in February of 1888. President Grover Cleveland, traveling by private train, stopped in the Northwest Township. An account of his visit was recorded in a local paper.

"At Farmers Turnout (later named Maco), in Brunswick, before reaching Wilmington, the train bearing the Presidential party stopped ten or more minutes. A large arch of holly and cedar had been placed over the track bearing the words, 'Our honored President is welcome to North Carolina,' and a large gathering of ladies and gentlemen were present. Major Reilly did the honors of the occasion, and after shaking hands with the President introduced him to the crowd. The President seemed well pleased with the attentions he received, and said that he would be back again in North Carolina next year. Mrs. Cleveland was welcomed, and hearty cheers followed the party as the train moved off."

The train later stopped in Wilmington, hoping to garner votes in the upcoming election. He lost the next election.

Supply

Supply is a small unincorporated community located around the intersection of US 17 (Ocean Highway) and NC 211 (Southport-Supply Road/Green Swamp Road). Its name is derived from the hardware stores and other supply shops found within the community. Old Georgetown Way had its' name changed to Supply in the late 1800's. As early as the 1820's a trading post sat on the site of highway 17 and 211. The keen eye on the banks of the Lockwood Folly River can still see faint remains of the original trading post buildings, as it intersects Supply.

The house was named from a hickory tree stump, sanded, that became the dining room table. About 1841, the Frink family owned the home and plantation. Dr. Lorenzo Frink is reported to have conducted unsavory "experimental operations" on slaves at the house in the mid 19th century. As a result, the ghosts of these unfortunate slaves still haunt the structure.

According to Robert Simmons, while he was a boy living in the home, ghostly footsteps were heard on the stairs and doors opened and shut alone. Even recently, footsteps have been heard climbing the stairs along with doors slamming. No one was in the house but the individual relaying this lore; some say the slaves are still there. This isn't the only location where former residents make themselves known to modern day visitors.

In the late 1800's, the area was called Pea Landing because of the peanut crops sent to Wilmington. A post office was opened in 1883 with the name "Calabash".

Around 1890 Samuel Thomas purchased the Hickory Hall Plantation, the site of reported hauntings. The Hickory Hall House, the oldest known home in Brunswick County, is located in the Calabash area. For two hundred years (established circa 1807), it has stood the neglect of owners who have redecorated and refurbished it. Now starting to show her age, the home is in a state of being restored to its original condition and design at a cost of over $200,000.

Hidden behind the Calabash Thrift Store on a former plantation that once overlooked the Calabash River, it is a piece of Brunswick County history. Former resident Robert Simmons and his siblings were born in this house, owned by his grandparents, Samuel Hemingway Thomas and Georgia Ann Jenrette Thomas who bought the 1,000-acre plantation in 1889 for $1000. Nine children were raised in this home and their descendents remained there through 1994.

1890 - Bolivia

The central portion of the county was established as Bolivia about 1890 and incorporated in 1911. In 1975, it became the county seat as it was the most centrally located. The community was named for the South American country. It is unclear why this name was chosen.

Bolivia is also home to the county's only Buddhist Temple, the Wat Carolina. It is a Thai Buddhist Monastery, located about 20 miles west of Wilmington. The Buddhist religion teaches that the greatest merit and blessing goes to those who study scripture and explain it to others. It is said that when this takes place, the location is sacred ground, an altar consecrated to Buddha.

Wat Carolina Buddhist Temple

Leland

Lucille Dresser Blake recorded the history of Leland in 1991 describing how it was established and formed after researching courthouse records. She described the location of Leland as the road, which crossed the Wilmington, Columbia and Augusta Railroads on the way to Summerville and Pheonix, and established about 1890. Mr. Joseph W. Gay petitioned for a post office in this area, calling the area Leland, in 1897. (Note: this was also the name of his nephew, Leland Adams and was one of three names submitted to the federal authorities.) The post office officially opened on February 10, 1898 in the corner of Gay's General Store.

Early families in the Leland area included the Joseph W. Gay family, Mr. Will G. Adams, Mr. Richard Williams, and the Reynolds, Krahnke, Murrell and Dickens families. Joseph Watters owned the Clarendon Plantation, one of the earliest in the area along the Cape Fear River, "the thoroughfare". Other plantations in the area included the Mallory Plantation, owned by the Hankins family and the Forks Plantation – owned by the Eagles family (after which Eagle Island is named). The Eagles plantation was located where the Brunswick River runs into the Cape Fear River. The Buchoi Plantation was once owned by Judge Alfred Waddell, now known as the Old Towne area.

The nearby Belvedere Plantation was once the home of William Dry and the late Governor Benjamin Smith. The Woodburn Plantation was also a part of the Belvedere Plantation at one time. However, in 1815, the Bank of the Cape Fear foreclosed on the mortgage of Benjamin Smith and in 1816, John F. Burgwin purchased the land. In 1818, Mr. Burgwin sold it to John Swann. The land circulated through five different owners until in 1904, A. M. Chinnis purchased it.

Mr. Chinnis had the land surveyed and divided into ten farms of about ten acres each, and built a new sand, clay road, now Village Road. He built a bridge over the "Ricefield Branch" (now designated Sturgeon Creek). He subsequently sold this land in 1905 and by 1923 the road from the Brunswick River, through Leland, was paved and became state road #20.

Additional plantations known to have been in the Leland area include: the Cobham Plantation (Dr. Thomas Cobham of Wilmington), Shawfields Plantation (Robert Shaw family), Sauchie Plantation (Schaw family), the Prospect Plantation (unknown owner but perhaps a Moore family member), the Mulberry Plantation (owned by the Watters and Hall families), the Dollison Plantation (owned by John Dallison), the Hailpoint Plantation (owned first by Dollison and later by Samuel Watters), the Auburn Plantation (owned by the Hall family), and Magnolia Plantation (also owned by the Hall family). Both Auburn and Magnolia Plantations were located on the current Dupont Plant land.

Louisiana Plantation was located near the current Goshen Baptist Church land and was owned by the Lock and Robbins families. The Rowell family later owned the Rowan Plantation, owned by the Rowan's about 1760.

Roger Moore first owned The Blue Banks Plantation about 1735. Later William Dry and his son-in-law Benjamin Smith owned the property. A. A. Wannet owned this plantation in the mid 1800's.

Drury Allan owned the Green Banks Plantation in 1765. The Bryan and Green families later owned it. Also along the river, Ephraim Vernon owned the Port Vernon Plantation in 1760.

Leland was considered a transportation center, as was nearby towns established along the Brunswick River. There were ferries across both the Brunswick and Cape Fear Rivers to assist travelers. By 1923 the main road through Leland (now Village Road) was paved. The town was officially incorporated in 1989 with natural boundaries of the Brunswick River to the east and Sturgeon Creek to the north. Its population has grown to about 5,189 by the end of 2004, expanding to become the largest municipality in Brunswick County. Currently the population has exploded to 9,642 residents with the addition of several new residential areas.

Malmo

Malmo was named after Malmo, Sweden. In December of 1885, it opened its own post office but later closed it around 1911. Postal service was continued by Leland.

Hoods Creek

The Point Repose Plantation is known to have been located in the Hoods Creek area and was the first home of James Murray, and Revolutionary War General Thomas Clark. General Clark is buried on the property in an unmarked grave.

Chapter 9

The Twentieth Century

1900

The turn of the century brought about many changes for Brunswick County. Slavery had ended and the depression was not far behind. Most families faced a daily challenge with financial difficulties during the early years. However, Brunswick County continued to grow and develop, incorporating many areas into towns.

About 1930 the US Army Corps of Engineers dredged the US Intercoastal Waterway. This project drew attention to the barrier islands, now popular vacation destinations. By the 1950's and 60's Ocean Isle, Holden Beach, Sunset Beach, Long Beach, Yaupon Beach and Caswell Beach (home to loggerhead turtles who nest there from mid-May until mid-August) had been established and began to become more populated. During the late 60's and 70's other Brunswick County towns were incorporated adding Waccamaw, Ash, Exum, Longwood, Grissettown, Calabash, Hickman's Crossroads, Lockwood's Folly, and Thomasboro as named communities of southern Brunswick County.

Northern Brunswick County grew to establish the Leland, Maco, Bishop, Belville, Boiling Springs, Northwest, and the Winnabow communities. The north continued to be connected to the south part of the county by the Green Swamp encompassing thousands of acres of natural preserves (17,800 acres). Additional towns, such as St. James and Varnamtown, continue to increase the number of named communities of our county.

Located at the southeastern tip of North Carolina, Brunswick County is the 15th fastest growing county in the nation. It continues to welcome visitors and new residents alike. It contains 856 square miles and ranks 6th in total land area of the 100 North Carolina counties. As of 2006, the population of Brunswick County totaled about 95,000 up from 73,000 in the year 2000.

As of 2007, the following incorporated areas and communities were noted in Brunswick County:

Ash	Bald Head Island	Belville
Bishop	Boiling Spring Lakes	Bolivia
Calabash	Carolina Shores	Caswell Beach
Exum	Freeland	Grissettown
Hickman's Crossroads		Holden Beach
Lanvale	Leland	Lockwood's Folly
Long Beach	Longwood	Maco
Malmo	Navassa	Northwest
Ocean Isle	Phoenix	Sandy Creek
Shallotte	Southport	St. James
Sunset Beach	Thomasboro	Varnamtown
Waccamaw	Winnabow	Yaupon Beach

Boiling Spring Lakes

There are over 50 lakes, one a 150-acre lake that forms the centerpiece for Boiling Spring Lakes. The largest one is fed by five springs and Allen Creek, is 2.5 miles long and has ten miles of shoreline. The conglomeration of lakes formed when in 1961 the developers discovered a natural spring. They built a four-foot brick wall to encompass this phenomenon. Almost immediately the spring stopped running and erupted in another location, about fifteen feet from the wall. Over time multiple lakes were formed and the spring returned to its former self, still boiling. At one time this was known as the Bouncing Log Spring where a piece of petrified wood was tossed by the spring in the pool of water. State geologists estimate the spring emits over 43 million gallons of water per day. Legend says that long ago Indians camped at the spring and hold tribal council meetings at that location on their annual trip to the ocean to replenish food supplies. They drank from the spring believing that all who drank from it would always return.

St James

St. James began as a planned development in the early 1990's. It is located near Southport on Highway 211. The Town of St. James was officially incorporated on July 1, 1999 as a "Council/Manager" form of government.

The first official population estimate provided by the State of North Carolina was 695. In 2004 the Town requested that the Census Bureau conduct a special census count because there was a very strong feeling that rapid development and growth contributed to a much higher population count than the State's estimate at that time, which was 857. The resulting statistics from the special census count indicated that St. James had a population of 1,831 with over 1,361 dwelling units. Today, in 2007, St. James covers approximately 6.5 square miles and the Town is currently completing its second Special Census Count. Current population counts are over 2,500 in this gated community.

Ocean Isle Beach

Ocean Isle Beach was incorporated in 1959. It spans seven miles in length. It's current population of about 425 expands to around 25,000 during peak summer months, as do other Brunswick County beaches.

OIB Plane Crashes

The east end of Ocean Isle Beach has a history of plane crashes. One resident removed a machine gun from one of those crashes in the early 1940's, proud of their loot from the unfortunate accident. After being warned that the FBI and authorities were looking for the machine gun, those young lads quickly and quietly returned that machine gun. However, occasional machine gun casings are still found in the area surrounding those crashes and surrounding woods on the "land side" of the east end of Ocean Isle.

Sam of Ocean Isle Beach

At Ocean Isle Beach, the coastal shores provide a serene and beautiful setting for the nearby cottage, just one street back from the Winds Beach Resort where a man named Sam died of a heart attack while on vacation there. Strange happenings in this cottage include cold spots and shades opening and shutting. Some think Sam is still among the OIB residents.

Caswell Beach

The Town of Caswell Beach was incorporated on the 4th of May 1975. The permanent population is 478 which expands to over 3,000 during the peak summer months.

Caswell Beach protects and enables the loggerhead turtles as they nest. In 2006, Caswell Beach recorded 75 nests that were tended and protected.

Caswell Beach, like the rest of the Brunswick County beaches has been the recipient of many hurricanes and major storms causing untold damages to the beach communities. Their records indicate the following official notes regarding intense weather events that have occurred on the coast of Brunswick County.

October 15, 1954	Hurricane Hazel	
	Category 2 at Landfall	
1955	Hurricane Connie	Cat 4
1955	Hurricane Ione	Cat 3
1960	Hurricane Donna	Cat 5
1971	Hurricane Ginger	Cat 2
Sept. 13, 1984	Hurricane Diane	Cat 4
1985	Hurricane Gloria	Cat 4
1986	Hurricane Charley	Cat 1
Dec. 19878	Snow Storm	
1993	Hurricane Emily	Cat 3
July 12, 1996	Hurricane Bertha	Cat 3
September 6, 1996	Hurricane Fran	Cat 3
February 11, 1998	Nor'easter	
August 26, 1998	Hurricane Bonnie	105-115.mph
	winds	
September 2, 1998	Hurricane Bonnie Lingers	
August 1999	Hurricane Dennis	Cat 2
September 16, 1999	Hurricane Floyd	Cat 4
(twenty inches of rain and ten foot storm surges)		
July 31, 2004	Hurricane Alex	Cat 3
August 14, 2004	Hurricane Charley	Cat 4
September 25, 2005	Hurricane Ophelia	Cat 2
October 2005	Tropical Storm Tammy	

Fort Caswell

Fort Caswell was one of the strongest forts at the time. It originally encompassed over 2,800 acres and was located at the east end of Oak Island. It was built in 1838. The main compound was made of earthen ramparts in a pentagonal brick-and-masory style. Ft. Caswell saw very little action during the Civil War, perhaps because of its heavy fortification. It was abandoned about January 1865 after the fall of Fort Fisher to Union troops. It was deliberately destroyed except for the citadel and surrounding earthworks.

A battery and a seawall were built after the Civil War from 1885 to 1902.

Liberty Ships

The Liberty Ships were important during World War II because these ships carried supplied to military forces overseas. The largest shipyard was located in Wilmington. However security was crucial along the southeastern North Carolina coast, trying to protect it's coastal residents from the German submarines patrolling the seas. Several of the liberty ships were sunk before they reached 100 miles out to sea. The 1966 photo below shows the Liberty Ships lined up on the Brunswick River in the northern end of the county.

Sunset Beach

Three miles of coastline comprise the quaint Sunset Beach that is connected to the mainland by a swinging bridge. It is the smallest of the three barrier islands collectively forming the Brunswick Isles and home to the swinging bridge, the last of the non-high rise bridges in Brunswick County.

The Green Swamp

The Green Swamp Nature Preserve consists of 15, 907 acres located in Brunswick County. (Other estimates are over 17,000 acres). The Federal Paper board donated 13,850 acres of this preserve in 1977 and an additional 2, 577 acres in the 1980's. The Nature Conservancy has since purchased more land. The management of the land is supported by the estate of Harry Patrick gold and Erma Green Gold. It is located 5.5 miles north of Supply on NC highway 211.

This ecological area contains many examples of longleaf pine savannas, morchids and insectivorous plants. However, more than 13, 000 acres is comprised of a dense evergreen shrub bog (pocosin), dominated by gallberry, titi, and sweetbay. It contains at least 14 different species of insectivorous plants including extensive protected populations of the Venus flytrap, Sundew and four different species of pitcher plants. It is also home to alligators, fox squirrels,

Henslow's sparrow, Bachman's sparrow, the endangered red-cokaded woodpecker, and the Hessel hairstreak butterfly. There are over twenty-four rare plants and nineteen rare animals in the swamps.

Management activities of the Green Swamp include periodic burning, installing woodpecker nest boxes and restoring pine plantation to longleaf pine savannas.

Local Legends

Throughout the 20th century, legends and stories continue to be told about more recent events and situations related to the southeastern coast of North Carolina. Among them are:

The Spirit of Gore Lake Road

Joyce Jacobs and her family lived near the Gore Lake Road, in the northern section of the county at one time. Rumor had it that near the home where she lived, there was a man who had been killed on the railroad track. This man's ghost was seen on more than one occasion in the dark of the hallway of their home. He never seemed to bother anything or anyone, just suddenly appeared and as quickly as he materialized, faded away. It seems that railroad accidents are not uncommon in this part of Brunswick County.

Turtle Nests Luck

The endangered loggerhead turtles have a special place in the hearts of Brunswick County residents and visitors alike. These small hatchling creatures need protection from crowded sunsets and beach home lights. From May to October, nesting and hatching sea turtles are protected to ensure their proliferation and safety. During nesting lays, "nest parents", volunteers, watch nests nightly during their expected hatch times and assist the babies into the surf. It has been said that good luck will follow those who protect our coastal endangered species of sea turtles.

Residents and visitors alike are encouraged to turn off their porch lights, especially those shining on the beach strand during hatching times. Baby hatchlings will follow the moonlight to the sea. They do not need to be confused with the porch lights guiding them in opposite directions. Visitors to the Brunswick Isles are encouraged to be extremely cautious around turtle mounds and identified nests so as not to disturb the natural progression of birth. Your cooperation in protecting the nests helps to preserve the turtle-patrol tradition for future generations of visitors and turtles alike. Blessings are bestowed upon all turtle nest protectors.

The Bolivia Beast

Residents in the Bolivia area have recently reported a predator that has reportedly killed at least three family dogs (Fall 2007). The dogs left in the yard were found dead in the morning, a victim of some wild creature. No barking, no whimper or other sounds were heard giving their owners a warning that something was amiss. Tracks of a "big cat" were reported and measured three inches in diameter. While *the* predator has not actually been spotted, residents are leery of what may be a very large cougar or other feline. However, if the predator is as large as reported, it will certainly be an endangered species and may be difficult to capture. Visitors and residents should be ever vigilant in their nature treks. (October 2007).

Alligator Attacks

No book about the coast would be complete without a mention of the alligators. Ah, the alligators in Brunswick County. Yes, there are 'gators' in the county, practically the entire county. Avid golfers, especially in the Ocean Isle, Sunset and Calabash areas, are well aware of the hazards of the courses. Gators are often spotted sunning on the banks of the many ponds on local fairways. A ball hit near a gator, regardless of size, is a ball "lost". The gators are afforded their natural rights as the golfer bows to their clout.

Alligator "re-homed" from a Brunswick County Golf Course

Recently, the alligators in Brunswick County have exalted their innate behaviors endangering local pets. In the southern end of the county, an alligator recently attacked and killed a 114-pound dog as it swam in a pond at Sea Trail Golf Resort. It was removed and found to be an 11-foot gator, weighing about 500 pounds. Earlier that week a Labrador retriever was killed in the same pond. Two gators were known to reside in the pond.

Another gator-incident occurred in the northern end of the county, on Town Creek. Young boys were fishing, accompanied by their dog. After several evenings of fishing, it was too much for the local gators of Town Creek. Their dog suffered the same horrible fate.

While this type of incident must have surely occurred in the past, perhaps the increased urban development has decreased the food supply of these natural predators, the southern gators. Should this be a warning to the leaders and developers of Brunswick County?

Mrs. Calabash

"Good Night, Mrs. Calabash, wherever you are." Jimmy Durante was well known for his closing statement on his entertaining radio show. The origin of this national catch phrase remained a mystery. Mr. Durante never revealed the meaning. However, locals of Calabash are convinced that it originated in a restaurant in the area when his troupe stopped to eat enroute to a performance. Mr. Durante was so taken with the food, service, and conversation of the owner, that he vowed to make her famous. Not knowing her name, he began referring to her, as Mrs. Calabash and she became known to the nation.

Interestingly, Mr. Durante married his late first wife on the 19th of June in 1921 and remained married to her until her death on Valentine's Day in 1943. The word Calabash was a typical verbal mangle of Durante as he said the word "Calabasas", the southern California location where the couple made their home for the last years of her life. Regardless of its origin, the world recognized the infamy of the famous Calabash Seafood and continues to come for the cuisine, much to the delight of the local shrimpers and fishermen.

Sometime in the late 40's and 50's, Calabash became known for its seafood and was named "Seafood Capital of the World". It was incorporated in 1973 and in 1989 consolidated Carolina Shores Village into the town. However in 1998, the Town of Calabash voted for the removal of Carolina Shores from the corporate limits of the town, and both areas continue to develop and expand independently.

Long Beach

Long Beach grew from a few prewar cottages to a community of over 300 near-shore habitations after World War II and then was practically destroyed by Hurricane Hazel in 1954. Only five houses remained where they were built, and everyone in the small population was homeless. Yet in 1955 the town incorporated, development spurred by E. F. Middleton and developer G. V. Barbee. The community was laid out in a different fashion than its neighbors, with major residential roadways running perpendicular to the beach rather than parallel. Because of this feature, the town was considered more of a permanent than resort community.

The Gray Man of Long Beach

Further up in the northern end of the county, The Gray Man "shows himself". He was seen before the infamous Storm of 1893 struck the coast, wiping out the settlement at Magnolia Beach just north of Pawley's Island. He has also been seen in Brunswick County at Oak Island, and the former Long Beach area. Long Beach is said to host "the gray man" who walks along the beach just prior to hurricanes. He is said to be visible prior to all hurricanes, sometimes in South Carolina and sometimes at Long Beach/Oak Island. Those persons who have seen him seem to be mysteriously spared the storm's destructive power. The Gray Man was the subject of an episode of the popular television program Unsolved Mysteries. Was he a casualty of a hurricane? A tourist? A long time resident? We may never find the answer to his nocturnal beach treks.

The story of the Gray Man is a tragic love story. As the soldier returned home to marry his sweetheart, riding on horseback, he was killed in an accident. His spirit, however, lived on, and he was able to warn his lover of an approaching hurricane and save her life. Since that time, many people have reported seeing the Gray Man before a hurricane and heeded his ghostly warning to seek safety.

Fort Fisher Hermit – Robert E. Harrell

With a tyrant for a father and an overly strict mother, Robert E. Harrell grew up in the mountains of North Carolina. After living in an abusive home he went to live with relatives, but grew into an adult who found his peace in the woods and streams of western Carolina. Disappointing careers and a failed marriage did not help him find his inner tranquility. Even a brief stay in a psychiatric facility in Morganton, NC, could not help Mr. Harrell find his "way" after relatives committed him. He escaped the facility and the suicide of his oldest son, Robert, as he sought a simpler lifestyle. Born on February 2, 1893 in Gaffney, South Carolina, he became a hermit in 1955.

At sixty-two years old, he left the mountains and traveled to the coastal waters landing in the Carolina Beach locale. Soon after arriving at Fort Fisher, Robert Harrill was arrested as a vagrant and sent to his hometown of Shelby by the sheriff's department. The following summer he returned to Carolina Beach. With no house, no job, no means of support, and no friends, he found himself living among the bunkers of Fort Fisher providing for himself from the environment around him. Living under the stars, and sustaining himself on the local flora and fauna, he soon became a tourist attraction sharing his personal philosophies with thousands of visitors through his "School of Common Sense."

Many of the visitors were simply curious, others were attracted to his wisdom and words, but others went out of their way to harass him or to try to steal his money. Rumor was that he had thousands of dollars hidden in his bunker. He was arrested several times for vagrancy but successfully defended himself in a court of law. Once, a group of men who assaulted him were convicted on the testimony against them by the hermit.

Robert was warm and friendly to the visitors lured to the site by its rich Civil War history. Here amid the scrub oaks, the mosquitoes, the summer suns, he provided for himself, often accepting donations from tourists and locals alike. Although his death left many questions, his legacy remains as the Fort Fisher Hermit. He was attributed to the following quote: "My life here goes up and down like the tides of this old sea out here... Only nature determines my existence."

Sadly, in June of 1972, his body was found by a group of teens on an early Sunday morning. Some believed he was murdered. The coroner ruled the cause of death a heart attack. Others believe it was a prank gone wrong. His legacy remains.

Varnamtown

Varnamtown is a quaint fishing village. It population was reported as 481 in the year 2000. The estimated population in July 2006 was 560 showing a 16.4% growth. Varnamtown is the home of the annual Dixon Chapel Oyster Roast, a festive November activity attended by many surrounding community members who enjoy the local oysters cooked on the grounds and nestling waters welcome many local shrimp boats, shrimpers, fishermen, and clammers who continue to collect the food treasures of the sea, enjoyed by the local residents and tourists alike.

Battery Island

Battery Island is owned by the North Carolina Department of Environment and Natural Resources and is leased to the National Audubon Society. It is home to the blue heron, snowy egret, tricolored heron and glossy ibis. It is one of the largest heronries on the east coast.

Bluff Island and East Beach

Bluff Island contains a rare Interdune pond and several rare plant species including dune bluecurls. Part of the site is owned by the North Carolina Wildlife Resources Commission and part owned by the North Carolina Division of Parks and Recreation. Other areas such as the Lower Cape Fear Bird Nesting Area, Bird Island, Middle Island, Brantley Island, and Zeke's Island Estuarine Sanctuary encompass islands, marshes, tidal flats and shallow estuaries throughout the coast of Brunswick County, some owned by agencies of North Carolina and some privately owned.

The Future

Regardless of any rumors, legends, lore, history, or legacy of Brunswick County or its residents, each person has left his or her mark in one fashion or another. Whether through volunteer service, spiritual leadership, political activities, or social duties, our churches, schools and businesses have continued to preserve our heritage, coastal regions and resources, ever mindful of its historic past. With a full heart, we honor our past, pay tribute to our history, and look forward to the future.

Stained glass window at Sabbath Home Church

Bibliography

Alcock, John P. "What Genealogists should know about 18th Century Virginia Law" in 18th Century Virginia Law. Friends of the Virginia State Archives. Speech presented November 17, 1999. http://home.hiwaay.net/~woliver/Virginia_Law.html

Biographical Directory of the Governors of the United States, 1789-1978, Robert Sobel and John Raimo, eds. Westport, CT: Meckler Books, 1978.

Brickell, John. Volume Title Unknown. Dublin, Ireland, 1737.

Colonial Williamsburg: 18th Century Clothing http://www.history.org/history/clothing/index.cfm

Curtis, Walter Gilman, Reminiscences of Wilmington and Smithville-Southport, 1848-1900. 1905.

Eastern North Carolina Digital Library. A collection of historical documents and artifacts. http://digital.lib.ecu.edu/historyfiction/subjects.aspx?sort=A

Georgia Historical Papers, Vol. 2, page 54.

"James Gwyn Family Papers 1653-1946," Series J Volumes 1844-1804, Folder 31, Manuscripts Department, CB#3926, Wilson Library, University of North Carolina at Chapel Hill, Phone: 919/962-1345

Henry, Nathan C. Assistant State Archaeologist and Conservator. Underwater Archaeology Branch of the NC Office of State Archaeology. http://www.arch.dcr.state.nc.us/default.htm

Hill, Jerry. Blackbeard's Last Stand, Cordingly, David "Life among the Pirates" 1995. Exquemelin. A.O."The Buccaneers of America" 1923. Ocracoke Island Web Site www.ocracokeislan.d.com.)

Holden, John F. The Beginning and Development of Holden Beach 1756-2000. New Hanover Printing and Publishing, Inc., Wilmington, NC. C. 2000 by John F. Holden.

Holden, J. M. M. Heartening Heritage on a Carolina Crescent. New Hanover Printing and Publishing Company, Wilmington, NC. C. 1989 by J. M. M. Holden.

Lawrence, Richard. NC State Deputy Archaeologist, Underwater Branch. http://www.arch.dcr.state.nc.us/default.htm

Lee, Lawrence. The History of Brunswick County, North Carolina. Published by Brunswick County, NC. 1978.

Meredith, Hugh. AN ACCOUNT OF THE CAPE FEAR COUNTRY 1731. Edited by EARL GREGG SWEM Librarian of College of William and Mary. CHARLES F. HEARTMAN, Perth Amboy, N. J.
1922

North Carolina Encyclopedia, www.carolinacuzins.org/brunswic.html

North Carolina Government 1585-1979, A narrative and statistical history, Thad Eure-Secretary of State, North Carolina Department of Secretary of State-Raleigh, North Carolina.Ash

"Order in the Court: Juvenile Justice in the 18th Century: An Electronic Field Trip" in Colonial Williamsburg Foundation and PBS Teacher Resource Service. http://www.cwf.org/history/teaching/eft.cfm

Rattroy, Jeannette Edwards. East Hampton History. Country Life Press, Garden City, NY, c 1953.

Sprunt, James. Chronicles of the Cape Fear 1660-1916, Second Edition. Raleigh, 1916.

Waddell, Alfred Moore. History of New Hanover County.

Watters, Fanny C. Plantation Memories of the Cape Fear River Country. C. 1944 by Fanny C. Watters. Stephens Press, Asheville, NC.

Wilford, J. A New Voyage to Georgia, by a Young Gentleman, giving an Account of his trip to South Carolina, and part of North Carolina. A curious account of the Indians, by an honorable person and a poem to Jame Oglethorpe, Esq. on his arrival from Georgia. London. 1735.

Personal Interviews with:

Herman R. Faircloth, Ouida Hewett, Woody Fulford, Lynn Holden, Judy Holden, Joyce Jacobs, Nathan C. Henry, and Richard Lawrence, and many other wonderful Brunswick County residents.

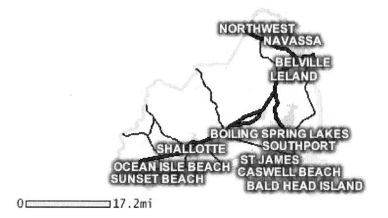

0 ☐════════☐17.2mi

Appendix

Municipal Population in Brunswick County

Municipality	1990	2000	2004
Bald Head Island	78	173	217
Belville	66	285	427
Boiling Spring Lakes	1,650	2,972	3,580
Bolivia	228	148	154
Calabash	1,210	711	1,346
Carolina Shores	1,031	1,482	2,439
Caswell Beach	175	370	443
Holden Beach	626	787	861
Leland	1,801	1,938	4,786
Navassa	445	479	1,600
Northwest	n/a	671	746
Oak Island ***	4,550	6,571	7,369
Ocean Isle Beach	523	426	462
Sandy Creek	243	246	267
Shallotte	965	1,381	1,704
Southport	2,369	2,351	2,595
St. James	n/a	804	1,833
Sunset Beach	311	1,824	1,985
Varnamtown	404	481	527
Unincorporated Brunswick County	34,310	49,043	51,693
Totals	50,985	73,143	85,034

Brunswick County totals increased by 67% from 1990 to 2004.

***Long Beach and Yaupon Beach merged into Oak Island on 7/1/99.
Sources: US Census Bureau for 1990, 2000 and 2004.

The following Last Will and Testaments and assorted legal documents are some of those available at the Brunswick County Courthouse. These were selected to present samples of the types of Wills that our former residents wrote in order to give us a glimpse into their lives and deaths. Many more are also available. Words are spelled as closely as originally written.

Last Will and Testament of *Richard Ransom*

IN THE NAME OF GOD AMEN: the twenty -seventh day of June in the year of our Lord One Thousand seven hundred and forty eight. I Richard Ransom of Saint Andrew Parrish in the County of Brunswick being sick and weak but of sound and perfect memory do made and ordain this my last Will and Testament. IMPREMIS, I desire that my body may have a decent and Christian burial at the discreition of my Exores hereafter   named.

ITEM, it s my will and desire that my slaves Andrew and Lucy and my slave peter now in the possession of my Father in Glauchester County may be sold and that the money arising them from be applied towards the payment of my just debts.

ITEM: I give and bequeath unto my beloved wife Frances Ransom during her natural life the use of the plantation whereon I now live with all my other slaves and estate of what kind   forever.

ITEM: I give and bequeath unto my son James Ransom and his heirs after his Mothers decease two slaves named Caesar and   Hannah.

ITEM: I give and bequeath unto my son Robert Hicks Ransom and to his heirs after the death of his Mother two salves named Joe and Jeffry. ITEM All the rest of my estate not hereinbefore mentioned I desire may be equally divided between my three children James Robin & Elizabeth and lastly I do hereby constitute appoint and ordain my trusty friends Col. John Wall and Col Nathaniel Edwards to be joynt Executors of this my last Will and Testament, and do also appoing them and the survivor of them to be Guardian to my two sons James and Robin whom I desire they may be bound Apprentics's to such trade or calling as the think they shall think fit when they come to the age of sixteen years.

And I do hereby utterly revoke and make void all other Will or Wills by me in any manner heretofore made.

IN WITNESS whereof I have hereunto set my hand and affixed my seal the day and year herein first above written.

Richard   Ransom.   (SS)

Source: "James Gwyn Family Papers 1653-1946," Series J Volumes 1844-1804, Folder 31, Manuscripts Department, CB#3926, Wilson Library, University of North Carolina at Chapel Hill, Phone: 919/962-1345.

Last Will and Testament of *James C. Stanland*

I JAMES C. STANLAND of the County of Brunswick and State of North Carolina

Being of Sound mind and memory, but Considering the uncertainty of my earthly existence, do make and declare this my last will and testament, in manner and form following that is to Say: first that my Executrix, hereinafter named Shall provide for my body a decent burial, Suitable to the wishes of my relations and friends, and pay all funeral expenses, together with my just debts, howsoever and to whomsoever owing, out of the monies that may first come into her hand, as apart or parcel of my estate.

Item I give and devise to my beloved wife twenty acres of land so as to include the plantation in the north end of the tract whereon i now live So as to include my mansion house, all out houses and other improvements, to have and to hold to her, the Said MIMMA for and during the term of her natural life in Satisfaction for, and in lieu of, her dower and thirds of and in all my real estate

Item I give and devise to my Eldest Son ASA, all of that tract of land whereon he now lives, twenty acres to have and to hold to him and [repeated on new page] his heirs in fee Simple forever

Item I give and devise to my Son JOHN D all of that tract of land whereon he now lives twenty acres to have and to hold to him and his heirs, in fee simple forever.

Item I give and devise to my youngest Son STEWARD twenty acres of land a joining his Brother JOHN D. STANLAND to have and to hold to him and his heirs in fee simple forever

Item I give and devise to my daughter all the tract of land whereon I now live, twenty acres   [inserted here above line] except the life estate of my wife, devised in a former Item of this my will, to have and to hold to her and her heirs, in fee simple forever

Item I give and bequeath to my Said beloved wife all my beds and furniture, all the household and kitchen furniture all of my cattle: hogs and one sorrel mare and cart: All the crop of Every description that may be upon the plantation were on I now live and all the provisions on hand at the time of my death

Item I give and bequeath to MARY SIMMONS after my wifes death my mare crop stock and plantation and tools during and assign absolutely forever and lastly I do hereby constitute and appoint my wife MIMMA my lawful Executrix to all intents and purposes, to Execute this my last will and testament, according to the true in tent and meaning of the Same, and Every part and Clause thereof hereby revoking and declaring uterly voyd all other wills and testaments by me heretofore made
In witness whereof, I, the Said JAMES C. STANLAND, do hereunto set my hand and seal this [word repeated on new line] Feby 2^{cond}-A. D. 1860

James   C. Stanaland (Seal)

Signed Sealed, published and declared by the Said JAS C. STANLAND to be his last will and testament, in the presence of us who at his request and in his presence do subscribe our names as witnesses thereto

John H. Brooks
Thomas X (his mark)
Simmons

Last Will and Testament of *Joel Reaves*

Recorded in Book D Page 16
Brunswick County, North Carolina

State of North Carolina

260

In the name of God Amen! I Joel Reaves of the County of Brunswick and State of North Carolina, being of sound disposing mind, and considering the uncertainty of this life, do make, publish and declare the following and no other to be and contain my last Will and Testament. That is to say

First It is my will and desire and I so direct that my Executors hereinafter named shall provide for my body a decent burial suitable to the wishes of my relations and friends; and pay all funeral expenses together with my just debts out of the moneys that shall first come into their hands as part and parcel of my Estate.

Secondly I give, devise, and bequeath unto my beloved wife Sarah Reaves to have and to hold for and during the term of her natural life and no longer the following described property. Real and personal. viz. My plantation on Cape Fear River where I now reside, My negro slaves Nancy, Henry, & Betty, one horse, one yoke of oxen, two carts, and my Barouche; all my stock of hogs and cattle marked with a crop and two splits in the right ear, and a split in the left ear; also as many of my tools, and farming utensils as my Executors shall think necessary for her use; also one half of my house hold and Kitchen furniture, the division of said furniture to be fairly made between

my said wife and my daughter Mary by my Executors.

Thirdly - I give, devise and bequeath unto my daughter Mary Reaves my Negroes Lucy and Ned. One half of my household & Kitchen furniture, also my mare named Eliza. And from and after her mothers death the following propety, viz; one horse, one yoke of Oxen. One Barouche, Stock of Hogs and Cattle, marked with a crop and two splits in the right ear and a split in the left ear. the other half of my house hold & kitchen furniture, and the following slaves viz; Nancy, Henry and Betty. The foregoing negro slaves to be held by my said daughter Mary for and during her natural life and after her death to such child or children as she may leave her surviving, But in case she die without leaving any surviving child or children then Nancy and Henry to be the property of my wifes children (by her former husband) viz; Sarah E. Moore, wife of Revd WM. D Moore, Charlotte

Robbins, wife of Enoch Robbins, and William Hankins, and the other slaves above named to wit. Lucy Betty and Ned to be the property of my other Children hereinafter named share and share alike

Fourthly. I give, devise, and bequeath unto my son Samuel F. Reaves a tract of land containing One hundred & Seventy five acres on Daws' Creek, being the tract purchased of John Willets; also all my tock of hogs and cattle marked with a poplar leaf in the right ear and an overbi? in the left ear and also my slaves. Celia and James

Fifthly I give, devise and bequeath unto my daughter Prudence Catharine Wells my slaves Susan and her children

Sixthly. I give, devise and bequeath unto my daughter Patience Ward my slaves Elsy and her children except her child Tom hereinafter given to my daughter Annie Ward. and her youngest child name not known. His Executors & administrators in trust for the sole and seperate use of my daughter Annie Ward wife of James Ward for and during her natural life, and not in anywise subject to the debts, contracts or control of her said present or any future husband and at her death to be equally divided among her children, share and share alike.

Tenthly. It is not my intention in making the forgoing disposition of my slaves to do any injustice to my children. I wish the slave to go to the persons named, but at the same time I hereby direct that they be fairly valued by my Executors excepting expressly those given to my daughter Mary. To be more specific for certain good reasons, I have given my daughter Mary a larger share than my other children The bequest to her is not to be disturbed; but I wish the Shares of my other Children to be equal in value. My Executors will therefore fairly estimate the value of the slaves given to each and those having more that a fair proportion, or one Sixth of the value of the whole, shall pay over to the other so as to make the share of each equal.

262

Eleventhly. It is my will and I so direct that all my property Real and personal not herein devised or bequeathed be sold by my Executor on such terms as they shall think best, the proceeds thereof as also what money, I may have at the time of my death to be applied to the payment of my debts, and the charges in and about the execution of this will, The overplus if any to be equally divided among all my Children share and share alike, But before such sale, I direct that a sufficient portion of the crop stock and provisions be set apart for the support of my wife and family for one year. At the death of my wife I also direct that my Executor sell my plantation on Cape Fear upon such terms as they may think best. The proceeds, to be equally divided among all my children

Lastly. I appoint my friends Robert M. McRacken, William M. D. Moore and my son Joel my Executors to carry into effect this my last Will & Testament.

Given under my hand & Seal this
13th of November A.D. 1858

Signed Sealed published & declared by the testator to be his last will and Testament in presence of　　　Joel Reaves (seal) who in his presence and in the presence of each other do at his request hereunto

set our names as subscribing witnesses the words " and my stock of cattle & hogs" on this page erased before signing

Jesse G. Drew
James Langdon

Last Will and Testament of *Elisa Sellers*, 1801

Brunswick Will Book B Page 69

In the name of God, Amen, I, Elisha Sellers, of Brunswick County　　　　in　　　　　　the State of North Carolina, being weak of body but perfect mind and sound memory, calling to mind the mortality of my flesh, and that it is appointed unto all men once to die, do make and ordain this my last Will and Testament in the form and manner following. First and principally, I recommend my soul to God who gave it, trusting in the merits of Christ for a Glorious Resurrection, and my body to be buried after a Christian manner at the discretion of my executors hereinafter named, nothing doubting but I shall receive the same again through the mighty power of God, and touching such worldly goods wherewith it hath pleased God to bless me with, I give, devise, and bequeath in manner & form following: First, I give unto my beloved wife, Mary Sellers, the use of the plantation whereon I now live, during her life or widowhood and after her death or marriage to revolve to my son John Bryant Sellers. Secondly, I give unto my daughters Sarah McClelland and Mary Singletary and my sons William Sellers, Thomas Sellers, Matthew Sellers, and Willets Sellers, and also to my daughter Ann Peoples Mints one shilling to each of them. Thirdly, I give unto my wife Mary Sellers her equal part of the remaining part of my property not hereinbefore given. I mean one child's part. Fourthly, it is my will and desire that the remaining part of my property may be equally divided between all the children which I have had or may hereafter have by said wife Mary, share and share alike. Fifthly, I give to my grandsons Elisha and William Sellers one heifer calf to each of them. Lastly, I nominate, constitute, and appoint my beloved wife Mary Sellers Executrix, my dutiful son Thomas Sellers and my friend John Conyers as executors to this my last Will and Testament hereby revoking all former wills by me heretofore made and ratifying and confirming this to be my last Will and Testament. In witness whereof I have hereunto set my hand and affixed my seal this sixteenth day of November one thousand eight hundred and one.

Elisha [X is mark] Sellers

Signed, sealed, published and declared to be the last will and testament
of the testator in presence of us.

264

Mary (X) Ramsay
Drucilla (X) Churis(?)
J. Gause, Jr.

Last Will and Testament of *John Sullavind*

Brunswick County
N. C. 20 September 1782

In the Name of God Amen, I John Sullavind of North
Carolina Brunswick County being very Sick and Weak in
Body, but of perfect Mind and Memory, Thanks be given unto
God Calling unto Mind the Mortality of my Body and
knowing that it is appointed for all men once to die, do make
and ordain this my last Will and Testament that is to Say,
Principally and first of all, I Give and Recommend my Soul
into the Hand of Almighty God that gave it and my body I
Recommend to the Earth, to be buried in decent Christian
Burial, at the Discretion of my executor: nothing doubting but
at the General Resurrection I Shall receive the Same again, by
the Mighty Power of God, and as touching Such Worldly
Estate Wharewith it has pleased God to bless me in this Life I
Give divise and dispose of the Same in the following Manner
and form: First I Give and bequeath to Agga my beloved wife
one mare Cauled Fan and bridle and Saddle allso I Give to my
well beloved son Hamtonn Sullavind one Shilling Sterling
also I give to my beloved son John Sullavind one Shilling
Sterling allso I give to my beloved son William Sullavind one
Shilling Sterling also I give to my beloved daughter Nanny
Sullavind and my son Calib, and my son Robbin, and my son
Archer, and my son Elcany, and my Daughter Paully, all my
stock of Cattle and what Cattle'some of them had before to be
Equally devide with my stock and for every child to have a
part not one to have more than the other - also I give to my son
Mical Campeal one Hundred acre of land joining Bengamin
Outlaw old_ part of the land that I bought of John Sullavind
and for him to pay to the Estate five hard dollars on the
account _____ Sullavind and my son _____n and my

265

Son Archer and my son Elcany and my daughter Paully all my
_____ that the said lands may be sold and the money
to be Equally divided among them and all the Dets thats Dew
to me, I will that fore horses may be sol for the Use of the
family, I will that three Guns may be devided among the four
youngest Boys, and all my houshold furniture to be the the
property of my Loving wife Agga Sullavind to make yuse of
and dispose of it at her own descretion further I will that if
Either of the five youngest Children above mentioned should
die, what Estate thay have shall be Equally devided amung the
Rest of the Same Youngest Children,

in Witness Whareof I halve hereunto put my name and Seal
this twentieth day of September one thousand seven Hundred
Eighty Two
John Sulavint seal
Request (Abraham N (ott? Miller?) [William Sullav-
Executors] Will'am

Sullavint Exetor
Signed Sealed and Delivered in the Presence of his mark
Richard(i Harriss
Peter Hanseli +0 his mark
Ann(I)Harriss
(bracketed words crossed out)

Last Will and Testament of *John Galloway*

State of North Carolina – Brunswick County
In the name of God, Amen! I, John Galloway, on my XXX,
do, with all obedience to the Almighty God, make my last
Will and Testament. I hereby give unto my well beloved
wife's hands three hundred acres, one negro fellow named Jo,
also one negro wench named Serier (?), a XXX Terier, and
one negro fellow named Manuel, and a boy negro, Tom, and a
girl named Hannah, and also all my household and after my
wife's decease, to be equally divided amongst my four
266

youngest children which are Alfred and Cornelius and Mary and Amelia: and also I give unto my well beloved son, Nathan, onehundred acres of land that he now lives on and one negro named Jeepister to be his full and just portion of all my estate and I hereby acknowledge this to be my last will and testament whereunto I do hereby set my hand and seal this 17th day of September, 1788.

John Galloway

Witnesses: Samuel Bell, Henry Goodware, William Galloway.

The written will was proved agreeably to law and ordered to be registered in Brunswick County on April 1, 1798.

Last Will and Testament of *Miles Potter* – 1798

In the name of God, Amen! I, Miles Potter, in the State of North Carolina, and of the County of Brunswick, being weak of body, but perfect in memory and having my understanding, do make, ordain, constitute, and appoint this my Last Will and Testament, and I do hereby disxxxx all former Will or Wills and declare this above to be my Last Will and Testament. First, I recoxxxx my soul to Almighty God, from whence it came and my body to the grave to be buried in a decent, Christian burial at the discretion of my Executors. XXXX, I desire that my negro woman, Chloe, may serve my son, Miles Potter, the xxx of two years from the day of my death and also her child, Maney, and then to be freed, if agreeable to the laws of the Country; if inconsistent with the law, then to be sold at Vendue to the highest bidder, the money to be equally divided between my four sons, Miles, James, John & Robert Potter, my son in law, Abraham Skipper, my daughter in law Margaret McMurray. XXX, I desire Margaret McMurray may have my cow named Martha two years. XXX, I desire Miles Potter may have my other cattle two years and at the exxxuration of said two years the aforesaid cattle to be sold and the money equally divided as before mentioned. XXX I desire James Potter may have my two red sows and one barrow. XXX, I desire Abraham Skipper may have one barrow and one sow. XXX, I desire Miles Potter may have one barrow. XXX, I desire my Negro woman may have the two sows called hers. XXX, I desire John Potter may have my gxxx. XX, I desire my Executors raise six dollars at or before the exXuration of two years to fray my debts it being a just estimate of what I owe. XX, I desire Miles Potter may discharge my vote offhand of Eight Pounds fifteen shillings owe Thomas Leonard. I having paid xxx for a discharge of the same, and I do aolemnly hereby appoint Miles Potter and John Potter Executors to this my Will and testament for the faithful fulfilling thereof. Signed sealed and acknowledged this tenth of October 1798.

Miles Potter

Witnesses: Nathan Christie
              Abraham Skipper

ABSTRACTS OF NORTH CAROLINA WILLS
Which mention Brunswick County

DOWNER, WILLIAM.

Brunswick, New Hanover County.

December 10, 1745. March Court, 1745. *Executors:* CAPT. HUGH BLANING and CAPT. RICHARD QUINCE. The will directs the executors to sell so much of the estate as may be necessary to pay the debts of the testator and to pay to themselves 80 pounds each in addition to their legal fees of seven and one-half per cent, and to ship the remainder to WILLIAM WYNN and wife RUTH at ALDGATE in the City of London, and BENJAMIN and MARY SANDWELL in Wapping, London. *Witnesses:* HUGH MACKAY, RALPH SUGNION, THOMAS CAMPBELL. *Clerk of the Court:* JAMES SMALLWOOD.

EAGLE, RICHARD.

Brunswick County.

March 23, 1769. March 31, 1769. *Son:* JOSEPH ("House, plantation, saw and grist mills"). *Daughter:* SUSANNAH EAGLE. *Wife:* MARGARET HENRIETTA EAGLE (formerly BUGNION). *Cousins:* JEAN and ELIZABETH DAVIS. *Sister:* ELIZABETH DAVIS. *Other legatees:* JEANET MCFARLING, JOHN EAGLESON. *Executors:* JOHN GIBBS, ROBERT SHAW, JOHN ANCRUM and THOMAS OWEN. *Witnesses:* JOHN WALKER, JOHN FERGUS, MARY WALKER. Will proven before WM. TRYON. Codicil to this will, of even date. Confirms title to MR. WM. DRY in and to a tract of land "bought of my father, RICH'D EAGLES."

DOBBS, ARTHUR.

Brunswick, in New Hanover County.

"Governor and Captain General of the Province of North Carolina." August 31, 1763. April 24, 1765. *Sons:* CONWAY RICHARD DOBBS, EDWARD BRICE DOBBS. *Wife:* JUSTINA. *Brother:* REVEREND DOCTOR RICHARD DOBBS. *Witnesses:* JAMES HASELL, LEWIS DEROSSET, JOHN SAMPSON. Proven before WM. TRYON. The following items are of interest: "instead of immoderate funeral expenses I desire that one hundred pounds Sterling money may be paid and distributed proportionately among the housekeepers of the Parishes of Ballynure and Kilroot in the County of Antrim and Kingdom of Ireland, and one other hundred pounds of like money among the poor freemen House-keepers who reside within the county of the town of Carrick-fergus to be paid — — — — — out of my Demesnes at Castle Dobbs or out of the arrears of rents I reserved out of a Moiety of lands in that Kingdom during my life." All slaves, plate, etc., is bequeathed to wife, together with "the money

and interest due to me by the General Assembly for the lands
called Tower hill in Johnston County, purchased from me by
the publick." "Whereas, I have a right to the Moiety of two
hundred thousand acres of land granted to me by the Crown in
Sixteen patents of twelve thousand five hundred acres each in
Mecklinburgh (late Anson) County as one of the associates of
HUEY and CRYMBLE—etc." To each of children is
bequeathed fifty pounds and to brother twenty pounds. "Item.
Whereas I am entitled to a Moiety of Twelve Thousand acres
of land by a purchase from MR. PATRICK SMITH of
Waterford, merchant, for which a patent was granted to him as
an associate of HUEY and CRYMBLE, subdivided from the
great tract No. 4, the heirs and assigns of MR. JAMES
BENNING of Lisburn, Ireland, being entitled to the other
moiety." "I give and bequeath to my son CONWAY
RICHARD DOBBS

EATON, WILLIAM.

Granville County.

February 19, 1759. March 20, 1759. Saint Johns Parish in the
County of Granville. *Sons:* WILLIAM (lands in Dinwiddie
and Brunswick counties in Virginia, except land received of
William Scoggan), THOMAS, CHARLES RUST. *Daughters:*
JANE, wife of COLO. NATHANIEL EDWARDS; ANNE
HAYNES, relict of ANDREW HAYNES; MARY, wife of
ROBERT JONES; SARAH, wife of CHARLES JOHNSON;
ELIZABETH, wife of DANIEL WELDON; MARTHA
EATON. *Grandson:* EATON HAYNES. *Wife and Executrix:*
MARY. The following lands devised: plantation in Granville
"whereon I now live"; land in Granville called Bowsers; land
where LEWIS BALLARD and CORMELIAL EARLS live;
land in Northampton called Cumboes; lots in the town of
Halifax; land "where Granville Court house is built"; land on
Tabbs Creek; lot in the town of Petersburg; land in Granville
called Gould's; land on Little Fishing Creek called Youngs;
land on Andersons Swamp; two tracts on Smiths Creek called
270

Hughes and Rayborn's; lot in Halifax adjoining the Market place and Main street. A large number of negroes bequeathed, some being on plantations at Tabbs Creek and others on Mush Island. *Witnesses:* WM. PERSON, JAS. PAINE, RICHD. COLEMAN. *Clerk of the Court:* DANIEL WELDON.

ESPY, JAMES.

Brunswick, in New Hanover County.

October 3, 1739. October 9, 1739. *Son:* USHER. *Daughter:* SARAH ESPY. *Wife:* MARGARET. *Executors:* JOHN MONTGOMERY and WILLIAM DRY. *Witnesses:* RICHARD HELLIER, WM. GRAY, JAMES LYON. Will proven before GAB. JOHNSTON at Newton.

IRBY, HENRY.

Brunswick County.

January 30, 1733. February 12, 1733-1734. *Sons:* WILLIAM, HENRY ("plantation up North West and House and Lott in Cape Fair to hold in common with ELIZABETH, his sister, and FORTUNE HOLEDERLEY their mother"). *Daughters:* ANN and ELIZABETH IRBY. *Executrix:* FORTUNE HOLEDERLEY. *Witnesses:* JAMES ESPY, ROBT. EATON, WILLIAM POWER. Will proven before GEO. BURRINGTON.

JOHNSON, JOHN.

Brunswick County.

March 1, 1750. February Court, 1752. St. Andrews Parish in Brunswick County. *Son and Executor:* WILLIAM ("my land and plantation"). *Daughters:* AMEY MITCHELL and ANN JELKS. *Granddaughters:* MARTHA and ANNE (daughters of WILLIAM). *Witnesses:* JOHN CARRELL, WILLIAM

HOLLOWAY and WILLIAM MOSELEY. *Clerk of Edgecombe Court:* BENJ'N WYNNS.

KINCE, CHRISTIAN.

Brunswick County.

December 24, 1761. January 19, 1762. *Sons:* JOHN, EDWARD, WILLIAM. *Daughter:* ELIZABETH. *Executors:* JOHN and JOSEPH KINCE and EDWARD WILLIAMS. *Wife:* mentioned, but not named. *Witnesses:* JOHN FILLYAW, SAMUEL KINCE, JOHN HOWARD. Proven before ARTHUR DOBBS.

LORD, WILLIAM.

Brunswick, in New Hanover County.

July 5, 1748. August Court, 1749. *Sons:* PETER, WILLIAM, THOMAS. *Daughters:* MARY, MARGARET, AMELIA. *Wife and Executrix:* MARGARET. *Witnesses:* RICH'D QUINCE, WILLIAM ROSS, GEO. NICHOLAS. *Clerk of Court:* ISAAC FARIES.

MCDOWELL, JOHN.

Brunswick County.

March 27, 1735. April 19, 1735. "Master of the scooner called the Jolly Batchelor, now riding at anchor in Cape Fear River, But of Brunswick * * *." Ten pounds is bequeathed to the Presbyterian church at Dover, Delaware, and five pounds to the Episcopal Church at the same place. *Brother:* JAMES MCDOWELL. *Sister:* ELEANOR NISBETT. *Friend:* LYDIA JONES. *Executors:* HUGH CAMPBELL and JAMES ESPY, of Brunswick. *Witnesses:* STEPHEN MOTT, A.

DELABASTIE, ANDW. BLYTH, MAGDALEN
CAMPBELL. Proven before GAB. JOHNSTON. Provision in
will that "a small brick wall be put around my grave wt two
marble stones sett up, one att the head and the other att the
foot, as is commonly us'd in such cases att Philadelphia."

MOORE, ROGER.

New Hanover County.

March 7, 1747-1748. May Court, 1758. Parish of St. Philips.
Sons: GEORGE, WILLIAM. *Daughters:* SARAH SMITH,
MARY and ANNE MOORE. *Wife:* MARY. The following
lands are devised: Plantation called Kendall; land on "Mr.
Allens Creek"; lands between Therofaire and Black River in
the Neck known by the name of Maultsby's Point and lands on
the Island opposite; land in fork of River known by name of
Mount Misery; 500 acres on So. West River; land between
JOB HOWE and MR. DALLISON; 3,025 acres near
Saxpahaw Old Fields, bought of JOHN PORTER; lot in
Brunswick where "Mr. Ross at present dwells"; plantation
called Orton where "I now dwell"; 640 acres at Rocky Point;
land on Smith Creek; 5,000 acres at Eno Old Fields. To
daughters, ANN and MARY MOORE, is bequeathed 3,600
pounds, 1,800 to each. To *son-in-law,* THOMAS SMITH, is
devised lot in Brunswick "where WILLIAM LORD at present
dwells." *Grandmother of daughters:* MRS. SARAH TROTT.
Aunt of daughters: MRS. SARAH ALLEN. About 250
negroes bequeathed. Will mentions mill at Brices Creek.
Executors: GEORGE and WILLIAM MOORE (sons).
Witnesses: WM. FORBES, RICH'D QUINCE, GEO.
LOGAN, WM. ROSS, REBECCA COKE. *Clerk of the Court:*
ISAAC FARIES. Coat of arms on seal.

MOSELEY, EDWARD.

New Hanover County.

March 20, 1745. August Court, 1749. *Sons:* JOHN (plantation at Rockey Point, on the west side of the northeast branch of Cape Fear River, about 3,500 acres; lot and houses in Brunswick "where my Habitation usually is at Present"; plantation below Brunswick commonly called Macknights), EDWARD (plantation in Chowan County containing 2,000 acres in fee tail; lot and house in Wilmington; 600 acres of land opposite Cabbage Inlet; 500 acres in Tyrrell called Coopers; 450 acres in Tyrrell called Whitemarsh), SAMPSON (land on the east side of the northeast branch of Cape Fear River, lying between Holly Shelter Creek and the bald white sandhills, containing 3,500 acres), JAMES (lands on the east side of the northeast branch of Cape Fear River opposite Rocky Point plantation, containing 1,650 acres), THOMAS (1,880 acres of land on northwest branch of Cape Fear River). TO SAMPSON, JAMES and THOMAS is devised "all my lands on the East side of Cape Fear River, on part whereof MR. BUGNION dwelleth." To five sons is devised "my large tract of Land in Edgecomb County called Clur, containing 10,000 acres," and fifty-six slaves. *Wife:* ANN (plantation on the Sound "whereon is a large Vineyard planted"; also 3,200 acres of land in Edgecomb called Alden of the Hill, lying on a branch of Fishing Creek, by "some called Irwins, by Other Butterwood"; also 1,650 acres on the west side of Neuse River, about twenty-four miles above Newbern; also twenty-one slaves, new chaise harness and pair of bay horses, ten cows and calves, ten steers and twenty sheep. *Daughter:* ANER (eleven slaves). *Friends:* SAMUEL SWANN, JOHN SWANN, JEREMIAH VAIL, ALEXANDER LILLINGTON, JAMES HASELL. *Mother-in-law:* MRS. SUSANNAH HASELL. *Brother-in-law:*

STUART, JOHN.

New Hanover Precinct.

June 27, 1736. July 9, 1736. *Legatees:* SARAH SMITH, HENRIETTA STUART (sister, of Inverness in North Britain).

274

Executors: THOMAS WARDROPER (Surveyor General of the Province) and JAMES MURRAY, of Brunswick.
Witnesses: JAMES FERGUS, WM. ELLISON. Proven before W. SMITH, C. J.

More NC Abstracts of Wills can be found at
http://digital.lib.ecu.edu/historyfiction/fullview.aspx?id=gra

Additional Last Will and Testaments available at the Brunswick County Government Complex, Clerk of Court and Register of Deeds Offices:
(does not include all wills, just the first few in the Will books.)

Most Wills will list many names of family, friends, and acquaintances as well as provide locations of land, homesteads and plantations.

P. 1	William Brinkly	1848
P. 2	Peter Finvri (sp?)	1854
P. 13	Jacob A. S. Price	1869
P. 14	Stephen D. Thurston	1869
P. 15	Isaac Reynold	1869
P. 16	Isaac D. Reynolds	1870
P. 17	John G. Grissett	1858
P. 18	D. K. Bennett	1870
	John B. Gause	1870
P. 19	Cornelius Galloway	1871
P. 20	Cornelius Galloway	1871
	Alexander Galloway	1871
P. 21	William Raymond Sellers	1869
P. 22	William Raymond Sellers	1869
P. 23	Dennis Cannon	1874
P. 24	Dennis Cannon	1874
P. 25	John A. Cannon	
P. 26	William E. Carr (Wilmington)	1869
P. 27	William B. Carr	1869
	William E. Carr	1869

P. 28	Eliza Lehew	1874
P. 29	W. G. Curtis	1874
P. 30	Charlotte Davis	1875
P. 31	Charlotte Davis	1875
P. 32	Mark Reynolds	1870
P. 33	Mark Reynolds	1870
P. 52	Stephen Spencer	1857
	John Galloway	1788
P. 53	Samuel Frink	1795
P. 54	Martha Frink	1795
P. 55	Sarah Daniel	1797
P. 56	James Bell	1793
P. 57	James Bell cont.	1793
	Thomas Neal	1796
P. 58	Thomas Neal cont.	1796
P. 59	Drury Allen	1797
P. 60	Drury Allen cont.	1797
	John Vernon	1781
P. 61	Henry Taylor	1799
P. 62	Miles Potter	1798
P. 63 written	Daniel Beery	Recorded 1908 but Earlier
P, 64	Daniel Beery cont.	
	William E. Lord	1799
P. 65	Needham Gause	1794
P. 66	Needham Gause cont.	1794
	Samuel Cox	1800
P. 67	John Hall	1801
P. 68	Ame Goodman	1800
P. 69		
P. 70	John Chairs	1781
P. 71	William Gause	1801
P. 72	William Gause cont.	1801
P. 73	William Gause cont.	1801

Index

Croatoan, 2, 4, 32

D

Daniel L. Russell, 111
Davis Rock, 111
DeSoto, Hernando, 3
Dickens, 234
Dollison, 235
Dollison Plantation, 235
Drake, Sir Francis, 3
Drury Allan, 236
Duke of Brunswick, xvi, 95
Dupont, 235

E

E. F. Middleton, 248
Eagles, 103, 235
East Beach, 251
Edward Teach, 57
Elaezar Allen, 109
Eleanor Dare, 32
Elizabeth A. Holden, 156
Elmira, the Death Camp of the North, 224
Eno,, 2
Ephraim Vernon, 236
Exum, 237

F

ferry, 78, 79, 82, 88, 93, 94, 208
Food, 134
Forks Plantation, 235
Fort Anderson, 216
Fort Caswell, 61, 209, 220, 221

Fort Fisher, 17, 74, 208, 213, 216, 221, 223, 224, 249
Fort Fisher Hermit, 249
Fort Johnson, 84
Frink-Long Cemetery, 149

G

G. V. Barbee, 248
Gale, Christopher, 47
Gause Landing, 22
Gause Manor, 122, 159
Gause's tomb, 122
George Washington, 93, 107, 121, 122, 142, 286
George Washington Holden, 93
George Washington Visits the Gause Manor, 160
Gordillo, Francisco, 2
Gore Creek, 22
Gore Lake Road, 244
Governor Arthur Dobbs, 5, 77, 109
Governor George Burrington, 67
Governors Point, 109
Gray Man of Long Beach, 248
Green, 33, 112, 232, 236, 237
Green Banks Plantation, 236
Green Swamp, 33, 232, 237
Grissett, Emmitt, 201, 202
Grissettown, 237

John F. Holden, 254
John Holden, Jr.,, 93
John Holden, Senior, 93
John Lawson, 4
John McDowell, 89
John Moore, 109
John Swann, 73, 187, 235
John Waddell, 110
John White, 19, 32, 34, 37,
    44, 46
Joseph W. Gay, 234
Joseph Watters, 234
Juan Vespucci, 30
Judge Hassell, 111
July 4th Toasts, 141

K

Keyauwee, 2
Keziah Memorial Park, 25
King Charles I, 48
King Phillip II of Spain, 30
Kinston Street Cemetery,
    194
Krahnke, 234
Krzysztof Wilczyski, 51

L

Land Grants, 48
Late Woodland, 19, 20
Late Woodland period, 19
Lawson, John, 9, 12
Lee, Lawrence, 7, 61
Legends, 244
Leland, 210, 234, 235, 236,
    237, 238
Leland Adams, 234
Leonard School, 78

Liberty Ships, 242
Little Charlotte River, 78
Live Oak Road Cemetery,
    152
Lockwood's Folly, 79, 81,
    82, 89, 237, 238
Long Beach, 24, 202, 208,
    237, 238, 248
Longwood, 237
Lost Colony, 4, 30, 33, 35
Lumbee, 6, 56
Lunenberg, xvi

M

M. Jennett Long,, 149
Machapunga, 2
Maco, 34, 211, 212, 231,
    237, 238
Maco Light, 211
Maco: The Maco Light,
    211
Magnolia Plantation, 235
Major General Robert
    Howe, 107
Mallory Plantation, 235
Malmo, 34, 236, 238
Marsden Campbell, 109
Mary Hemingway, xii,
    192, 195, 198, 199, 200,
    204
Mary Hemingway Last
    Will and Testament, 195
McFayden Mound, 14
Meherrin, 2
Middle Island, 251
Middle Woodland period,
    19

Polybius, 51
Port Vernon Plantation, 236
pottery types, 20
Poverty in Brunswick County, 112
Pre-Colonial Era, 1
Prices Creek Lighthouse, 207, 208
Privateers, 52
Prospect Plantation, 235
Punishment, 134

Q

Quakers, 73
Quexos, Pedro de, 2
Quince, 100, 105, 110, 117, 121
Quinces, 110

R

Rackham, Jack, 62
Raleigh, 32
Read, Mary, 62, 63, 64
Reuban Long, 149
Revolutionary War Period, 107
Reynolds, 234
Ricefield Branch, 235
Richard Eagles, 109
Richard Williams,, 234
Roanoke, 3, 4, 6, 30, 31, 32, 33, 34, 39, 41, 214, 215
Roanoke Island, 31
Robert E. Harrell, 249
Robert Hewett, 193

Robert Howe, 108, 109
Robert Shaw, 235
Roe Noakers, 33, 34
Roger Moore, 22, 70, 109
Rowan Plantation, 236
Rowell, 236

S

Sam of Ocean Isle Beach, 240
Samuel Ashe, 84, 85, 86
Samuel Frink, 68, 149
Samuel Frinks, 149
Samuel Swann, 86
Samuel Watters, 235
Saponi, 2
Saxapahaw, 7
Schencking Moore, 109
Scots, 83
Secotan, 2, 47
Shakori, 2
Shallotte, 24, 78, 93, 123, 211, 238
Shawfields Plantation, 235
Ships, 146, 242
Silver Hill, 23
Siouan, 7, 8, 13, 19
Sir Francis Drake, 31
Sir Walter Raleigh, 3, 30
Sissipahaw, 2
Slave Cemeteries, 200
Slave Cemetery, xi, xii, 188, 190, 201, 205, 229
slaves, xii, 3, 89, 188, 192, 200, 201, 204, 210, 232
Smith Island, 7, 13, 49, 74
Smith, John, 4, 32, 47

War of the Spanish
   Succession, 52
Watters, 102, 113, 235
Weapemeoc, 2
White, John, 4
William Ashe, 86
William Dry, 235, 236
William Soranzo Quince,
   110
Willie Fullwood, 202
Wilmington, 17, 18, 57, 64,
   68, 73, 82, 83, 88, 110,
   121, 122, 123, 146, 211,
   212, 213, 214, 215, 216,
   217, 221, 231, 233, 254
Wilmington Census
   Records, 83

Wilson County, 1
Winnabow, 52, 188, 190,
   200, 223, 237, 238
Winyaw Bay, 30
Woccon, 2, 7
Woodburn Plantation, 235
Woodland Culture, 1
Woody Fulford, 23

Y

Yahasee Wars, 11
Yamassee War, 21
Yaupon Beach, 237, 238

Z

Zeke's Island, 251

Quotable Quotes

I hope I shall always possess firmness and virtue enough to maintain what I consider the most enviable of all titles, the character of an Honest Man.

Let us raise a standard to which the wise and honest can repair; the rest is in the hands of God.
George Washington

Being unwanted, unloved, uncared for, forgotten by everybody, I think that is a much greater hunger, a much greater poverty than the person who has nothing to eat.

Kind words can be short and easy to speak, but their echoes are truly endless.
Mother Teresa

Come unto me, ye who are weary and overburdened, and I will give you rest.   **Matthew 11:28**

Let the name of the Lord be praised both now and forevermore.   **Psalms 113:3**

Printed in the United States of America.